A Garland Series

The English Stage
Attack and Defense 1577 - 1730

A collection of 90 important works
reprinted in photo-facsimile in 50 volumes

edited by
Arthur Freeman
Boston University

A Short View of the Immorality and Profaneness of the English Stage

by

Jeremy Collier

with a preface
for the Garland Edition by

Arthur Freeman

Garland Publishing, Inc., New York & London

1972

Library of Congress Cataloging in Publication Data

Collier, Jeremy, 1650-1726.
  A short view of the immorality and profaneness of
the English stage.

  (The English stage: attack and defense, 1577-1730)
  Reprint of the 1698 ed.
  "Wing C5263."
  1. Theater--Moral and religious aspects.
2. Theater--England. I. Title. II. Series.
PN2047.C6 1972   792'.013'0942   70-170438
ISBN 0-8240-0605-4

Preface

Jeremy Collier, the non-juring divine whose first assault on the stage is this celebrated Short View, *has been discussed and his argument described with and without sympathy by virtually every historian of Restoration drama. A balanced view is Joseph Wood Krutch's essential* Comedy and Conscience after the Restoration *(New York 1924; revised reprint 1949); a most useful summary of the controversy sparked by this book, with* précis *of most major contributions, remains Sister Rose Anthony,* The Jeremy Collier Stage Controversy *(Marburg, 1937). The fullest handlist up to 1700 is still that in Edward Niles Hooker's* The Critical Works of John Dennis *(two vols., Baltimore, 1939-1943), I, 468-70, followed mainly by Lowe-Arnott-Robinson, who add secondary editions and later works. T. J. Wise interested himself in some of the material, and additional bibliographical data and invention are to be found in the* Ashley Catalogue.

A Short View *collates A-T*[8], *A4 signed A5. Our*

PREFACE

*reprint is prepared from a copy of the first edition
in the possession of the Publishers, compared with
two copies in the British Museum (King's and
Grenville). The stamped "IE/NES" within squares
on the present title page is presumably the device
of an early owner, whom I have failed to identify.*

*The preface to the first edition is dated 5 March;
the book was advertised in* The Post Boy, *issue of
16-18 April 1698, and in* The Flying Post, *April
19-21, and it appears in the Easter (May) Term
Catalogues for 1698 (III, 66). Subsequent to this
edition appeared six insignificantly corrected re-
prints, two of which (1730 and 1738) are reissues
of* 1728, *comprising most of Collier's replies to the*
adversaria *as well.*

*Lowe-Arnott-Robinson 284; Hooker 1; Wing C
5623; Ashley X, 80.*

July, 1972   A. F.

6

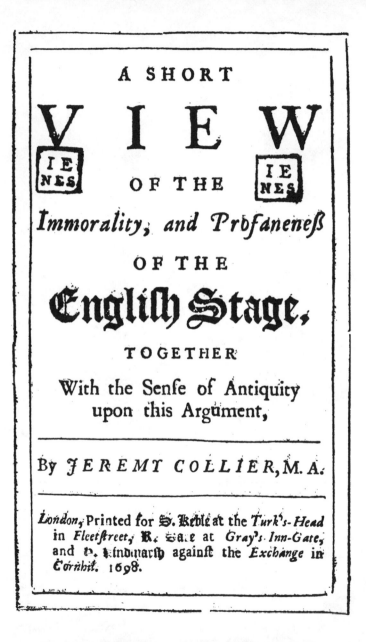

A SHORT VIEW

OF THE

Immorality, and Profaneneſſ

OF THE

Engliſh Stage,

TOGETHER

With the Senſe of Antiquity
upon this Argument,

By *JEREMY COLLIER*, M. A.

London, Printed for S. Keble at the *Turk's-Head*
in *Fleetstreet*, R. Sare at *Gray's-Inn-Gate*,
and H. Hindmarsh against the *Exchange* in
Cornhil. 1698.

THE

PREFACE

BEing convinc'd that no-
thing has gone farther
in Debauching the Age
than the Stage Poets, and
Play-House, I thought I could
not employ my time better than
in writing against them. These
Men sure, take Vertue and
Regularity, for great Enemies, why else is their Disaf-
fection so very Remarkable?

A 2   It

The Preface.

It must be said, They have made their Attack *with great* Courage, *and* gain'd *no inconsiderable* Advantage. *But it seems* Lewdness without Atheism, *is but* half their Business. Conscience *might possibly recover, and* Revenge *be thought on; and therefore like* Foot-Pads, *they must not only* Rob, *but* Murther. *To do them right their* Measures *are* Politickly taken : *To make sure work on't, there's nothing like* Destroying of Principles *; Practise must follow of* Course. *For to have no good* Principles, *is to have no*

Rea-

The Preface.

Reason to be Good. *Now 'tis not to be expected that people should* check *their* Appetites, *and* balk *their* Satisfactions, *they don't know why.* If Virtue *has no* Prospect, *'tis not worth the owning.* Who *would be* troubled *with* Conscience *if 'tis only a* Bugbear, *and has nothing* in't *but* Vision, *and the* Spleen .

My Collection *from the* English Stage, *is much short of what* They *are able to furnish.* An Inventory *of their* Ware-House *would have been a large* Work: *But being*

afraid

The Preface.

afraid of over charging the Reader, *I thought a* Pattern *might do.*

In Translating *the* Fathers, *I have endeavour'd to keep* close *to their* Meaning : *However, in* some few places, *I have taken the* Liberty of throwing in a Word or **two** ; *To* clear *the* Sense, *to* preserve *the* Spirit of the Original, *and keep the* English *upon its* Legs.

There's one thing more to acquaint *the* Reader *with* ; *'Tis that I have Ventured to*

change

The Preface.

change *the* Terms *of* Miſtreſs
and Lover, *for* others *ſomewhat more* Plain, *but much
more* Proper. *I don't look
upon This as any* failure *in*
Civility. *As* Good *and* Evil
are different *in* Themſelves,
ſo they ought to be differently
Mark'd. *To* confound *them
in* Speech, *is the way to* confound *them in* Practiſe. Ill
Qualities *ought to have* ill
Names, *to prevent their being*
Catching. *Indeed* Things
are in a great meaſure Govern'd *by* Words : *To* Guild
over a foul Character, *ſerves
only to perplex the* Idea, *to en-*

The Preface,

courage the Bad, *and mislead
the* Unwary. *To treat* Honour, *and* Infamy *alike, is
an* injury *to* Virtue, *and a
sort of* Levelling *in* Morality. *I confess, I have no*
Ceremony *for* Debauchery.
For to Complement Vice, *is
but* one Remove *from* worshipping *the* Devil.

March 5th. 169⅞.

THE

THE

CONTENTS.

CHAP. I.

The

The CONTENTS.

CHAP. II.

The *Profaneness* of the *Stage.*

THis Charge *prov'd upon them,*
   I. *By their* Cursing *and* Swearing.   p. 57

The English Stage *formerly less hardy in this re-*
  spect.   Ibid

The provokingness *of this Sin.*   p. 58.

This Offence punishable *by* Law, *and how far.* p. 59

Swearing *in the* Play House *an* Un-Gentlemanly,
  as well as an Un-Christian practise.

A Second *Branch of the* Profaness *of the* Stage,
  consisting in their Abuse of Religion, *and the* Holy Scriptures.   p. 60

Instances of this Liberty in the Mock Astrologer. Ib.

In the Orphan.   p. 62

                     In

The CONTENTS.

CHAP. III.

Immo-

The CONTENTS.

CHAP. IV.

To

The CONTENTS.

CHAP. V.

SECT. I.

SECT. II.

His

The CONTENTS.

SECT. III.

CHAP. VI.

The

The CONTENTS.

The Stage *Condemn'd by the* Primitive Church.

ERRATA.

PAge 31 Margin for Κᾶϛοϛ, r. Μᾶϛοϛ. p. 37. l. 1. for *by his*, r. *his*. l. 2. for *other*, r *his other*. l. 25. for *prætr*, r. *prater*. p. 39. l. 18. for *Poets, Knaves*, r. *Poets Knaves*. p. 44. l. 14. for *Concianotores*, r. *Concionatores*. p. 45. l. 25. for *Debaush*, r. *Debauchee*. p. 46. l. 9. for *Enterprizes*, r. *Enterprize*. p. 47. l. 9. for *ridicules*, r. *ridiculous*. p. 52. l. 1. for *justifying*, r. *and justifie*. p. 60. l. 2. for *tempestinous*, r. *tempestuous*. l. 31. for *pray*, r. *should pray*. p. 80. for *executed*, r. *exerted*. p. 108. l. 4. for *Antarkick*. r. *Antartick*. p. 117. l. 12. for *Angitia*. r. *Angitiæ*. p. 121. l. 24. for *Auger*, r. *Augur*. p. 135. margin, for *Heglins Cogmog*, r. *Heylins Cosmog*. p. 154. l. 22. dele up. p. 163. l. 28. for *then*, r. *therefore*. p. 183. l. 6. for *to*, r. *too*. p. 186. l. 6. dele *And*. p. 191. l. 18. for *Circumstance*, r. *Circumstances*. p. 222. l. 9. for *Cup*, r. *a Cup*. p. 237. l. 2. for *apon't*, r. *upon't*. 245. l. 25. for *Le*, r. *Les*. p. 257. l. 28. for *Correspondence* r. *this Correspondence*. p. 272. l. 9. for *himself*. r. *themselves*.

The Litteral mistakes the Reader is Desired to Correct.

———————————

Essays upon several Moral Subjects in two parts the Second Edition Corrected and Enlarged by Jeremy Collier, *M. A.*

Human Prudence, or the Art by which a man may raise himself and his Fortune to Grandure, the Seventh Edition.

An Answer to all the Excuses and Pretences that men usually make for their not coming to the Holy Communion, by a Divine of the Church of England : Fitted for Persons of the meanest Capacity, and proper to be given away by such as are Charitably Inclin'd. Price 3 pence.

THE

INTRODUCTION.

THE bufinefs of *Plays* is to reco-
mend Virtue, and difcountenance
Vice ; To fhew the Uncertainty of Humane Greatnefs, the
fuddain Turns of Fate, and the Unhappy Conclufions of Violence and Injuftice :
'Tis to expofe the Singularities of Pride
and Fancy, to make Folly and Falfe-
hood contemptible, and to bring every
Thing that is Ill Under Infamy, and
Neglect. This Defign has been oddly
purfued by the Englifh *Stage.* Our *Poets*
write with a different View, and are
gone into an other Intereft. 'Tis true,
were their Intentions fair, they might
be *Serviceable* to this *Purpofe.* They
have in a great meafure the Springs
of Thought and Inclination in their Power. *Show, Mufick, Action,* and *Rhetorick,* are moving Entertainments ; and
rightly employ'd would be very fignifi-
B cant.

cant. But Force and Motion are Things indifferent, and the Use lies chiefly in the Application. These Advantages are now, in the Enemies Hand, and under a very dangerous Management. Like Cannon seized they are pointed the wrong way, and by the Strength of the Defence the Mischief is made the greater. That this Complaint is not unreasonable I shall endeavour to prove by shewing the Misbehaviour of the *Stage* with respect to *Morality*, and *Religion*. Their *Liberties* in the Following Particulars are intolerable. *viz.* Their *Smuttiness* of *Expression*; Their *Swearing, Profainness*, and *Lewd Application of Scripture*; Their *Abuse* of the *Clergy*; Their *making* their *Top Characters Libertines*, and giving them *Success* in their *Debauchery*. This Charge, with some other Irregularities, I shall make good against the *Stage*, and shew both the *Novelty* and *Scandal* of the *Practise*. And first, I shall begin with the *Rankness*, and *Indecency* of their *Language*.

CHAP. I.

The Immodesty of the Stage.

IN treating this Head, I hope the Reader does not expect that I should set down Chapter and Page, and give him the Citations at Length. ·To do this would be a very unacceptable and Foreign Employment. Indeed the Passages, many of them, are in no Condition to be handled: He that is desirous to see these Flowers let him do it in their own Soil: 'Tis my business rather to kill the *Root* than *Transplant* it. But that the Poets may not complain of Injustice; I shall point to the Infection at a Distance, and refer in General to *Play* and *Person*.

Now among the Curiosities of this kind we may reckon Mrs. *Pinchwife*, *Horner*, and Lady *Fidget* in the *Country Wife*; Widdow *Blackacre* and *Olivia* in the *Plain Dealer*. These, tho' not all the exceptionable *Characters*, are the most remarkable. I'm sorry the Author should stoop his Wit thus Low, and use his Understanding so unkindly. Some People

ap-

appear Coarse, and Slovenly out of Poverty: They can't well go to the Charge of Sense. They are Offensive like Beggars for want of Necessaries. But this is none of the *Plain Dealer*'s case; He can afford his Muse a better Dress when he pleases. But then the Rule is, where the Motive is the less, the Fault is the greater. To proceed. *Jacinta, Elvira, Dalinda*, and *Lady Plyant*, in the *Mock Astrologer, Spanish Friar, Love Triumphant* and *Double Dealer*, forget themselves extreamly: And almost all the *Characters* in the *Old Batchelour*, are foul and nauseous. *Love* for *Love*, and the *Relapse*, strike sometimes upon this *Sand*, and so likewise does *Don Sebastian*.

I don't pretend to have read the *Stage* Through, neither am I Particular to my Utmost. Here is quoting enough unless 'twere better: Besides, I may have occasion to mention somewhat of this kind afterwards. But from what has been hinted already, the Reader may be over furnish'd. Here is a large Collection of Debauchery; such *Pieces* are rarely to be met with: 'Tis Sometimes painted at Length too, and appears in great Variety of Progress and Practise. It wears almost all sorts of Dresses to engage the Fancy, and fasten upon the

Me-

Memory, and keep up the Charm from Languishing. Sometimes you have it in Image and Description ; sometimes by way of Allusion ; sometimes in Disguise ; and sometimes without it. And what can be the Meaning of such a Representation, unless it be to Tincture the Audience, to extinguish Shame, and make Lewdness a Diversion ? This is the natural Consequence, and therefore one would think 'twas the Intention too. Such Licentious Discourse tends to no point but to stain the Imagination, to awaken Folly, and to weaken the Defences of Virtue : It was upon the account of these Disorders that *Plato* banish'd Poets his *Common Wealth* : And one of the *Fathers* calls *Poetry, Vinum Dæmonum* an intoxicating *Draught*, made up by the Devils *Dispensatory*.

I grant the Abuse of a Thing is no Argument against the use of it. However Young people particularly, should not entertain themselves with a Lewd Picture ; especially when 'tis drawn by a Masterly Hand. For such a Liberty may probably raise those Passions which can neither be discharged without Trouble, nor satisfyed without a Crime : 'Tis not safe for a Man to trust his Virtue too far, for fear it should give

him

him the flip! But the danger of such
an Entertainment is but part of the
Objection : 'Tis all Scandal and meanness
into the bargain : it does in effect degrade Human Nature, sinks Reason
into Appetite, and breaks down the
Distinctions between Man and Beast.
Goats and Monkeys if they could speak,
would express their Brutality in such Language as This.

To argue the Matter more at large.

Smuttiness is a Fault in Behaviour as
well as in Religion. 'Tis a very Coarse
Diversion, the Entertainment of those
who are generally least both in Sense,
and Station. The looser part of the
Mob, have no true relish of Decency
and Honour, and want Education, and
Thought, to furnish out a gentile Conversation. Barrenness of Fancy makes
them often take up with those Scandalous Liberties. A Vitious Imagination
may blot a great deal of Paper at this
rate with ease enough: And 'tis possible
Convenience may sometimes invite to
the Expedient. The Modern Poets seem
to use *Smut* as the Old Ones did *Machines*,
to relieve a fainting Invention. When
Pegasus is jaded, and would stand still,
he is apt like other *Tits*, to run into e-
very Puddle.

Ob-

Obſcenity in any Company is a ru-
ſtick uncreditable Talent ; but among
Women 'tis particularly rude. Such Talk
would be very affrontive in Converſation, and not endur'd by any Lady of
Reputation. Whence then comes it to
Paſs that thoſe Liberties which diſoblige
ſo much in Converſation, ſhould entertain upon the *Stage*. Do the Women
leave all the regards to Decency and
Conſcience behind them when they come
to the *Play-Houſe* ? Or does the Place
transform their Inclinations, and turn their
former Averſions into Pleaſure ? Or were
Their pretences to Sobriety elſewhere
nothing but Hypocriſy and Grimace ?
Such Suppoſitions as theſe are all Satyr
and Invective: They are rude Imputations upon the whole Sex. To treat the
Ladys with ſuch ſtuff is no better than
taking their Money to abuſe them. It
ſuppoſes their Imagination vitious, and
their Memories ill furniſh'd : That they
are practiſed in the Language of the Stews,
and pleas'd with the Scenes of Brutiſh-
neſs. When at the ſame time the Cu-
ſtoms of Education, and the Laws of
Decency, are ſo very cautious, and reſerv'd in regard to Women : I ſay ſo
very reſerv'd, that 'tis almoſt a Fault for
them to Underſtand they are ill Uſed.

They

They can't discover their Disgust without disadvantage, nor Blush without disservice to their Modesty. To appear with any skill in such Cant, looks as if they had fallen upon ill Conversation; or Managed their Curiosity amiss. In a word, He that treats the Ladys with such Discourse, must conclude either that they like it, or they do not. To suppose the first, is a gross Reflection upon their Virtue. And as for the latter case, it entertains them with their own Aversion; which is ill Nature, and ill Manners enough in all Conscience. And in this Particular, Custom and Conscience, the Forms of Breeding, and the Maxims of Religion are on the same side. In other Instances Vice is often too fashionable; But here a Man can't be a Sinner, without being a Clown.

In this respect the *Stage* is faulty to a Scandalous degree of Nauseousness and Aggravation. For

1*st*. The *Poets* make *Women* speak Smuttily. Of This the Places before mention'd are sufficient Evidence: And if there was occasion they might be Multiplyed to a much greater Number: Indeed the *Comedies* are seldom clear of these Blemishes: And sometimes you have them in *Tragedy*. For Instance. The

The *Orphans Monimia* makes a very improper Description ; And the Royal *Leonora* in the *Spanish Friar*, runs a strange Length in the History of Love *p.* 50. And do Princesses use to make their Reports with such fulsom Freedoms ? Certainly this *Leonora* was the first Queen of her Family. Such raptures are too Lascivious for *Joan* of *Naples*. Are these the *Tender Things* Mr. *Dryden* says the Ladys call on him for ? I suppose he means the *Ladys* that are too Modest to show their Faces in the *Pit*. This Entertainment can be fairly design'd for none but such. Indeed it hits their Palate exactly. It regales their Lewdness, graces their Character, and keeps up their Spirits for their Vocation : Now to bring Women under such Misbehaviour is Violence to their Native Modesty, and a Misprefentation of their Sex. For Modesty as Mr. *Rapin* observes, is the *Character* of Women. To represent them without this Quality, is to make Monsters of them, and throw them out of their Kind. *Euripides*, who was no negligent Observer of Humane Nature, is always careful of this Decorum. Thus *Phædra* when possess'd with an infamous Passion, takes all imaginable pains to conceal it. She is as regular

Reflect upon Aristot. &c.

Eurip. Hippolit.

gular

gular and reserv'd in her Language as the most virtuous Matron. 'Tis true, the force of Shame and Desire; The Scandal of Satisfying, and the difficulty of parting with her Inclinations, disorder her to Distraction. However, her Frensy is not Lewd; She keeps her Modesty even after She has lost her Wits. Had *Shakespear* secur'd this point for his young Virgin *Ophelia*, the *Play* had been better contriv'd. Since he was resolv'd to drown the Lady like a Kitten, he should have set her a swimming a little sooner. To keep her alive only to sully her Reputation, and discover the Rankness of her Breath, was very Cruel. But it may be said the Freedoms of Distraction go for nothing, a Feavour has no Faults, and a Man *non Compos*, may kill without Murther. It may be so: But then such People ought to be kept in dark Rooms and without Company. To shew them, or let them loose, is somewhat unreasonable. But after all, the Modern *Stage* seems to depend upon this Expedient. Women are sometimes represented *Silly*, and sometimes *Mad*, to enlarge their Liberty, and screen their Impudence from Censure: This Politick Contrivance we have in *Marcella*, *Hoyden*, and Miss *Prue*.

Hamlet.

*Don Quix-
ot. Relifse.
Love for
Lnc.*

How-

However it amounts to this Confession; that Women when they have their Understandings about them ought to converse otherwise. In fine; Modesty is the distinguishing Vertue of that Sex, and serves both for Ornament and Defence: Modesty was design'd by Providence as a Guard to Virtue; And that it might be always at Hand, 'tis wrought into the Mechanism of the Body. 'Tis likewise proportion'd to the occasions of Life, and strongest in Youth when Passion is so too. 'Tis a Quality as true to Innocence, as the Sences are to Health; whatever is ungrateful to the first, is prejudicial to the latter. The Enemy no sooner approaches, but the Blood rises in Opposition, and looks Defyance to an Indecency. It supplys the room of Reasoning, and Collection: Intuitive Knowledge can scarcely make a quicker Impression; And what then can be a surer Guide to the Unexperienced? It teaches by suddain Instinct and Aversion; This is both a ready and a powerful Method of Instruction. The Tumult of the Blood and Spirits, and the Uneasiness of the Sensation, are of singular Use. They serve to awaken Reason, and prevent surprize. Thus the Distinctions of Good and Evil are refresh'd, and the Temptation kept at proper Distance. 2ly.

2ly. They Represent their single Ladys, and Persons of Condition, under these Disorders of Liberty, This makes the Irregularity still more Monstrous and a greater Contradiction to Nature, and Probability : But rather than not be Vitious, they will venture to spoil a Character. This mismanagement we have partly seen already. *Jacinta,* and *Belinda* are farther proof. And the *Double Dealer* is particularly remarkable. There are but *Four* Ladys in this *Play,* and *Three* of the biggest of them are Whores. A Great Compliment to Quality to tell them there is not above a quarter of them Honest ! This was not the Roman Breeding, *Terence* and *Plautus* his Strumpets were Little people ; but of this more hereafter.

Mock Astrologer. Old Batchelour.

3dly. They have oftentimes not so much as the poor refuge of a Double Meaning to fly to. So that you are under a necessity either of taking Ribaldry or Nonsence. And when the Sentence has two Handles, the worst is generally turn'd to the Audience. The Matter is so Contrived that the Smut and Scum of the Thought rises uppermost ; And like a Picture drawn to *Sight,* looks always upon the Company.

4ly. And

4ly. And which is still more extraordinary: the *Prologues*, and *Epilogues* are sometimes Scandalous to the last degree. I shall discover them for once, and let them stand like Rocks in the Margin. Now here properly speaking the *Actors* quit the *Stage*, and remove from Fiction into Life. Here they converse with the *Boxes*, and *Pit*, and address directly to the Audience. These Preliminaries and concluding Parts, are design'd to justify the Conduct of the *Play*, and bespeak the Favour of the Company. Upon such Occasions one would imagine if ever, the Ladys should be used with Respect, and the Measures of Decency observ'd, But here we have Lewdness without Shame or Example: Here the *Poet* exceeds himself. Here are such Strains as would turn the Stomach of an ordinary Debauchee, and be almost nauseous in the *Stews*. And to make it the more agreeable, Women are Commonly pick'd out for this Service. Thus the *Poet* Courts the good opinion of the Audience. This is the Desert he regales the Ladys with at the Close of the Entertainment: It seems He thinks They have admirable Palats! Nothing can be a greater Breach of Manners then such Liberties as these. If a Man would stu-

dy

Mock Astrologer. Country Wife. Cleomenes. Old Batchelour.

dy to outrage *Quality* and Vertue, he could not do it more Effectually. But

5thly. Smut is still more insufferable with respect to Religion. The Heathen Religion was in a great Measure a *Mystery* of *Iniquity*. Lewdness was Consecrated in the Temples, as well as practised in the *Stews*. Their Deitys were great Examples of Vice, and worship'd with their own Inclination. 'Tis no wonder therefore their Poetry should be tinctured with their Belief, and that the *Stage* should borrow some of the Liberties of their Theology. This made *Mercurys* Procuring, and *Jupiters* Adultery

Plaut. the more passable in *Amphitrion* : Upon this Score *Gymnasium* is less Monstrous in

Cistellar. Praying the Gods to send her store of Gallants. And thus *Chærea* defends his Ad-

Terent. venture by the Precedent of *Jupiter* and

Eunuch. *Danae.* But the Christian Religion is quite of an other Complexion. Both its Precepts, and Authorities, are the highest discouragement to Licentiousness. It forbids the remotest Tendencies to Evil, Banishes the Follies of Conversation, and Obliges up to Sobriety of Thought. That which might pass for Raillery, and Entertainment in Heathenism, is detestable in Christianity. The Restraint of the Precept, and the Quality of the Deity,

Deity, and the Expectations of Futurity quite alter the Case.

But notwithstanding the Latitudes of Paganism, the Roman and Greek *Theatres* were much more inoffensive than ours. To begin with *Plautus*. This Comedian, tho' the most exceptionable, is modest upon the Comparison. For

1*st*. He rarely gives any of the above mention'd Liberties to Women ; And when these are any Instances of the contrary, 'tis only in prostituted and Vulgar People ; And even these, don't come up to the Grossness of the *Modern Stage.*

For the Purpose. *Cleæreta* the Procuris borders a little upon Rudeness: *Lena* and *Bacchis* the Strumpet are Airy and somewhat over-merry, but not *A l'Anglois* obscene. *Chalinus* in Womans Cloaths is the most remarkable. *Pasicompa Charinus* his Wench talks too freely to *Lysimachus* ; And so does *Sophroclidisca Slave* to *Lymnoselene*. And lastly : *Phronesiam* a Woman of the *Town* uses a double entendre to *Stratophanes*. These are the most censurable Passages, and I think all of them with relation to Women; which considering how the World goes is very moderate. Several of *our* Single*Plays* shall far out-do all This put together. And yet *Plautus* has upon the

Asinar.

Cistellar.

Bacchid.

Casin.

Mercat.
Act.3.

Persa.

Trucul.

mat-

matter left us 20 entire *Comedies*. So
that in short, these Roman Lasses are
meer *Vestal Virgins*, comparatively speaking.

2ly. The *Men* who talk intemperate-
ly are generally *Slaves*; I believe *Dor-*
dalus the Pandar, and *Lusiteles* will
be found the only exception: And
this latter young Gentleman; drops but
one over airy expression : And for this
Freedom, the Poet seems to make him
give Satisfaction in the rest of his
Character. He disputes very handsomly by himself against irregular Love ;
The Discourse between him and *Philto*
is instructive and well managed. And
afterwards he gives *Lesbonicus* a great
deal of sober advice, and declaims heartily against Luxury and Lewdness !
Now by confining his Rudeness to little People, the Fault is much extenuated.
For First, the representation is more
Naturall this way ; And which is still
better, 'tis not so likely to pass into
Imitation : Slaves and Clowns are not
big enough to spread Infection; and set
up an ill Fashion. 'Tis possible the
Poet might contrive these *Pesants Of-*
fensive to discountenance the Practise.
Thus the *Heilots* in *Sparta* were made
drunk to keep Intemperance out of
Credit

Persa.

Trinum.

Act. 2· 1.

Act. 2. 2.

Credit. I don't mention this as if I approv'd the Expedient, but only to show it a circumstance of Mitigation and Excuse.

Farther, These *Slaves* and Pandars, Seldom run over, and play their Gambols before Women. There are but Four Instances of this Kind as I remember, *Olympio, Palæstrio, Dordalus,* and *Stratilax* are the Persons. And the Women they discourse with, are two of them Slaves, and the third a Wench. But with our *Dramatists,* the case is otherwise. With us *Smuttiness* is absolute and unconfin'd. 'Tis under no restraint, of Company, nor has any regard to Quality or Sex. Gentlemen talk it to Ladies, and Ladies to Gentlemen with all the Freedom, and Frequency imaginable. This is in earnest to be very hearty in the cause! To give Title and Figure to Ill Manners is the utmost that can be done. If Lewdness will not thrive under such encouragement it must e'en Miscarry!

Casin
Mil. Glor.
Pers.
Trucul.

4ly. Plautus his *Prologues* and *Epilogues* are inoffensive. 'Tis true, *Lambinus* pretends to fetch a double *entendre* out of that to *Pænulus,* but I think there is a Strain in the Construction. His *Prologue* to the *Captivi* is worth the observing.

Fabulæ huic operam date.

Pray mind the Play. The next words give the reason why it deserves regarding.

Non enim pertractate facta est
Neque spurcidici insunt versus immemora-
biles.

We see here the Poet confesses Smut a scandalous Entertainment. That such Liberties ought to fall under Neglect, to lie unmention'd, and be blotted out of Memory.

And that this was not a Copy of his Countenance we may learn from his Compositions. His best *Plays* are almost alwaies Modest and clean Complexion'd. His *Amphitrio* excepting the ungenuine Addition is such. His *Epidicus* the Master-Piece of his whole Collection is inoffensive Throughout : And so are his *Menechmi*, *Rudens*, and *Trinummus*, which may be reckon'd amongst some of his next Best. His *Truculentus* another fine *Play* (tho' not entire) with a Heathen Allowance, is pretty Passable. To be short : Where he is most a Poet, he is generally least a Buffoon. And where the Entertainment is Smut, there is rarely any other Dish well dress'd : The Contrivance

vance is commonly wretched, the Sence lean and full of Quibbles. So that his Understanding seems to have left him when he began to abuse it.

To conclude, *Plautus* does not dilate upon the Progress, Successes, and Disappointments of *Love*, in the *Modern* way. This is nice Ground, and therefore He either stands off, or walks gravely over it, He has some regard to the Retirements of Modesty, and the Dignity of Humane Nature, and does not seem to make Lewdness his Business. To give an Instance. *Silenium* is much gone in Love, but Modest withall, tho' formerly debauch'd. *Cistellar. A. 1.*

She is sorry her Spark was forced from her, and in Danger of being lost. But then she keeps within compass and never flies out into Indecency. *Alcesimarchus* is strangely smitten with this *Silenium*, and almost distracted to recover her. He is uneasy and blusters, and threatens, but his Passion goes off in Generals. He Paints no Images of his Extravagance, nor descends to any nauseous particulars. *Ibid. A. 2.*

And yet after all, *Plautus* wrote in an Age not perfectly refin'd, and often seems to design his *Plays* for a Vulgar Capacity. 'Twas upon this view I suppose

pose

pose his *Characters* exceed Nature, and his ill
Features are drawn too large: His old
Men over credulous, his Misers Romantick, and his Coxcombs improbably
singular. And 'tis likely for this reason
his *Slaves* might have too much Liberty.

Terence appear'd when Breeding was
more exact, and the *Town* better polish'd ;
And he manages accordingly : He has
but one faulty bordering Expression,
which is that of *Chremes* to *Cliti-
pho*. This single Sentence apart, the rest
of his Book is (I think) unsullied and
fit for the nicest Conversation. I mean
only in referrence to the Argument in
Hand, for there are things in Him,
which I have no intention to warrant.
He is Extreamly careful in the Behaviour of his Women. Neither *Glycerium*
in *Andria*, *Pamphila* in *Eunuchus*, or
Pamphila in *Adelphi*, *Phanium* in *Phor-
mio*, or *Philumena* in *Hecyra*, have any
share of Conversation upon the *Stage*.
such Freedom was then thought too much
for the Reservedness of a Maiden-Cha-
racter. 'Tis true in *Heautontimoroumenos*
the *Poets* Plot obliged *Antiphila* to go
under the Disguise of *Bacchis* her Maid.
Upon this Occasion they hold a little
Discourse together. But then *Bacchis*

Heauton.

tho'

tho' she was a Woman of the *Town*, behaves her self with all the Decency imaginable. She does not talk in the Language of her Profession. But commends *Antiphila* for her Virtue : *Antiphila* only says how constant she has been to *Chinia*, seems surprised at his Arrival, and salutes him civilly upon't, and we hear no more from her. Mr. *Dryden* seems to refer to this Conduct in his Dramatick *Poesie*. He censures the *Romans* for making *Mutes* of their single Women. This He calls the *Breeding of the Old* Elizabeth *way, which was for Maids to be seen and not to be heard.* Under Favour the old Discipline would be very serviceable upon the *Stage.* As matters go, the *Mutes* are much to few. For certainly 'tis better to say nothing, than talk out of Character, and to ill purpose.

To return. The Virgin injured by *Chærea* does nothing but weep, and won t so much as speak her misfortune to the *Eunuch.* Women. But Comedy is strangly improved since that time ; For *Dalinda* has a great deal more Courage, tho' *Love Tri-* the loss of her Virtue was her own *ump.* Fault.

But *Terence* has that regard for Women, that he won't so much as touch upon an ill Subject before them. Thus

C 3

Chremes

Chremes was afhamed to mention any thing about his Sons Lewdnefs when his Wife was prefent.

Heauton.
A. 5. 4.   *Pudet dicere hac præfente verbum turpe.*

Eunuch.
A. 5. 4. 5.
Adelph.
A. 2. 3.

    The Slaves in this Comedian are kept in order and civilly bred. They Guard and Fence when occafion requires, and ftep handfomly over a dirty place. The Poet did not think Littlenefs and low Education a good Excufe for Ribaldry. He knew Infection at the weakeft, might feize on fome Conftitutions: Befides, the Audience was a Superior Prefence, and ought to be confidered. For how Negligent foever People may be at Home, yet when they come before their Betters 'tis Manners to look wholfom.

    Now tho' *Plautus* might have the richer Invention ; *Terence* was always thought the more judicious Comedian. His Raillery is not only finer, and his ftile better polifh'd ; but his *Characters* are more juft, and he feems to have reach'd farther into Life than the other. To take Leave of this Author, even his Strumpets are better behaved than our honeft Women, than our Women of Quality of the Englifh *Stage*. *Bacchis* in *Heautontimoroumenos*, and *Bacchis* in
Hecyra,

Hecyra, may serve for example. They are both modest, and converse not unbecoming their Sex. *Thais* the most accomplish'd in her way, has a great deal of Spirit and wheadling in her Character, but talks no Smut. *Eunuch.*

Thus we see with what Caution and Sobriety of Language *Terence* manages. 'Tis possible this Conduct might be his own Modesty, and result from Judgment and Inclination. But however his Fancy stood, he was sensible the Coarse way would not do. The *Stage* was then under Discipline, the publick *Censors* formidable, and the Office of the *Choragus* was originally to prevent the Excesses of Liberty.

To this we may add the *Nobless* had no Relish for Obscenity ; 'twas the ready way to Disoblige them. And therefore 'tis *Horaces* Rule. *Casaub. Annot. in Curcul Plauti.*

Nec immunda crepent ignominiosaque dicta. De A te Offenduntur enim quibus est Equus & Pater, Poet. & res.

The Old *Romans* were particularly carefull their Women might not be affronted in Conversation : For this reason the Unmarried kept off from Entertainments for fear of learning new Language. And in *Var. apud.. Nonium.*

Greece

Corn. Nep.

Greece no Woman above the degree of a *Slave*, was treated abroad by any but Relations. 'Tis probable the old Comedy was silenced at *Athens* upon this Score, as well as for Defamation. For as *Aristotle* observes the new Set of Comedians were much more modest than the former. In this celebrated Republick, if the *Poets* wrote any thing against Religion or Good Manners, They were tryed for their Misbehaviour, and lyable to the highest Forfeitures.

Arist. Lib. 4. de Mor. cap. 14.

Vit. Eu-rip. ed Cantab. 1694.

It may not be amiss to observe that there are no Instances of debauching Married Women, in *Plautus*, nor *Terence*, no nor yet in *Aristophanes*. But on our *Stage* how common is it to make a Lord, a Knight, or an Alderman a Cuckold? The Schemes of Success are beaten out with great Variety, and almost drawn up into a Science. How many Snares are laid for the undermining of Virtue, and with what Triumph is the Victory proclaim'd? The Finess of the *Plot*, and the Life of the Entertainment often lies in these Contrivances. But the *Romans* had a different sence of these Matters, and saw thro' the consequences of them. The Government was awake upon the Theatre, and would not suffer the Abuses of Honour, and Family, to pass into

Di-

Diverſion. And before we part with theſe *Comedians* we may take notice that there are no Smutty Songs in their *Plays*; in which the *Engliſh* are extreamly Scandalous. Now to work up their Lewdneſs with Verſe, and Muſick, doubles the Force of the Miſchief. It makes it more portable and at Hand, and drives it Stronger upon Fancy and Practice.

Love for Love. Love Triump. &c.

To diſpatch the *Latins* all together. *Seneca* is clean throughout the Piece, and ſtands generally off from the point of Love. He has no Courting unleſs in his *Hercules Furens* : And here the Tyrant *Lycus* addreſſes *Megara* very briefly, and in Modeſt and remote Language. In his *Thebais*, *Oedipus*'s Inceſt is reported at large, but without any choaking Deſcription. 'Tis granted *Phædra* ſpeaks her Paſſion plainly out, and owns the ſtrength of the Impreſſion, and is far leſs prudent than in *Euripides*. But tho' her Thoughts appear too freely, her Language is under Diſcipline.

p. 14. Ed Scriv.

Hipp. L.

Let us now Travel from *Italy* into *Greece*, and take a view of the Theatre at *Athens*. In this City the *Stage* had both its beginning and higheſt Improvement. *Æſchylus* was the firſt who appear'd with any Reputation. His Genius

ſeems

seems noble, and his Mind generous,
willing to transfuse it self into the Audience, and inspire them with a Spirit
of Bravery. To this purpose his Stile
is Pompous, Martial, and Enterprizing.
There is Drum and Trumpet in his
Verse. 'Tis apt to excite an Heroick
Ardour, to awaken, warm, and push
forward to Action. But his Mettal is
not always under Management. His Inclination for the *Sublime* ; carrys him too
far : He is sometimes Embarrass'd with
Epithites. His Metaphors are too stiff, and
far fetch'd ; and he rises rather in Sound,
than in Sence. However generally speaking, his Materials are both shining and
solid, and his Thoughts lofty, and un-
common. This Tragedian had always
a nice regard to Good Manners. He
knew corrupting the People was the
greatest disservice to the Commonwealth ;
And that Publick Ruine was the effect of
general Debauchery. For this reason he
declines the Business of Amours, and declares expresly against it. Now here we
can't expect any length of Testimony.
His aversion to the subject makes him
touch very sparingly upon it. But in this
case there is no need of much citation. His
very Omissions are Arguments, and his Evidence is the stronger for being short. That
little I meet with shall be produced. 1*st*.

Aristoph.
Ran.

1*st.* Or*estes* was obliged by the Oracle to revenge his Fathers Death in the Murther of his Mother. When he was going to kill her, he Mentions her Cruelty, but waves her Adultery. *Euripides* approv'd this Reservedness and makes his *Electra* practise it upon the same occasion *Æschylus* in his next Play complements his Country with a great deal of Address in the Persons of the *Eumenides.* They are very Gentile and Poetical in their Civilities: Among other things They wish the Virgins may all Marry and make the Country Populous: Here the *Poet* do's but just glance upon the Subject of Love; and yet he governs the Expression with such care, that the wishes contain a Hint to Sobriety, and carry a Face of Virtue along with them. *Χοηφορ. 263. Ed. Steph. Orest. 48. Ed Cantab. Ευμέν. 305.*

The *Double Dealer* runs Riot upon such an Occasion as this; and gives Lord *Touchwood* a mixture of Smut and Pedantry to conclude with, and yet this Lord was one of his best Characters: But *Poets* are now grown Absolute within themselves, and may put Sence and Quality upon what Drudgeries they please. To return. *Danaus* cautions his Daughters very handsomly in point of Behaviour. They were in a strange Country, and had Poverty and Dependance to *p. 79.*

struggle

struggle with: These were circumstances
of Danger, and might make him the more
pressing. He leaves therefore a solemn
Charge with them for their Security, bids
them never to subsist upon Infamy, but
to prefer their Virtue to their Life.

'Ικέτ.
340.

Μόνον φύλαξαι τάς δ' ὀπιςολὰς πατρὸς
Τὸ σωφρονεῖν τιμῶσα τε βίου πλέον.

Our *Poets* I suppose would call this
Preaching, and think it a dull Business.
However I can't forbear saying an ho-
nest Heathen is none of the worst Men:
A very indifferent Religion well Believ-
ed, will go a great way.

To proceed. *Sophocles* appear'd next
upon the *Stage*, and was in earnest an
Extraordinary Person. His Conduct is
more Artificial, and his Stile more just,
than that of *Æschylus*. His Characters
are well drawn, and Uniform with
themselves: His *Incidents*, are often surprising, and his *Plots* unprecipitated.
There is nothing but what is Great, and
Solemn Throughout. The Reasoning
is well Coloured. The Figures are sometimes Bold, but not Extravagant. There
are no Flights of Bombast, no Towring
above Nature and Possibility: In short,
nothing like Don *Sebastians* Reigning in
his *Atomes.*

Don
Sebast.
p. 12.

This

This Tragedian like *Æschylus* does not often concern himself with *Amours*, and when he does, nothing can be more temperate, and decent. For example where the Inceſt of *Oedipus* is deſcribed, the Offenſiveneſs of the Idea is ſcreen'd off and broken by Metaphorical and diſtant Expreſſions. In another *Play Creon* resolves to put *Antigone* to Death for preſuming to bury *Polynices.* This Lady and *Hæmon Creons* Son were very far engaged; *Hæmon* endeavours to diſſwade his Father from *Antigones* Execution: He tells him the burying her Brother tho' againſt his Order, was a popular Action. And that the People would reſent her being puniſh'd: But never ſo much as mentions his own Concern unleſs in one Line; which was ſo obſcure that *Creon* miſunderſtood him. *Antigone* amongſt her other Misfortunes laments her dying Young and Single, but ſays not one word about *Hæmon.* The *Poet* takes care not to bring theſe two Lovers upon the *Stage* together, for fear they might prove unmanagable? Had They been with us, they had met with kinder treatment. They might have had Interviews and Time and Freedom enough. Enough to mud their Fancy, to tarniſh their Quality, and make their Paſſion Scandalous. In the Relation of *Hæmons* Death, his Love is related too, and that with all the Life and *Pathos* imaginable.

Oedip. Tyran. Ed Steph.

Antig 242. 244.

aginable. But the Description is within
the Terms of Honour: The tendernesses
are Solemn, as well as Soft: They move
to Pity and Concern, and go no farther.

Ibdi. 264,

In his *Trachiniæ* the *Chorus* owns the Force
of Love next to irresistable; gently hints
the Intrigues of the Gods, and then passes

Tracb, 348.

on to a handsome Image of the Combat
between *Achelous* and *Hercules*. We see
how lightly the *Poet* touches upon an a-
morous Theme: He glides along like a
Swallow upon the Water, and skims the
Surface, without dipping a Feather.

Sophocles will afford us no more, let us
therefore take a view of *Euripides*. 'Tis
the Method of this Author to decline the
Singularities of the *Stage*, and to appear
with an Air of Conversation. He delivers
great Thoughts in Common Language,
and is dress'd more like a Gentleman than
a *Player*. His Distinction lies in the per-
spicuity of his Stile; In Maxim, and
Moral Reflection; In his peculiar Happiness for touching the Passions, especially
that of Pity: And lastly, in exhausting
the Cause, and arguing *pro* and *Con*, upon the streach of Reason. So much by
way of Character. And as for the Matter before us He is entirely Ours. We
have had an Instance or two already in
Electra and *Phædra*: To go on to the rest.
In his *Hippolitus* He calls *Whoring*, stupid-
nefs

ness and playing the Fool. And to be
Chast and regular, is with him, as well as
with *Æschylus*, Σωφρονᾶι. As much as to say
'tis the Consequence of Sence, and right
Thinking. *Phædra* when her Thoughts
were embarrass'd with *Hippolitus*, endeavours to disentangle her self by Argument.
She declaims with a great deal of Satyr a-
gainst intemperate Women; she conclud-
ed rather to die then dishonour her Husband and Stain her Family. The Blemishes of Parents, as she goes on, often
stuck upon their Children, and made them
appear with Disadvantage. Upon this,
the *Chorus* is transported with the Virtue of her Resolution and crys out

Μωεία τὸ
Κᾶϱϱν.
Ed Cant.
241:
250:
252.

Φεῦ Φεῦ. Τὸ σῶφϱον ὡς ἀπανταχῦ καλὸν
καὶ δὸ ξαν ἰσθλὴν ἐνϐϱοτοῖς κομίζεται.

Ibid.
232.
233.

How becoming a Quality is Modesty in all
  Places.
How strangly does it burnish a Character, and
  oblige ones Reputation?

The Scholiast upon these verses of *Hip-*
politus.

Σοὶ τὸν ἀ πλεκτὸν Στέφανον ἐξ ἀκηράτε
Λειμῶνθ, &c.

Makes this Paraphrase. 'That a *Poets*
'Mind should be clean and unsullied: And
                                                  'that

'that the Muses being Virgins their Per-
'formances should agree with their Con-
'dition.

To proceed. *Hermione* complains a-
gainst *Andromache* because she was entertain'd by her Husband: For this *Andro-*
mache tells her she talk'd too much for a
Young Woman, and discover'd her Opinion too far. *Achilles* at the first Sight of
Clytemnestra, lets her understand he was as
much taken with the Sobriety of her Air,
as with the rest of her fine Face and Person. She receives the Complement kindly, and commends him for commending
Modesty. *Menelaus* and *Helen* after a long
Absence manage the surprize of their
good Fortune handsomly. The Most tender Expressions stands clear of ill Meaning. Had *Osmin* parted with *Almeria* as
civilly as these Two met, it had been
much better. That Rant of smut and profainness might have been spared. The *Rea-*
der shall have some of it.

O my Almeria *;*
What do the Damn'd endure but to despair,
But knowing Heaven, to know it lost for ever.

Were it not for the *Creed*, these *Poets*
would be crampt in their Courtship, and
Mightily at a loss for a Simile! But *Os-*
min is in a wonderful Passion. And
truly

(margin notes:) Androm. p. 303. — Iphig in Aulid. p. 51. — Helen. 277, 278. — Mourning. Bride. p. 36.

truly I think his Wits, are in some danger, as well as his Patience. You shall hear.

What are all Wracks, and Whips, and Wheels
      to this ;
Are they not soothing softness, sinking Ease,
And wasting Air to this?

Sinking Ease, and *Wasting Air,* I confess are strange comforts ; This Comparison is somewhat oddly equip'd, but Lovers like sick People may say what they please ! *Almeria* takes this Speech for a Pattern, and suits it exactly in her return.

O I am struck, thy words are Bolts of Ice?
Which shot into my Breast now melt and
    chill me.

Bolts of Ice? Yes most certainly ! For the Cold is struck up into her Head, as you may perceive by what follows.

I chatter, shake, and faint with thrilling
    Fears.

By the way 'tis a mighty wonder to hear a Woman Chatter ! But there is no jesting, for the Lady is very bad. She won't be held up by any Means, but Crys out.

——*lower yet, down down* ;

One would think she was learning a Spa-
nel to *Sett*. But there's something behind.

——*no more we'll lift our Eyes,*
But prone and dumb, Rot the firm Face of
    Earth,
With Rivers of inceffant scalding Rain.

¶These Figures are some of them as stiff as
Statues, and put me in mind of *Sylvesters*
Dubartas.

Now when the Winters keener breath began
To Cryftallize, the Baltick Ocean,
To glaze the Lakes, to bridle up the Floods,
And periwig with Snow the bald pate woods.

I take it, the other Verses are somewhat
of Kin to These, and shall leave them to
Mr. *Dryden's* Reflection. But then as for
Soothing Softness, Sinking Eafe, Wafting
Air, thrilling Fears, and inceffant scalding
Rain ; It puts me to another stand. For
to talk a little in the way of the *Stage.*
This Litter of *Epithetes* makes the *Poem*
look like a Bitch overstock'd with Pup-
pies, and sucks the Sence almost to skin
and Bone. But all this may pass in a *Play-*
house : False Rhetorick and false Jewells,
do well together. To return to *Euripides.*
Cassandra in reporting the Misfortunes of
                                        the

Spanish
Fryar.
Ep. Ded.

the *Greeks* ftops at the Adulteries of *Cly-temneſtra* and *Ægiala* And gives this hand-ſome reaſon for making a Halt.

Σιγᾶν ἄμεινον τἀισχεᾷ, μηδὲ μῦσα μοι
Γένοιτ ἀοιδὸς ἥτις ὑμνήσει κακά. *Troad. p. 146.*

*Foul Things are beſt unſaid, I am for no Muſe,
That loves to flouriſh on Debauchery.*

Some Things are dangerous in report, as well as practiſe, and many times a Diſeaſe in the Deſcription. This *Euripides* was aware of and manag'd accordingly, and was remarkably regular both in ſtile, and Manners. How wretchedly do we fall ſhort of the Decencies of Heatheniſm! There's nothing more ridiculous than Modeſty on our *Stage*. 'Tis counted an ill bred Quality, and almoſt ſham'd out of Uſe. One would think Mankind were not the ſame, that Reaſon was to be read Backward, and Vertue and Vice had changed Place. *Plain Dealer. p. 21.* *Provok'd Wife. p. 41.*

What then? Muſt Life be huddled over, Nature left imperfect, and the Humour of the Town not ſhown? And pray where lies the Grievance of all This? Muſt we relate whatever is done, and is every Thing fit for Repreſentation? is a Man that has the Plague proper to make a

Sight of? And muſt he needs come Abroad
when he breaths Infection, and leaves the
Tokens upon the Company? What then
muſt we know nothing? Look you! All
Experiments are not worth the making.
'Tis much better to be ignorant of a Diſeaſe then to catch it. Who would wound
himſelf for Information about Pain, or
ſmell a Stench for the ſake of the Diſcovery? But I ſhall have occaſion to en-
counter this Objection afterwards, * and
therefore ſhall diſmiſs it at preſent.

*Remarks
upon Quix-
ot.*

The *Play-houſe* at *Athens* has been hitherto in Order, but are there no Inſtances
to the contrary? Do's not *Ariſtophanes*
take great Liberties and make Women
ſpeak extraordinary Sentences? He do's
ſo. But his Precedent ſignifies nothing in
the caſe. For

1ſt. We have both the Reaſon of the
Thing, and all the Advantage of Authority on the other ſide. We have the Practiſe and Opinion of Men of much greater
Sence, and Learning then Himſelf. The
beſt Philoſophers and Poets; Criticks and
Orators, both Greek and Latin, both Antient and Modern, give the Cauſe againſt
him. But *Ariſtophanes* his own *Plays* are
ſufficient to ruin his Authority. For

1ſt, He diſcovers himſelf a downright
Atheiſt. This Charge will be eaſily Made
good

good againſt him by his Comparing his *Nubes* with other *Plays*. The Deſign of his *Nubes* was to expoſe *Socrates*, and make a Town jeſt of him. Now this Philoſopher was not only a Perſon of great Sence and Probity, but was likewiſe ſuppos'd to refine upon the Heathen Theology, to throw off the Fabulous part of it, and to endeavour to bring it back to the Standard of Natural Religion. And therefore *Juſtin Martyr* and ſome others of the *Fathers*, look'd on him as a Perſon of no Pagan Belief, and thought he ſuffer'd for the Unity of the God-Head. This Man *Ariſtophanes* makes fine ſport with as he fancies: He puts him in a Fools Coat, and then points at him. He makes *Socrates* inſtruct his Diſciple *Strepſiades* in a new Religion, and tell him that *he did uot own the Gods in the vulgar Notion.* He brings him in elſwhere affirming that the *Clouds are the only Deities.* Which is the ſame Laſh which *Juvenal* gives the *Jews*, becauſe they worſhip'd but one ſingle Soveraign Being.

Nub. Act. 1. Sc. 3. p. 104. Ed.Amſtel.

Nil praetr Nubes & Cæli numen adorant. Sat. 14

Socrates goes on with his Lecture of Divinity and declares very roundly that there is no ſuch thing as *Jupiter.* Afterwards he advances farther, and endeavours

p. 106.

to get *Strepsiades* under Articles to acknow-
ledge no other Gods, but *Chaos*, the *Clouds*,
and the *Tongue*. At last the *Poet* brings
the Philosopher to publick Pennance for
his Singularities. He sets fire to his *School*
for teaching Young People (as he pretends)
to dispute against Law and Justice; for
advancing Atheistick Notions, and bur-
lesquing the Religion of the Country.

That *Socrates* was no Atheist is clear
from Instances enough. To mention but
one. The Confidence he had in his *Dæ-
mon*, or *Genius* by which he governed his
Affairs puts it beyond all dispute. However 'tis plain *Aristophanes* was not of his
Religion. The *Comedian* was by no means
for correcting the Common Perswasion.
So that he must either be an Orthodox
Heathen or nothing at all. Let us see then
with what Respect he treats the Receiv'd
Divinities. This *Play*, where one would
not expect it, discovers somewhat of his
Devotion. In the beginning of it *Phidip-
pides*, who was a sort of *New-Market* Spark,
swears by *Jocky Neptune*, that he had a
strange Kindness for his Father *Strepsiades*.
upon this the old Man replies; *No Jocky,
if you love me ; that Deity has almost undone
me*. This was making somewhat bold
with *Neptune* who was *Jupiters* Brother,
Soveraign of a whole *Element*, and had no
less

Nub.
p. 110.

Act. 5.
p. 176.

Plat. Apol.
Socrat.

Nub. p. 86.

lefs than the Third Share of the Univerfe!
Certainly *Ariftophanes* had no Venture at
Sea, or elfe muft think the *Trident* figni-
fied but very little. But this is meer Ceremony to what follows. In his firft *Play*
Plutus pretends he had a mind to oblige
only Men of Probity, but *Jupiter* had
made him blind on purpofe that he might
not diftinguifh Honeft men from Knaves:
For to be plain *Jupiter* had a Pique againft
Good people. Towards the end of this
Comedy Mercury is abufed by *Cario*, and *Plut. A. 1.*
afts a ridiculous, and leffening part him- *Sc. 2.*
felf. Afterwards he complains heavily
that fince *Plutus* was cured of his Blind-
nefs, the bufinefs of Sacrifing fell off, and
the Gods were ready to ftarve. This *Mer-*
cury has the fame ill Ufage with the *Poets*,
Knaves, Informers, and Lewd Women;
From all this ftuff put together, his meaning is pretty plain, *viz.* That Religion
was no better than an Impofture fuppor-
ted by Art, and Ignorance: And that
when Men's Underftandings were awake,
and their Eyes a little open, they would
have more difcretion than to be at any
expence about the Gods.

This I take to be part of the Moral of
his Fable. If we look farther into him we
fhall fee more of his Mind. His *Ranæ*
makes Merry with the Heathen Scheme of

Heaven

Heaven and Hell. Here *Charon* and the *Stygian Frogs* are brought in Comically enough. And that you may understand his opinion more perfectly we are told, that He that Bilks his *Catamite* after a *Sodomitical* Abuse, is thrown into the Common shore of *Hades*. And what Company do you think he is lodg'd with? Why with those who Perjure themselves, with those who Kick their Fathers and Mothers?

Ran.
p. 188. It seems in the *Poets* Justice a Man might as good be false to his Oath, as to his Lewdness. To disappoint the *Stews*, is every jot as great a Crime; as to fly in the Face of Nature, and outrage our Parents. His Quartering his Malefactors thus critically, was without question on purpose to Banter the perswasion of future Punishment. In the same *Play Xanthias* bids *Æacus* answer him by *Jove*, Ὅς ἡμὶν ἐσὶν ὁμομασγίας. This little Scoundrel of a Slave has the Manners to make *Jupiters* Quality no better than his own. To go on with him: In his *Aves* he speaks out to purpose. Here *Pisthetærus* tells *Epops* that if the *Birds* would build a Castle in the Air, they might intercept the Fumes of the Sacrifices, and starve the Gods unless they would come too, and be Tributary. It seems the *Birds* had very good Pretences to execute this project; for they

were

were ancienter than *Jupiter* and *Saturn*, and
Govern'd before the Gods. And to fpeak
truth were more capable of the Function.
Their Advifer goes on to inform 535. 538.
them, that after they had built 546.
their penfile City, and fortifyed the Air,
their next bufinefs was to demand their
ancient Soveragnity : If *Jupiter* refufed
to quit, they were to declare a Holy War
againft Him, and the reft of the Confederate Gods, and to cut off the Commu-
nication between Heaven and Earth.
Piſthæterus grows very warm in his 542.
new Intereft, and fwears by *Jove* that
Men ought to Sacrifice to the *Birds*, and
not to *Jupiter*. And if things came
to a Rupture, and *Jupiter* grew Trouble- 582.
fome, he undertakes to fend a Detache-
ment of Eagles againft Him ; with Orders
to ftorm his Palace with Flambeaux, and
fire it about his Ears. At laft to
prevent the Calamities of a War, *Hercules* Ibid.
propofes an Accomodation, and is willing
Jupiter fhould Refign. *Neptune* calls him
a Block-head for his pains, becaufe he was
Heir at *Law*, and after *Jupiters* Deceafe
was of Courfe to fucceed in his Domini-
ons : Once more, and I have done :
In *Eirene*, *Trygæus* fpeaks in a menacing 602.
way. That unlefs *Jupiter* gave him Satisfaction in his bufinefs, he would inform
againft

Eiren.
616.

againſt Him as a diſaffected Perſon, and a betrayer of the Liberties of *Greece.* I might add many other Inſtances, and ſome more Scandalous than any I have mentioned ; But theſe are ſufficient to ſhew the Authors Sentiment : And is it any wonder an Atheiſt ſhould misbehave him-ſelf in point of Modeſty ? What can we expect leſs from thoſe who laugh at the Being of a God, at the Doctrines of Pro-vidence, and the Diſtinctions of Good and Evil ? A *Sceptick* has no notion of Con-ſcience, no Reliſh for Virtue, nor is under any Moral reſtraints from Hope or Fear. Such a one has nothing to do but to con-ſult his Eaſe, and gratifie his Vanity., and fill his Pocket. But how theſe Ends are compaſſed, he has no ſqueamiſhneſs, or Scruples about it. 'Tis true when the Methods of Lewdneſs will Take, they are generally moſt agreeable. This way ſuits their Talent, and ſcreens their pra-ctiſe, and obliges their Malice. For no-thing is a greater Eye-ſore to theſe Men, then Virtue and Regularity. What a pleaſure is it then to be admired for Miſ-cheif, to be reveng'd on Religion, and to ſee Vice proſper and improve under our Hands ! To return : Beſide *Ariſtophanes* ; Atheiſme, I have a Second objection to his Authority, and that is want of Judg-ment

ment. If we examine his *Plays* we shall
find his Characters improper, or ununi-
form; either wrong at first, or unsteady
in the Right. For the purpose. In his
Nubes. A. 3. S. 3. p. 146. 150. He puts
dirty expressions in the Mouth of his Man
of Probity, makes him declaim vitiously a-
gainst Vice, and Corrects scurrility with Impudence; Now what can be more idle
and senceless, than such Conduct as this?
Epecially when this *Juſtus* as he calls
him had told them in the beginning of
his speech, that People used to be well
flash'd for such Fooling, when Government and Discipline were in their due
Force. The *Chorus* of his *Ranæ* slides *p.* 142.
into the same Inconsistency of Pre- *p.* 200.
cept, and Practise. Farther, in the
Progress of this *Play*; *Æschylus* falls a
rallying contrary to his Humour, and jests
away his own Arguments at a very unseasonable Juncture, when he was disputing
for no less prize than the Laureatship.
This *Tragedian* after he had play'd 242.
a little with the Story of *Bellerophon*, goes
on in the same strain; And charges *Euripides* that he had furnish'd all sorts of People with Sawciness and Prattle. The
Schools and *Academies* were spoil'd by
this means; So that the Boys were often
whip'd, aud the Boatswains drubb'd, for

their

p. 244, their Chattering. These Comical Levities come with an ill Grace from *Æschylus*. His Character was quite different both in Reality, and in the *Play* before us. He is all along represented as a Person of a serious Temper, of a reserv'd Loftiness, Cholerick, and tender of his Honour to an Excess, and almost in a rage at the Affront of a Rival, and being forc'd to enter the Lists with *Euripides*. The case standing thus, neither the Man, nor the Business, would admit of Drolling. Another Instance of his want of Conduct we have in his *Concianotores*. Here *Blepyrus* and some others of his Legislative Assembly, talk at a very dirty insipid rate. The Lowest of the *Mob*, can hardly jest with less Wit, and more Lewdness. And to make their Discourse more remarkable; These douty Members were just going to the *House*, and had their Heads full of the Good of the Nation, when they entertain'd themselves thus decently. And are these little Buf- p. 700,
p. 708. foons fit to consult *de Arduis Regni, &c.* to give Authority to Law, and Rules for publick Life? Do's Ribaldry and Nonsence become the Dignity of their Station, and the Solemnity of their Office ? To make his *Parliament-Men* play the Fool thus egregiously, must needs have a great deal of Decorum, and State-Policy in the

Con-

Contrivance; And is juſt as wiſe as if a
Painter ſhould have Drawn them in the
Habit of *Jack-Puddings*, and *Merry-Andrews*.
But *Ariſtophanes* has ſtill higher Flights
of Abſurdity. He won't ſo much as ſpare
the Gods but makes them act theſe little
Parts of Clowniſhneſs and Infamy. *Bacchus* and *Hercules* in his *Ranæ* are forced to
talk Smut and rally like *Link-boys*, and
do almoſt all the Tricks of *Bartholomew-
Fair*. To mention ſomething that will
bear the quoting. *Bacchus* enquires of *Hercules* the readieſt way to *Hades*, or the o-
ther World. He bids him either Hang,
or Poyſon himſelf, and he can't miſs the
Road. This is *Hercules*'s Humour to a
Tittle ! And repreſents him as much to
the Life, as an *Ape* would do the *Grand* Ranæ
Signior at a publick Audience ! This p. 186.
with a ſhort Sentence or two of Lewd- p. 182.
neſs, is the hardeſt of *Hercules* his
Uſage : And 'tis well he eſcaped ſo;
for *Bacchus* is treated much worſe. He
appears under the diſadvantages of a
Clowniſh Debauſh, and a Coward. And
is terribly afraid of a *Spectre*. When p. 192.
he comes before *Æacus*, this Judge is ve- 194, 196.
ry rough with him ; and tries his pretences to a Deity by Baſtinado : *Bacchus* howls
in the drubbing and had almoſt ſpoil'd all. Act 2. Sc.
6.

Now

Now do's this paultry Behaviour agree
with the Heathen Theology, with the
Common Opinion concerning *Bacchus* and
Hercules ? Do's a *Blew-Cap* and a *Ladle*,
become the Sons of *Jupiter* and the Ob-
jects of Religious Worship ? Those who
at the lowest, were counted the Conque-
rors of the World, and more than Men
both by Birth and Enterprizes ? *Sopho-*
cles and *Euripides* make these two Persons manage at a quite different rate of
Decency. 'Tis no defence to say *Aristo-*
phanes wrot Comedy, and so was obliged
to make his Scenes more diverting. This
excuse I say is defective; for a Comedian
ought to imitate Life and Probability, no
less than a Tragedian. To Metomorphose
Characters, and present Contradictions to
Common Belief, is to write, *Farce* instead
of *Plays*. Such Comedians like *Thespis*
ought to have a travelling *Stage*, and take
the Air with *Porcupines* and *Dromedaryes*.
If 'tis said that Gravity and greatness
do's not suit the Compleaction and Entertainment of Comedy. To this I answer,
that therefore the *Persons* should be chosen accordingly. They should have nothing in their known Humour, and Condition too Noble, and solemn for Trifling. 'Tis *Horaces* advice.

Aut

Aut famam sequere, aut convenientia fingé
Scriptor. De. Art. Poet.

Let us remember that Operations always
refemble the Nature from whence they
flow. Great Perfons fhould therefore
have a correfpondent Behaviour affign'd
them. To make *Beings* much Superior
to the Biggeft of Mankind, talk below
the Leaft, is abfurd and ridicules. This
Ariftophanes feems fenfible of in his defence of *Æfchylus*. Here *Euripides* objeéts *Ranæ*
to *Æfchylus*, that he was too rumbling, *p. 242.*
noify, and bombaftick, over affeéting
that which *Horace* calls

Ampullas, & fefquipedalia Verba.

To this *Æfchylus* Anfwers, that the
Thoughts, and Defigns of *Heroes* muft be
deliver'd in Expreffions proportioned to
their Greatnefs. It being likely that the
Demi-Gods fpoke up to their Dignity
and Stature: And as they were diftinguifh'd by the richnefs of their Habit,
fo they had a more Magnificent Language
than other Mortals. To this *Euripides*
replys nothing ; from whence you may
conclude the *Poet* thought the Apology
not unreafonable. In fhort *Ariftophanes*
had

had Sense but he does not always use
it.　He is not equal, and uniforme. Sometimes you have him flat and foolish a good
while together. And where he has Spirit, 'tis
oftentimes lavished away to little purpose.
His Buffoonery is commonly too strong
for his Judgment. This makes him let
fly his jests without regard to Person
or occasion : And thus by Springing the
Game too soon, the Diversion is lost.
I could make several other Material Ob-
jections against the Conduct of his *Plays*;
But this being not necessary I shall observe in the

Ranæ A. 1.
Sc. 1. *Con-*
cionat.

3*d*. Place. That notwithstanding the
scandalous Liberty for which *Aristophanes*
is so remarkable ; yet in his Lucid In-
tervalls, when Sence and Sobriety return
upon him, he pronounces against his own
Practise. In the contest between *Æschylus*
and *Euripides, Bacchus* is made the Um-
pire of the Controversie. *Æschylus* begins
with a Question, and asks *Euripides*
what 'tis which makes a *Poet* admired? He answers. 'Tis for the address of his Conduct, and the handsome
Turns of Morality in his Poems. 'Tis
because his performance has a tendency
to form the Audience to Virtue, and Improvement. *Æschylus* demands of him
farther

Ranæ
p. 238.

farther ; But suppose you debauched the Age, and made an Honest and a brave People Lewd, and good for nothing, what do you deserve then? Here *Bacchus* interposes, and crys out, what does he deserve? A Halter! pray don't ask so plain a question. And afterwards we are told, that *Poets* are valuable only for describing Things useful, in Life and Religion, for polishing Inventions, and setting off great Examples with Lustre, and Advantage. In the progress of the Dispute, *Æschylus* taxes *Euripides* with being too uncautious in his Representations ; And tells him that Poets ought to conceal that which is vicious in Story ; And entertain with nothing but Virtue, and Sobriety : He goes on reprimanding *Euripides* for his Dramatick Incests, Strumpets, and Amours : And as for himself, to his best remembrance, He never brought any Love-Intrigues upon the Stage.

p. 240.

p. 242. 244.

This is very significant expostulation : and contains very good Rules for the Trial of the *Muses* : But if the English *Stage*, should be obliged to this Test ; *Aristophanes* must set fire to it, and that with much more reason than to *Socrates* his *School*. Now that *Æschylus* spoke *Aristophanes*'s Sense is pretty plain: For first ; As to the Business of Love, *Aristophanes* always

E

ways declines it; He never patches up a *Play* with *Courtship*, and *Whining*, tho' he wrote nothing but *Comedy*. In the next place the *Chorus* which is usually the *Poets* Interpreter, speaks honourably of *Æschylus* even to a Preference; And at last Judge *Bacchus* gives Sentence for him.

255. 267.

Thus we see *Aristophanes* Confutes his own Lewdness, and comes in Evidence against himself. This with the other two Exceptions I have made good against him, are sufficient to take off the Force of the *Precedent*, and make him an insignificant Authority.

To what I have observ'd from the *Stage* of the Antients, I could add the Authorities of *Aristotle*, and *Quintilian*, both extraordinary Persons, but I shall reserve their Testimony till Afterwards.

To come Home, and near our own Times: The English Theatre from Queen *Elizabeth* to King *Charles* II. will afford us something not inconsiderable to our purpose.

As for *Shakespear*, he is too guilty to make an Evidence : But I think he gains not much by his Misbehaviour ; He has commonly *Plautus*'s *Fate*, where there is most Smut, there is least Sense.

Ben. Johnson is much more reserv'd in his *Plays*, and declares plainly for

for Modesty in his *Discoveries*, some of his Words are these.

A just Writer whom he calls a *True Artificer*, will avoid *Obscene* and *Effeminate Phrase. Where Manners and Fashions are Corrupted, Language is so too. The excess of Feasts and Apparel, are the Notes of a Sick State, and the Wantonness of Language of a sick Mind.* A little after he returns to the Argument, and applies his Reasoning more particularly to the Stage. *Poetry,* (says he) *and Picture, both behold Pleasure, and profit, as their common Object, but should abstain from all base Pleasures, least they should wholly Err from their End ; And while they seek to better Men's Minds, Destroy their Manners, Insolent and obscene Speeches, and Jests upon the best Men, are most likely to excite Laughter. But this is truly leaping from the Stage to the Tumbrill again, reducing all Wit to the Original Dung-Cart.* More might be cited to this purpose, but that may serve for an other Occasion : In the mean time I shall go on to *Beaumont* and *Fletcher.*

Fletchers Faithfull Shepheardess is remarkably Moral, and a sort of Exhortation to Chastity. This *Play* met with ill Judges, 'twas Hiss'd before half *Acted,* and seems to have suffer'd on the account of its Innocence. Soon after *Ben. Johnson*

Discov. p. 700.

p. 701.

p. 706. 717.

Beaumont, &c. Works.

E 2   and

and *Beaumont* appear justifying the Author in a Copy of Verses. And as *Beaumont,* commends Modesty in *Fletcher,* so he is commended himself by Mr. *Earl* for the same Quality.

Ibid.

Such Passions, Such Expressions meet my Eye, Such Wit untainted with Obscenity.

Ibid.

And as I remember *Jasper Main* has some stroaks to the same purpose. *Fletcher* is still more full for the Cause. Indeed nothing can be more express. He delivers himself by way of *Prologue*; where the *Poet* speaks in his own Person. The *Prologue* to the *Woman-Hater,* very frankly lets the Audience know what they are to expect. *If there be any amongst you, (says he) that come to hear Lascivious Scenes, let them depart; For I do pronounce this, to the utter discomfort of all two-penny Gallery Men, you shall no Bawdry in it.* We find in those days Smut was the expectation of a Coarse Palate, and relish'd by none but two-penny Customers. In the *Knight* of the *Burning Pestle,* part of the *Prologue* runs thus. *They were banish'd the Theatre at* Athens, *and from* Rome *hiss'd, that brought Parasites on the Stage with Apish Actions, or Fools with uncivil Habits, or Courtezans with immodest words.* Afterwards *Prologue,* who represents a Person, gives us more to the same purpose.

——— *Fly*

—————Fly far from hence
All private taxes, immodeſt phraſes,
Whatever may but look like Vitious.
For wicked mirth, never true Pleaſure brings;
For honeſt Minds, are pleas'd with honeſt things.

I have quoted nothing but Comedy in this Author. The *Coronation* is another. And the *Prologue* tells you there is

No Undermirth ſuch as does lard the Scene,
For Coarſe Delight, the Language here is clean,
And confident our Poet bad me ſay,
He'll bate you but the Folly of a Play.
For which altho' dull Souls his Pen deſpiſe;
Who think it yet too early to be wiſe.
The Nobles yet will thank his Muſe, at leaſt
Excuſe him, cauſe his Thought aim'd at the
    Beſt.

Thus theſe *Poets* are in their Judgments clearly ours. 'Tis true their Hand was not always ſteady. But thus much may be aver'd, that *Fletcher's* later *Plays* are the moſt inoffenſive. This is either a ſign of the *Poets* Reformation; or that the exceptionable Paſſages belong'd to *Beaumont,* who dyed firſt.

To theſe Authorities of our own Nation, I ſhall add a conſiderable Teſtimony out of Mr. *Corneille.* This Author was

E 3   ſenſi-

sensible that tho' the Expression of his *Theodore* was altogether unsmutty, 'Yet 'the bare Idea of Prostitution uneffected, 'shock'd the Audience, and made the Play 'miscarry. The *Poet* protests he took great 'care to alter the natural Complexion of 'the Image, and to convey it decently to 'the Fancy ; and deliver'd only some 'part of the History as inoffensively as pos- 'sible. And after all his Screening and Con- 'duct, the Modesty of the Audience would 'not endure that little, the Subject forced 'him upon. He is positive 'the Comedies St. '*Augustine* declaim'd against, were not 'such as the *French*. For theirs are not spe- 'ctacles of Turpitude, as that Father justly 'calls those of his Time. The *French* ge- 'nerally speaking, containing nothing but 'examples of Innocence, Piety and Virtue.

In this Citation we have the Opinion of the *Poet*, the Practise of the *French* The-atre, and the Sense of that *Nation*, and all very full to our purpose.

To conclude this *Chapter*. By what has been offer'd, it appears that the *Present English Stage* is superlatively Scandalous. It exceeds the Liberties of all Times and Coun-tries : It has not so much as the poor plea of a *Precedent*, to which most other ill Things may claim a pretence. 'Tis most-ly meer Discovery and Invention : A new World

World of Vice found out, and planted with all the Induſtry imaginable. *Ariſto-phanes* himſelf, how bad ſoever in other reſpects, does not amplyfie, and flouriſh, and run through all the Topicks of Lewdneſs like theſe Men. The *Miſcellany Poems* are likewiſe horribly Licentious. They are ſometimes Collections from Antiquity, and often, the worſt parts of the worſt *Poets*. And to mend the Matter, the Chriſtian*Tranſlation*, is more nauſeous than the *Pagan* Original. Such ſtuff I believe was never ſeen, and ſuffer'd before. In a word, If Poverty and Diſeaſes, the Diſhonour of Families, and the Debauching of Kingdoms, are ſuch valuable Advantages, then I confeſs theſe Books deſerve encouragement. But if the Caſe is otherwiſe, I humbly conceive the Proceeding ſhould be ſo too.

CHAP. II.

The Profaneſs of the Stage.

AN other Inſtance of the Diſorders of the *Stage* is their *Profaneſs* : This Charge may come under theſe two particulars.

1ſt. *Their Curſing and Swearing.*

2dly. *Their Abuſe of Religion and Holy Scripture.*

1ſt *Their Curſing and Swearing.*

What is more frequent then their wiſhes of Hell, and Confuſion, Devils and Diſeaſes, all the Plagues of this World, and the next, to each other ? And as for Swearing ; 'tis uſed by all Perſons, and upon all Occaſions: By Heroes, and Paltroons ; by Gentlemen, and Clowns : Love, and Quarrels, Succeſs, and Diſappointment, Temper, and Paſſion, muſt be varniſh'd, and ſet off with *Oaths*. At ſome times, and with ſome *Poets* Swearing is no ordinary Releif. It ſtands up in the room of Senſe, gives Spirit to a flat Expreſſion, and makes a Period Muſical and Round. In ſhort, 'tis almoſt all the Rhetorick,

rick, and Reason some People are Masters
of: The manner of performance is different. Some times they mince the matter ;
change the Letter, and keep the
Sense, as if they had a mind to steal

Gad for God.

a Swearing, and break the Commande-
ment without Sin. At another time the
Oaths are clipt, but not so much within the Ring, but that the *Image and
Superscription* are visible. These expedients, I conceive are more for variety,
then Conscience: For when the fit comes
on them, they make no difficulty of
Swearing at Length. Instances of all these
kinds may be met with in the *Old Batchelour*, *Double Dealer*, and *Love for Love*.
And to mention no more, *Don Quixot*,
the *Provok'd Wife*, and the *Relapse*, are
particularly rampant and scandalous. The
English Stage exceed their predecessors
in this, as well as other Branches of
immorality. *Shakespear* is comparatively
sober, *Ben Jonson* is still more regular ;
And as for *Beaument* and *Fletcher*, In their
Plays they are commonly Profligate Persons that Swear, and even those are re-
prov'd for't. Besides, the Oaths are not
so full of Hell and Defiance, as in the
Moderns.

So much for matter of Fact: And as
for point of Law, I hope there needs not
many

many words to prove Swearing a Sin: For what is more provoking than contempt, and what Sin more contemptuous than commonSwearing? what can be more Insolent and Irreligious, than to bring in God to atteſt our Trifles, to give Security for our Follies, and to make part of our Diverſion? To Play with Majeſty and Omnipotence in this manner, is to render it cheap and deſpicable. How can ſuch Cuſtomes as theſe conſiſt with the belief of Providence or Revelation? The *Poets* are of all People moſt to blame. They want even the Plea of *Bullies* and *Sharpers*. There's no Rencounters, no ſtarts of Paſſion, no ſuddain Accidents to diſcompoſe them. They ſwear in Solitude and cool Blood, under Thought and Deliberation, for Buſineſs, and for Exerciſe: This is a terrible Circumſtance; It makes all *Malice Prepence*, and enflames the Guilt, and the Reckoning.

And if Religion ſignifies nothing, (as I am afraid it does with ſome People) there is Law, as well as Goſpel againſt *Swearing*. 3d, *Jac.* 1. *cap.* 21. is expreſly againſt the *Playhouſe*. It runs thus.

FOR the preventing and avoiding of the great abuſe of the holy Name of God, in Stage Plays, Enterludes &c. Be it enacted by our Sovereign Lord &c. That if at any time, or times, after

after the End of this present Session of Parliament ; any Person or Persons do, or shall, in any Stage Play, Enterlude, Shew &c.   Jeastingly or Profanly, speak or use the holy Name of God, or of Christ Jesus, or of the holy Ghost, or of the Trinity, which are not to be spoken, but with Fear and Reverence ; shall forfeit for every such offence, by him or them committed, ten pounds: The one Moity thereof to the King's Majesty, his Heirs ; and Successors, the other Moity thereof to him, or them, that will sue for the same in any Court of Record at Westminster, wherein no essoin, protection, or wager of Law shall be allow'd.

By this *Act* not only direct Swearing, but all vain Invocation of the Name of God is forbidden.   This *Statute* well executed would mend the *Poets,* or sweep the *Box :* And the *Stage* must either reform, or not thrive upon Profaneß.

3dly Swearing in the *Playhouse* is an ungentlemanly, as well as an unchriftian Practice. The *Ladies* make a considerable part of the *Audience.* Now Swearing before Women is reckon'd a Breach of good Behaviour, and therefore a civil Atheift will forbear it.   The cuftom feems to go upon this Presumption ; that the Impreffions of Religion are ftrongeft in Women, and more generally fpread.   And that it muft be very difagreeable to them, to hear the Majefty of God treated with ſo little reſpect. Beſides : Oaths are a boiſtrous and tempeſtiuous ſort of Converſation ; Generally the effects of Paſſion, and ſpoken with Noiſe, and Heat. Swearing looks like the beginning of a Quarrel, to which Women have an averſion : As being neither armed by Nature, nor diſciplin'd by Cuſtome for ſuch rough Diſputes. A Woman will ſtart at a Soldiers Oath, almoſt as much as at the Report of his Piſtol : And therefore a well Bred Man will no more Swear, than Fight in the Company of Ladies.

A *Second* Branch of the Profaneſs of the *Stage* is their Abuſe of Religion, and *Holy Scripture*. And here ſometimes they don't ſtop ſhort of Blaſphemy. To cite all that might be Collected of this kind would be tedious. I ſhall give the *Reader* enough to juſtifie the Charge, and I hope to abhor the Practice.

To begin with the *Mock-Aſtrologer.* In the Firſt *Act* the *Scene* is a *Chappel* ; And that the Uſe of ſuch Conſecrated places may be the better underſtood, the time is taken up in Courtſhip, Raillery, and ridiculing Devotion. *Jacinta* takes her turn among the reſt. She Interrupts *Theodoſia*, and cries out : *why Siſter, Siſter —— will you pray ? what injury have I ever done you that you pray in my Company?*
Wild

Wildblood Swears by *Mahomet*, rallies smuttily upon the other World, and gives the
preference to the Turkiſh Paradiſe! This *p.* 31.
Gentleman to incourage *Jacinta* to a Com-
plyance in Debauchery, tells her *Heaven* p. 37.
is all Eyes and no Tongue. That is, it ſees
Wickedneſs but conceals it. He Courts
much at the ſame rate a little before.
When a Man comes to a great Lady, he is
fain to approach her with Fear, and Reve-
rence, methinks there's ſomething of Godli- p. 24.
neſs in't. Here you have the Scripture
burleſqu'd, and the Pulpit Admonition ap- *Hebr.* 12.
ply'd to Whoring. Afterwards *Jacinta*
out of her great Breeding and Chriſtianity, ſwears by *Alla*, and *Mahomet*, and 34. 36.
makes a Jeſt upon Hell. *Wildblood* tells
his Man that *ſuch undeſigning Rogues as*
he, make a Drudge of poor Providence. And
Maskall to ſhow his proficiency under his
Maſters, replies to *Bellamy*, who would
have had him told a Lie. *Sir upon the* 55.
Faith of a Sinner you have had my laſt Lie
already. I have not one more to do me Cre-
dit, as I hope to be ſaved Sir.

In the cloſe of the *Play*, They make
ſport with Apparitions and Fiends. One
of the Devils ſneezes, upon this they give
him the Bleſſing of the Occaſion, and conclude *he has got cold by being too long out* 59.
of the Fire.

The

The *Orphan* lays the Scene in Christen-
dom, and takes the same care of Religion.
Castalio Complements his Mistress to
Adoration.

Orph. p.
20.

> *No Tongue my Pleasure and my Pain can tell:*
> *'Tis Heaven to have thee, and without thee Hell.*

Polydor when upon the attempt to debauch *Monimia* puts up this ejaculation.

p. 31.

> *Blessed Heaven assist me but in this dear Hour:*

Thus the *Stage* worships the true God in
Blasphemy, as the *Lindians* did *Hercules*
Lactan.   by Cursing and throwing stones. This
Polydor has another Flight of Profaness,
but that has got a certain *Protection*, and
therefore must not be disturb'd.

In the *Old Batchelour*, *Vain-love* asks *Belmour, could you be content to go to Heaven?*

p. 19.

Bell. Hum, not immediatly in my Con-
science, not heartily. —— This is playing I
take it with Edge-Tools. To go to Heaven in jeast, is the way to go to Hell in
earnest. In the Fourth *Act*, Lewdness is
represented with that Gaity, as if the
Crime was purely imaginary, and lay only in ignorance and preciseness. *Have you*
throughly consider'd (says Fondlewife) how
detestable, how Heinous, and how crying a Sin

the

*the Sin of Adultery is ? have you weighed I
say ? For it is a very weighty Sin : and altho'
it may lie——yet thy Husband must also bear
his part* ; *For thy iniquity will fall on his Head.*
I suppose this fit of Buffoonry and profaness, was to settle the Conscience of young
Beginners, and to make the Terrors of
Religion insignificant. *Bellmour* desires
*Latitia to give him leave to swear by her Eyes.
and her Lips* : He kisses the Strumpet, and
tells her, *Eternity was in that Moment.*
Latitia is horibly profane in her Apology
to her Husband ; but having the *Stage-
Protection* of Smut for her Guard, we
must let her alone. *Fondlewife* stalks under the same shelter, and abuses a plain
Text of Scripture to an impudent Meaning.
A little before, *Latitia* when her Intrigue
with *Bellmour* was almost discover'd, supports her self with this Consideration. *All
my comfort lies in his impudence, and Heaven be prais'd, he has a Considerable Portion.*
This is the *Play-house* Grace, and thus
Lewdness is made a part of Devotion !
Ther's another Instance still behind : 'Tis
that of *Sharper* to *Vain-Love,* and lies
thus.

*I have been a kind of God Father to you,
yonder : I have promis'd and vow'd something
in your Name, which I think you are bound
to Perform.* For Christians to droll upon
their

p. 28.

p. 31.

33.

p. 39.

p. 39.

Ib.
49.

their Baptism is somewhat extraordinary ;
But since the *Bible* can't escape, 'tis the
less wonder to make bold with the *Ca-*
techisme.

In the *Double Dealer*, Lady *Plyant* cries
out *Jesu* and talks Smut in the same Sentence. Sr. *Paul Plyant* whom the Poet
dub'd a Fool when he made him a Knight,
talks very Piously ! *Blessed be Providence,*
a Poor unworthy Sinner, I am mightily be-
holden to Providence : And the same word
is thrice repeated upon an odd occasion.
The meaning must be that *Providence* is
a ridiculous supposition, and that none
but Blockheads pretend to Religion. But
the Poet can discover himself farther if
need be. Lady *Froth* is pleas'd to call *Jehu*
a *Hackney Coachman.* Upon this, *Brisk* replies, *If Jehu was a Hackney Coachman,*
I am answer'd —— you may put that into
the Marginal Notes tho', to prevent Criti-
cisms —— only mark it with a small Aste-
risme and say, —— Jehu was formerly a
Hackney Coachman. This for a heavy Piece
of Profaness, is no doubt thought a lucky
one, because it burlesques the Text, and
the Comment, all under one. I could go
on with the *Double Dealer* but he'll come
in my way afterwards, and so I shall
part with him at present. Let us now
take a veiw of *Don Sebastian.* And here
the

Double
Dealer.
34.

36.

55.

p. 40.

the *Reader* can't be long unfurnifh'd. *Dorax* fhall fpeak firft.

   Shall I truft Heaven
With my revenge ? then where's my fatis-
   faction ?   *Sebaft.*
No, it muft be my own, I fcorn a Proxy. *p. 9.*

But *Dorax* was a Renegado, what then? He had renounc'd Chriftianity, but not Providence. Befides ; fuch hideous Sentences ought not to be put in the Mouth of the Devil. For that which is not fit to be heard, is not fit to be fpoken. But to fome People an Atheiftical Rant is as good as a Flourifh of Trumpets. To proceed. *Antonio* tho' a profefs'd Chriftian, mends the matter very little. He is looking on a Lot which he had drawn for his Life : This proving unlucky, after the preamble of a Curfe or two, he calls it,

As black as Hell, an other lucky faying !
I think the Devils in me :——good again,
I cannot fpeak one fyllable but tends   *Id. p. 10.*
To Death or to Damnation.

Thus the Poet prepares his Bullies for the other World ! Hell and Damnation are ftrange entertaining words upon the *Stage* ! Were it otherwife, the Senfe in thefe
               F.   Lines,

Lines, would be almoſt as bad as the Conſcience. The *Poem* warms and riſes in
the working : And the next Flight is extreamly remarkable :

p. 47.

Not the laſt ſounding could ſurprize me more,
That ſummons drowſy Mortals to their doom,
When call'd in haſt they fumble for their Limbs:

Very Solemnly and Religiouſly expreſs'd !
Lucian and *Celſus* could not have ridiculed the Reſurrection better ! Certainly the
Poet never expects to be there. Such a
light Turn would have agreed much better to a Man who was in the Dark, and
was feeling for his Stockings. But let
thoſe who talk of *Fumbling* for their
Limbs, take care they don't find them too
faſt. In the Fourth *Act Muſtapha* dates
his *Exaltation to Tumult, from the ſecond*
Id. p. 83.
Exod. 12,
13. *Night of the Month* Abib. Thus you have
the Holy Text abuſed by Captain *Tom* ;
And the Bible torn by the Rabble ! The
Deſign of this Liberty I can't underſtand,
unleſs it be to make *Muſtapha* as conſiderable as *Moſes* ; and the prevalence of a
Tumult, as much a Miracle as the Delive-
rance out of *Ægypt.* We have heard this Author hitherto in his *Characters,* let us hear
him now in his own Perſon. In his *De-*
dication of *Aurenge Zebe* he is ſo hardy as
to

to affirm that *he who is too lightly reconciled after high Provocation, may Recommend himself to the World for a Christian, but I should hardly trust him for a Friend.* And, why is a Christian not fit to make a Friend of? Are the Principles of Christianity defective, and the Laws of it Ill contriv'd? Are the Interests and Capacities of Mankind overlook'd? Did our Great Master bind us to Disadvantage, and make our Duty our Misfortune? And did he grudge us all the Pleasures and Securities of Friendship? Are not all these horrid Suppositions? Are they not a flat Contradiction to the *Bible*, and a Satyr on the Attributes of the Deity? Our Saviour tells us we must *forgive until Seventy times Seven*; That is, we must never be tired out of Clemency and Good Nature. He has taught us to pray for the Forgiveness of our own Sins, only upon the Condition of forgiving others. Here is no exception upon the Repetition of the Fault, or the Quality of the Provocation. Mr. *Dryden* to do him right, do's not dispute the Precept. He confesses this is the way to be a Christian: But for all that he *should hardly trust him for a Friend.* And why so? Because the Italian Proverb says, *He that forgives the second time is a Fool.* This Lewd Proverb comes in for Authority,

Ibid.

F 2 and

and is a piece of very pertinent Blaſphemy! Thus in ſome Peoples *Logick* one
proof from Atheiſm, is worth Ten from
the *New Teſtament*. But here the *Poet* argues no better than he Believes. For moſt
certainly, a Chriſtian of all others is beſt
qualifyed for Friendſhip. For He that loves
his Neighbour as himſelf, and carries Be-
nevolence and Good Nature beyond the
Heights of Philoſophy: He that is not
govern'd by Vanity, or Deſign; He that
prefers his Conſcience to his Life, and
has Courage to Maintain his Reaſon; He
that is thus qualified muſt be a good Friend;
And he that falls ſhort, is no good Chriſtian. And ſince the *Poet* is pleas'd to find
fault with Chriſtianity, let us examine his
own Scheme. *Our Minds (ſays he) are
perpetually wrought on by the Temperament of
our Bodies, which makes me ſuſpect they are
nearer Allyed than either our Philoſophers,
or School Divines will allow them to be.* The
meaning is, he ſuſpects our Souls are nothing but Organiz'd Matter. Or in plain
Engliſh, our *Souls* are nothing but our Bodies. And then when the Body dies you may
gueſs what becomes of them! Thus the
Authorities of Religion are weaken'd, and
the proſpect of the other World almoſt ſhut
up. And is this a likely Suppoſition for Sin-
cerity and good Nature? Do's Honour
uſe

Ibid.

ufe to rife upon the Ruines of Confcience?
And are People the beft Friends where
they have the leaft Reafon to be fo?
But not only the Inclinations to Friend-
fhip muft Languifh upon this Scheme,
but the very Powers of it are as it were
deftroy'd. By this Syfteme no Man can
fay his Soul is his own. He can't be
affured the fame Colours of Reafon and
Defire will laft. Any little Accident
from *without* may metamorphofe his Fancy, and pufh him upon a new fet of
Thoughts. *Matter* and *Motion* are the
moft Humorfom Capricious Things in Nature; and withall, the moft Arbitrary and
uncontroll'd. And can Conftancy proceed
from Chance, Choice from Fate, and Virtue from Neceffity? In fhort a Man at
this rate muft be a Friend or an Enemy in
fpite of his Teeth, and juft as long as
the *Atoms* pleafe and no longer. Every
Change in *Figure* and *Impulfe*, muft alter
the Idea, and wear off the former Impref-
fion. So that by thefe Principles, Friend-
fhip will depend on the *Seafons*, and we
muft look in the *Weather Glafs* for our
Inclinations. But this 'tis to Refine upon
Revelation, and grow wifer than Wif-
dom! The fame Author in his Dedication of *Juvenal* and *Perfius*, has thefe words:
My Lord, I am come to the laft Petition of Ded. ⁂. 51.
F 3 Abraham;

Abraham; *If there be ten Righteous Lines in this vaſt Preface, ſpare it for their ſake; and alſo ſpare the next City becauſe it is but a little one.* Here the Poet ſtands for *Abraham*; and the Patron for God Almighty: And where lies the Wit of all this? In the Decency of the Compariſon? I doubt not. And for the *next City* he would have ſpared, he is out in the Alluſion. 'Tis no *Zoar*, but much rather *Sodom* and *Gomorrah*, Let them take care the Fire and Brimſtone does not follow: And that thoſe who are ſo bold with *Abraham*'s Petition, are not forced to that of *Dives*. To beg Protection for a Lewd Book in *Scripture Phraſe*, is very extraordinary! 'Tis in effect to Proſtitute the Holy Rhetorick, and ſend the *Bible* to the *Brothell*! I can hardly imagin why theſe Tombs of Antiquity were raked in, and diſturb'd? Unleſs it were to conjure up a departed Vice, and revive the Pagan Impurities: Unleſs it were to raiſe the Stench of the Vault, and Poyſon the Living with the Dead. Indeed *Juvenal* has a very untoward way with him in ſome of his Satyrs. His Pen has ſuch a Libertine ſtroak that 'tis a Queſtion whether the Practiſe, or the Reproof, the Age, or the Author, were the more Licentious. He teaches thoſe Vices he would correct

correct, and writes more like a Pimp,
than a *Poet*. And truly I think there is
but little of Lewdness loft in the *Tran-
flation*. The Sixth and Eleventh *Satyrs*
are Particularly remarkable. Such nau-
feous ftuff is almoft enough to debauch
the *Alphabet*, and make the Language
fcandalous. One would almoft be forry
for the privilege of *Speech*, and the Invention of *Letters*, to fee them thus wretchedly abufed. And fince the Bufinefs muft
be undertaken, why was not the Thought
Blanched, the Expreffion made remote,
and the ill Features caft into fhadows ?
I'm miftaken if we have not Lewdnefs
enough of our own Growth, without Im-
porting from our Neighbours. No. This
can't be. An Author muft have Right
done him, and be fhown in his own fhape,
and Complexion. Yes by all means *!*
Vice muft be difrobed, and People poy-
fon'd, and all for the fake of Juftice *!*
To do Right to fuch an Author is to burn
him. I hope Modefty is much better
than Refemblance. The Imitation of an
ill Thing is the worfe for being exact :
And fometimes to report a Fault is to
repeat it.

To return to his *Plays*. In *Love Triumphant*, *Garcia* makes *Veramond* this Compliment :

Love Tri-
umph. p. 3. *May Heaven and your brave Son, and a-
bove all,*
Your own prevailing Genius guard your Age.

What is meant by his Genius, in this
place, is not eaſy to Diſcover, only that 'tis
ſomething which is a better Guard than
Heaven. But 'tis no Matter for the Senſe,
as long as the Profaneſs is clear. In this
Act, Colonel *Sancho* lets *Carlos* know the
old Jew is dead, which he calls good
news.

Carl. *What Jew?*
Sanch. *Why the rich Jew my Father, He
is gone to the Boſom, of* Abraham *his Father,*
Id. p. 11. *and I his Chriſtian Son am left ſole Heir.*
A very mannerly Story! But why does
the Poet acquaint us with *Sanchos* Religion? The caſe is pretty plain: 'tis to give
a luſtre to his Profaneſs, and make him
burleſque St. *Luke* with the better Grace.
Id. p. 11. *Alphonſo* complains to *Victoria* that *Nature doats with Age.* His reaſon is, becauſe
Brother and Siſter can't Marry as they
did at firſt: 'Tis very well! We know
what *Nature* means in the Language of
Chriſtianity, and eſpecially under the Notion of a Law-giver. *Alphonſo* goes on,
and compares the Poſſeſſion of Inceſtuous
Love to Heaven. Yes, 'tis *Eternity in*
P. 34. *Little.*

It

It seems Lovers must be distracted or there's no diversion. A Flight of Madness like a Faulcons *Lessening*, makes them the more gaz'd at! I am now coming to some of the Poets Divinity. And here *Vengeance is said to be so sweet a Morsel,*

That Heaven reserves it for its proper Tast. 58.

This belike is the meaning of those Texts, *that God is good and Gracious, and slow to anger, and does not willingly afflict the Children of Men!* From expounding the Bible he goes to the *Common Prayer.* And as *Carlos* interprets the *Office* of *Matrimony,* **For Better, for Worse,** is *for Virgin for Whore*; And that the Reference might not be mistaken, the Poet is careful to put the Words in *Italick,*and great Letters. And by the way, He falls under the *Penalty* of the Statute for Depraving the *Common Prayer.* p. 62. 1st. Eliz. cap. 2.

Sancho upon reading a Letter which he did not like, cries *Damn it, it must be all Orthodox. Damn* and *Orthodox* clapt together, make a lively Rant, because it looks like Cursing the *Creed.* The most extraordinary Passage is behind; *Sancho* was unhappily Married: *Carlos tells him, For your Comfort, Marriage they say is Holy.* *Sancho* replies: *Ay, and so is Martyrdom as they say, but both of them are good for just nothing, but to make an end of a Mans Life.* p. 63.

p. 72.

I

I ſhall make no Reflections upon This:
There needs no Reading upon a Monſter : 'Tis ſhown enough by its own
Deformity. *Love for Love* has a Strain
like this, and therefore I ſhall put them
together : *Scandal* ſolicits Mrs. *Foreſight* ;
She threatens to tell her Husband. He

Love for
Love.
P. 49.

replys, *He will die a Martyr rather then
diſclaim his Paſſion.* Here we have Adultery dignified with the ſtile of Martyrdom : As if 'twas as Honourable to periſh
in Defence of Whoring, as to dye for the
Faith of Chriſtianity. But theſe *Martyrs.*
will be a great while in burning, And
therefore let no body ſtrive to grace the
Adventure, or encreaſe the Number. And
now I am in this *Play* the Reader ſhall
have more. *Jeremy* who was bred at the
Univerſity, calls the Natural Inclinations
to Eating and Drinking, *Whoreſon Appetites.* This is ſtrange Language ! The
Manicheans who made Creation the work

26.

of the Devil, could ſcarcely have been thus
Coarſe. But the *Poet* was *Jeremy's* Tutor,
and ſo that Myſtery is at an end. Sr.
Samſon carries on the Expoſtulation, rails
at the Structure of Human Bodies, and

P. 27.

ſays, *Nature has been Provident only to
Bears, and Spiders* ; This is the Authors
Paraphraſe on the 139 *Pſalm* ; And thus
he gives God thanks for the Advantage
of

of his Being ! The *Play* advances from
one wickedneſs to another, from the *Works*
of God, to the Abuſe of his Word.
Foreſight *confeſſes 'tis Natural for Men to
miſtake.* Scandal *replies, You ſay true,* Man
will err, meer Man will err——*but you are
ſomething more*—— *There have been wiſe
Men ; but they were ſuch as you*—— *Men
who conſulted the Stars, and were obſervers
of Omens*—— Solomon *was wiſe but how ?*
—— *by his Judgment in Aſtrology.* 'Tis
very well ! *Solomon* and *Foreſight* had their
Underſtandings qualified alike. And pray
what was *Foreſight* ? Why an *Illiterate
Fellow. A pretender to Dreams, Aſtrology,
Palmiſtry* &c. This is the *Poets* account
of *Solomon's* Supernatural Knowledge !
Thus the wiſeſt Prince is dwindled into
a *Gypſie !* And the Glorious Miracle re-
ſolved into Dotage, and Figure-flinging !
Scandal continues his Banter, and ſays, the
*wiſe Men of the Eaſt owed their Inſtruction
to a Star ; which is rightly obſerv'd by* Gre-
gory *the Great in favour of Aſtrology.* This
was the Star which ſhone at our Saviour's
Birth. Now who could imagine by the
Levity of the occaſion, that the Author
thought it any better than an *Ignis Fa-
tuus,* or *Sydrophel's* Kite in *Hudibras ?* Sr.
Sampſon and the fine *Angelica,* after ſome
lewd raillery continue the Allegory, and
drive

p. 47.

vid. Per-
ſon. Dram.

drive it up into Profaneſs. For this reaſon the Citation muſt be imperfect.

Sr. Sampſ. Sampſon*'s a very good Name
for*——*your* Sampſons *were ſtrong Dogs from
the Beginning.*

p. 80. Angel. *Have a care*—— *If you remember the ſtrongeſt* Sampſon *of your Name, pull'd
an old Houſe over his Head at laſt.* Here
you have the Sacred Hiſtory burleſqu'd,
and *Sampſon* once more brought into the
Houſe of *Dagon*, to make ſport for the
Philiſtines! To draw towards an end of
this *Play.* *Tattle* would have carried off
Valentine's Miſtreſs. This later, expreſ-
ſes his Reſentment in a moſt Divine manner! Tattle *I thank you, you would have in-
terpoſed between me and Heaven, but Providence has laid Purgatory in your way.*
p. 91. Thus Heaven is debas'd into an Amour,
and Providence brought in to direct the
Paultry concerns of the *Stage* ! *Angelica*
concludes much in the ſame ſtrain. *Men
are generally Hypocrites and Infidels, they pretend to Worſhip, but have neither Zeal, nor
Faith; How few like* Valentine *would per-
ſevere unto Martyrdom? &c.* Here you
p. 92. have the Language of the *Scriptures,* and
the moſt ſolemn Inſtances of Religion,
proſtituted to Courtſhip and Romance!
Here you have a Miſtreſs made God Almighty, Ador'd with Zeal and Faith,
and

and Worſhip'd up to Martyrdom! This
if 'twere only for the Modeſty, is ſtrange
ſtuff for a Lady to ſay of her ſelf. And
had it not been for the profane Alluſion,
would have been cold enough in all Conſcience.

The *Provok'd Wife* furniſhes' the Audience with a Drunken Atheiſtical Catch:
'Tis true this Song is afterwards ſaid to
be *Full of Sin and Impudence.* But why Prov. Wife
then was it made? This Confeſſion is p. 38.
a miſerable *Salvo*; And the Antidote is
much weaker than the Poyſon: 'Tis juſt
as if a Man ſhould ſet a Houſe in a Flame,
and think to make amends by crying *Fire*
in the Streets. In the laſt *Act Raſor* makes
his Diſcovery of the Plot againſt *Belinda*
in *Scripture* phraſe. I'le give it the *Rea-*
der in the Authors Dialogue.

Belind. *I muſt know who put you upon* Id. p. 77.
all this Miſchief.

Raſor. *Sathan and his Equipage. Wo-*
man tempted me, Luſt weaken'd, —— *And*
ſo the Devil overcame me: As fell Adam
ſo fell I.

Belind. *Then pray Mr.* Adam *will you*
make us acquainted with your Eve?

Raſor unmasks⎫ *This is the Woman*
Madamoſelle and ⎬ *that tempted me: But*
ſays, ⎭ *this is the Serpent*
(meaning Lady *Fanciful*)
that

that tempted the Woman; *And if my Prayers might be heard, her punishment for so doing should be like the Serpents of old, &c.* This *Rasor* in what we hear of him before, is all Roguery, and Debauch : But now he enters in *Sackcloth*, and talks like *Tribulation* in the *Alchemist.* His Character is chang'd to make him the more profane ; And his Habit, as well as Discourse, is a Jest upon Religion. I am forced to omit one Line of his Confession. The Design of it is to make the *Bible* deliver an obscene Thought : And because the Text would not bend into a Lewd Application ; He alters the words for his purpose, but passes it for Scripture still. This sort of Entertainment is frequent in the *Relapse.* Lord *Foplington* laughs at the publick Solemnities of Religion, as if 'twas a ridiculous piece of Ignorance, to pretend to the Worship of a God. He discourses with *Berinthia* and *Amanda* in this manner : *Why Faith Madam,*———*Sunday is a vile Day, I must confess. A man must have very little to do at Church that can give an account of the Sermon.* And a little after : *To Mind the Prayers or the Sermon, is to mind what one should not do.* *Lory* tells young *Fashion, I have been in a lamentable Fright ever since that Conscience had the Impudence to intrude into your Company.* His

Relapse.
p. 32, 33.

His Mafter makes him this Comfortable Anſwer. *Be at peace, it will come no more :*——*I have kick'd it down ſtairs.* A little before he breaks out into this Rapture. Now Conſcience I defie thee ! By the way P. 44, 45. we may obſerve, that this young *Faſhion* Vid. I. fra. is the *Poets* Favorite. *Berinthia* and *Worthy*, two *Characters* of Figure, determine the point thus in defence of Pimping.

Berinth. *Well, I would be glad to have no Bodies Sins to anſwer for but my own. But* P. 51. *where there is a neceſſity*——

Worth. *Right as you ſay, where there is a Neceſſity, a Chriſtian is bound to help his Neighbour.*

Nurſe, after a great deal of ProfaneStuff concludes her expoſtulation in theſe words: *But his Worſhip: (Young* Faſhion *) over-flows with his Mercy and his Bounty ; He is not only pleas'd to forgive us our Sins*——*but which is more than all, has prevail'd with me* P. 96, 97. *to become the Wife of thy Boſom :* This is very heavy, and ill dreſs'd. And an Atheiſt muſt be ſharp ſet to reliſh it. The Vertuous *Amanda* makes no ſcruple to charge the Bible with untruths.

Ibid.

——*What Slippery ſtuff are Men compos'd of ? Sure the Account of their Creation's falſe, And 'twas the Womans Rib that they were form'd of.*

Thus

Thus this Lady abuses her self, together with the Scripture, and shews her Sense, and her Religion, to be much of a Size.

*Berinthia,*after she has given in a Scheme for the debauching *Amanda,* is thus accosted by *Worthy : Thou Angel of Light, let me fall down and adore thee!* A most Seraphick Compliment to a Procuress! And 'tis possible some Angel or other, may thank him for't in due time.

I am quite tired with these wretched Sentences. The sight indeed is horrible, and I am almost unwilling to shew it. However they shall be Produced like Malefactors, not for Pomp, but Execution. Snakes and Vipers, must sometimes be look'd on, to destroy them. I can't forbear expressing my self with some warmth under these Provocations. What Christian can be unconcern'd at such intolerable Abuses? What can be a juster Reason for indignation than Insolence and Atheism? Resentment can never be better shown, nor Aversion more seasonably executed! Nature made the Ferment and Rising of the Blood, for such occasions as This. On what unhappy Times are we fallen! The Oracles of Truth, the Laws of Omnipotence, and the Fate of Eternity are Laught at and despis'd! That the *Poets*
should

p. 91.

should be suffer'd to play upon the *Bible*, and Christianity be Hooted off the *Stage!* Christianity that from such feeble beginings made so stupendious a progress! That over-bore all the Oppositions of Power, and Learning; and with Twelve poor Men, outstretch'd the Roman Empire. That this glorious Religion so reasonable in its Doctrine, so well attested by Miracles, by Martyrs, by all the Evidence that *Fact* is capable of, should become the Diversion of the Town, and the Scorn of Buffoons! And where, and by whom is all this Out-rage committed? why not by *Julian*, or *Porphirie*, not among Turks or Heathens; but in a Christian Country, in a Reform'd Church, and in the Face of Authority! Well! I perceive the Devil was a Saint in his *Oracles*, to what he is in his *Plays*. His Blasphemies are as much improv'd as his Stile, and one would think the Muse was *Legion*! I suppose the *Reader* may be satisfied already: But if he desires farther proof, there's something more flamingly impious behind.

The Christian *Almeida* when *Sebastian* was in danger, Raves and Foames like one Possess'd,

But is there Heaven, for I begin to doubt?
Now take your swing ye impious Sin unpunish'd,

Don. Sebastian.
p. 51.

G   Eter-

Eternal Providence ſeems over watch'd,
And with a ſlumbring Nod aſſents to Murther.

In the next *page*, ſhe bellows again much after the ſame manner. The *Double Dealer* to ſay the leaſt of him, follows his Maſter in this Road, *Paſſibus æquis.* Sr. *Paul Plyant* one would think had done his part: But the ridiculing *Providence* won't ſatisfie all People : And therefore the next attempt is ſomewhat bolder.

Double Dealer. p. 19.

Sr. Paul. *Hold your ſelf contented my Lady Plyant,——I find Paſſion coming upon me by Inſpiration.* In *Love Triumphant,* *Carlos* is by the Conſtitution of the *Play* a Chriſtian ; and therefore muſt be conſtrued in the ſenſe of his Religion. This Man blunders out this horrible expreſſion. *Nature has given me my Portion in Senſe with a P—— to her. &c.* The Reader may ſee the Helliſh Syllable at Length if he pleaſes. This Curſe is borrow'd for *Young Faſhion* in the *Relapſe.* The *Double Dealer* is not yet exhauſted. *Cynthia the Top Lady grows Thoughtful.* Upon the queſtion ſhe relates her Contemplation.

p. 17.

p. 44.

Double Dealer. p. 18.

Cynth. *I am thinking (ſays ſhe) that tho' Marriage makes Man and Wife one Fleſh, it leaves them two Fools.* This Jeſt is made upon a Text in *Geneſis,* and afterwards applyed by our Saviour to the caſe of Divorſe

Gen. 2. St. Math. 19.

vorfe, *Love for Love* will give us a farther account of this Authors Proficiency
in the *Scriptures*. Our Bleſſed Saviour affirms himſelf *to be the Way, the Truth, and
the Light , that he came to bear witneſs to
the Truth, and that his Word is Truth.*
Theſe expreſſions were remembred to
good purpoſe. For *Valentine* in his pretended Madneſs tells *Buckram* the Law-
yer ; *I am Truth,——I am Truth.——
Who's that, that's out of his way, I am Truth,
and can ſet him right.* Now a *Poet* that *Love, &c.*
p. 59. 61.
had not been ſmitten with the pleaſure
of Blaſphemy, would never have furniſh'd
Frenſy with Inſpiration ; nor put our Saviours Words in the Mouth of a Madman. *Lady Brute*, after ſome ſtruggle
between Conſcience and Lewdneſs, declares in Favour of the later. She ſays the
part of a downright Wife is to Cuckold *Provok'd*
Wife.
p. 3.
p. 4.
her Husband. And tho' this is *againſt the
ſtrict Statute Law of Religion, yet if there
was a Court of Chancery in Heaven, ſhe
ſhould be ſure to caſt him.*

This Braſs is double guilt. *Firſt,* It
ſuppoſes no Equity in Heaven. And *Secondly,* If there was, *Adultery* would not be puniſh'd ! The *Poet* afterwards acquaints us
by this Lady, that Blaſphemy is no Wo- *p.* 65.
mans Sin. Why then does ſhe fall into
it? Why in the mid'ſt of Temper and

Reasoning ? What makes him break in upon his own Rules ? Is Blasphemy never unseasonable upon the Stage, And does it always bring its excuse along with it ? The *Relapse* goes on in the same strain. When Young *Fashion* had a prospect of cheating his Elder Brother, he tells *Lory*, *Providence thou see'st at last takes care of Men of Merit.* *Berinthia* who has engag'd to corrupt *Amanda* for *Worthy*; attacks her with this Speech, *Mr.* Worthy *used you like a Text, he took you all to peices,* and it seems was particular in her Commendation, Thus she runs on for several Lines, in a Lewd, and Profane Allegory. In the Application she speaks out the Design, and concludes with this pious Exhortation ! *Now consider what has been said, and Heaven give you Grace to put it in practise*; that is to play the Whore. There are few of these last Quotations, but what are plain Blasphemy, and within the *Law.* They look reeking as it were from *Pandæmonium*, and almost smell of Fire and Brimstone. This is an Eruption of Hell with a witness ! I almost wonder the smoak of it has not darken'd the Sun, and turn'd the Air to Plague and Poyson ! These are outrageous Provocations ; Enough to arm all Nature in Revenge ; To exhaust the Judgments, of Heaven, and

Relapse. p. 19.

p. 96.

and sink the *Island* in the Sea! What a
spite have these Men to the God that made
them. How do They Rebell upon his
Bounty, and attack him with his own
Reason? These Giants in Wickedness,
how would they ravage with a Stature
Proportionable? They that can Swagger
in Impotence, and Blaspheme upon a Mole-
Hill, what would they do if they had
Strength to their Good-Will? And what
can be the Ground of this Confidence, and
the Reason of such horrid Presumption?
Why the *Scripture* will best satisfie the question. *Because sentence against an Evil work
is not excuted speedily, therefore the heart
of the Sons of Men, is fully set in them to
do Evil.*

Eccles. 8. 11.

Clemency is weakness with some People; *And the Goodness of God which should
lead them to Repentance, does but harden
them the more.* They conclude he wants
Power to punish, because he has patience
to forbear. Because there is a Space between Blasphemy and Vengeance; and
they don't perish in the Act of Defiance;
Because they are not blasted with Lightning, transfixt with Thunder, and Guard-
ed off with Devils, they think there's no
such matter as a day of Reckoning. *But
let no Man be Deceiv'd, God is not mock'd*;
not without danger they may be assur'd.
Let them retreat in time, before the *Floods*

Gal. 6.

run over them: Before they come to that place, where Madness will have no Mufick, nor Blafphemy any Diverfion.

And here it may not be amifs to look a little into the Behaviour of the *Heathens*. Now 'tis no wonder to find them run riot upon this Subject. The Characters of their Gods were not unblemifh'd. Their profpect of the other World, was but dim; neither were they under the Terrors of *Revelation*. However, they are few of them fo bad as the *Moderns*.

Terence does not run often upon this rock. 'Tis true *Chærea* falls into an ill Rapture after his Succefs. *Chremes* bids his Wife not tire the Gods with Thanks: And *Æfchinus* is quite fick of the Religious part of the Weding. Thefe Inftances, excepting his Swearing, are the moft, (and I think near all the) exceptionable Paffages of this *Author*.

Eunuch.

Heauton.
A. 5. 1.
Adelp.
A. 5. 7.

Plautus is much more bold. But then his fally's are generally made by *Slaves* and *Pandars*.

This makes the Example lefs dangerous, and is fome fort of extenuation. I grant this imperfect excufe wont ferve him always. There are fome Inftances where his *Perfons* of better Figure are are guilty of lewd Defences, Profane Flights, and Sawcy Expoftulation. But the *Roman* Deities were *Beings* of ill Fame,

Lycoides.
Aulular.
A. 2. 4.
Palæftra.
Rud. A. 1.
3.
Dinarchus.
Tincul.
A. 2. 4.

'tis

'tis the less wonder therefore if the *Poets*
were familiar with them. However,
Plautus has something good in him, and
enough to condemn the Practise. *Pleusides*
would gladly have had the Gods changed the
method of Things, in some Particulars. He
would have had frank good Humour'd People
long live'd, and close-fisted Knaves die Young.
To this *Periplectimenes* Gravely answers,
That 'tis great Ignorance, and Misbehaviour Mil.
to Censure the Conduct of the Gods, or speak Glor.
dishonorably of them. In his *Pseudolus* the
Procurer *Ballio* talks Profanely. Upon
which *Pseudolus* makes this Reflection.
This Fellow makes nothing of Religion, how
can we trust him in other matters? For the
Gods whom all People have the greatest rea- Pseud.
son to fear, are most slighted by him. A. 1. 3.

The Greek Tragedians are more staunch,
and write nearer the Scheme of Natural
Religion. 'Tis true, they have some bold
expressions : But then they generally re-
prove the Liberty, and punish the Men.
Prometheus in *Æschylus* blusters with a
great deal of Noise, and Stubborness. He Prom.
is not for changing Conditions with *Mer-* vinct.
cury : And chuses rather to be miserable, 57.
than to submit even to *Jupiter* himself.
The *Chorus* rebuke him for his Pride, and
threaten him with greater Punishment.
And the *Poet* to make all sure brings him

to Execution before the end of the *Play*.
He diſcharges Thunder and Lightning at
his Head ; ſhakes his Rock with an Earth-
quake, turns the Air into Whirl-wind,
and draws up all the Terrors of Nature
to make him an example.   In his *Expedi-*
tion againſt Thebes, *Eteocles* expects *Ca-*
paneus would be deſtroy'd for his Blaſ-
phemies.   Which happen'd accordingly.
On the other hand ; *Amphiaraus* being a
perſon of Virtue, and Piety, they are afraid
leaſt he ſhould ſucceed.   *For a Religious*
Enemy is almoſt invincible.   *Darius*'s Ghoſt
lays *Xerxes*'s ruin upon the exceſs of his
Ambition.   *'Twas, becauſe he made a Bridge*
over the Helleſpont, *uſed* Neptune *contume-*
liouſly, and thought himſelf Superiour to Hea-
ven.   This Ghoſt tells the *Chorus that the*
Perſian Army miſcarried for the out-rages
they did to Religion, for breaking down the
Altars, and plundering the Gods.

Ajax's Diſtraction is repreſented as ju-
dicial in *Sophocles*.   'Twas inflicted for
his *Pride* and *Atheiſm*.   'When his Fa-
'ther bid him be brave but Religious
'withall, he haughtily replyed that 'twas
'for Cowards to beg the Aſſiſtance of the
'Gods ; as for his part, he hoped to Con-
'quer without them.   And when *Miner-*
'*va* encouraged him to charge the Ene-
'my.

'He

p. 92.

p. 101.

Περσ.
161.

164.

Ajax.
Flagell.

Τότ ἀντιφωνεῖ δεινὸν ἀῤῥητόντ ἔπ⊙,

'He made her this Lewd and insuffer-
'able Answer. Pray withdraw, and give
'your Countenance elswhere, I want no
'Goddesses to help me do my Business.
'This Insolence made *Minerva* hate him;
'and was the cause of his Madness and
'self Murther. To proceed. The *Cho-*
rus condemns the Liberty of *Jocasta*, who
obliquely charged a Practise upon the *Ora-* *Oedip.*
cle : Tho' after all, she did not tax *Apollo,* *Tyran.*
but his Ministers. *p.* 187.

The same *Chorus* recommends Piety, and
Relyance upon the Gods, and threatens
Pride and Irreligion with Destruction.
In *Antigone, Tiresias* advises *Creon* to wave *p.* 188.
the Rigour of his *Edict,* And not let the
Body of *Polynices* lie unburied, and ex-
pos'd. He tells him the Altars were al-
ready polluted with Humane Flesh. This
had made the Language of the Birds un- *Antig.*
intelligible, and confounded the marks of *p.* 255.
Augury. *Creon* replies in a rage, and says
he would not consent to the Burial of
Polynices: No, tho' 'twere to prevent the
Eagle's throwing part of the Carkass in
Jove's Chair of *State.* This was a bold
Flight; but 'tis not long before he pays
for't. Soon after, his Son, and Queen, kill
them-

themselves. And in the close the Poet who speaks in the *Chorus*, explains the Misfortune, and points upon the Cause, and affirms that *Creon* was punish'd for his Haughtiness and Impiety. To go on to his *Trachiniæ*. *Hercules* in all the extremity of his Torture does not fall foul upon Religion. 'Tis true, He shows as much Impatience as 'tis possible. His Person, his pain, and the Occasion of it, were very extraordinary. These circumstances make it somewhat natural for him to complain above the common rate. The Greatness of his Spirit, the Feavour of his Blood, and the Rage of his Passion, could hardly fail of putting Force, and and Vehemence into his Expressions. Tho' to deal clearly he seems better furnish'd with Rhetorick, than true Fortitude. But *Trach.* *p.* 368. after all, his Disorders are not altogether ungovern'd. He is uneasy, but not impious, and profane.

I grant *Hercules Oeteus* in *Seneca*, swaggers at a strange Rhodomontading rate. But the Conduct of this Author is very indifferent. He makes a meer *Salamander* of his *Hero*, and lets him declaim with too much of Length, Curiosity and Affectation, for one in his Condition: He harangues it with great plenty of Points, and Sentences in the Fire, and lies frying, and

Phi-

Philosophizing for near a hundred Lines
together. In fine, this Play is so injudi-
ciously manag'd, that *Heinsius* is confident 'twas written by neither of the *Se-*
neca's, but by some later Author of a lower
Class. To return to *Sophocle*'s *Trachiniæ.*
Hyllus reproaches the Gods with Neglect,
because they gave *Hercules* no Assistance,
and glances upon *Jupiter* himself. This *Trach.* *p. 375.*
sally is not so throughly corrected as for-
merly. 'Tis true the *Chorus* make some
little satisfaction immediately after. They
resolve all surprizes of Misfortune, all Re-
volutions of States or Families, into the
will and Permission of *Jupitur*. This by
implication, They make an argument for
acquiescence. Besides, the Poet had laid
in a sort of caution against Misconstructi-
on before. For the *Messenger* tells *De-*
janeira that we ought not to Murmur at *Trach.*
the Conduct of *Jupiter.* *p. 340.*

—— Τὰ λόγᾳ δ' ὃ χρὴ Φθόνον
Γόναι περσῶναι ζῶς ὅτε περάκ]ωρ φανῆ.

This for a Heathen is something tho'
not enough, *Cleomenes*'s Rant seems an imitation of *Hyllus*. Only 'tis bolder, and *Cleom.*
has nothing of the rashness of Youth to *p. 54.*
excuse it. Besides *Sophocles* throws in
somewhat by way of Preservative.
Where-

Whereas in *Cleomenes* the Boy *Cleonidas* has the better on the wrong fide, and feems to carry the caufe of Atheifm a-gainft his Father. This *Scene* of a *Famine* Mr. *Dryden* calls a Beauty; and yet Me-thinks *Cleora* is not very Charming! Her part is to tell you the Child fuck'd to no purpofe.

Id.
P. 55.

> *It pull'd and pull'd but now but nothing came,*
> *At laft it drew fo hard that the Blood follow'd.*
> *And that Red Milk I found upon its Lips,*
> *Which made me fwoon for Fear.*

P. 54.

There's a Defcription of Sucking for you! And truly one would think the Mufe on't were fcarfely wean'd. This Lady's fancy is juft *Slip-Stocking-high*; and fhe feems to want Senfe, more than her Breakfaft. If this Paffage would not fhine, the Poet fhould have let it alone. 'Tis *Horace's* advice.

Dr.
Art.
Poet.

> ——— *et qua*
> *Defperes tractata nitefcere poffe relinquas.*

The greateft part of the Life of this *Scene* is fpent in impious Rants, and Athei-ftical Difputes. To do the Author right, his *Characters* never want Spirits for fuch Service, either full or Fafting. Some peo-ple

ple love to say the worst Things in the
best manner ; To perfume their Poysons,
and give an Air to Deformity.

There is one ill Sentence in *Sophocles*
behind. *Philoctetes* calls the Gods Κακοἰ, *Philoct.*
and Libells their Administration. This 402.
Officer we must understand was left upon
a Solitary Island, ill used by his Friends,
and harrass'd with Poverty and Ulcers,
for Ten years together. These, under
the Ignorance of Paganism, were trying
Circumstances, and take off somewhat
of the Malignity of the Complaint. Afterwards He seems to repent, and declares 419.
his Assurance that the Gods will do Justice, and prays frequently to them. The
Conclusion of this Play is remarkably
Moral. Here *Hercules* appears in *Machine*; aquaints *Philoctetes* with his own
glorious Condition ; That his Happiness
was the Reward of Virtue, and the Purchase of Merit. He charges him to pay
a due regard to Religion ; For Piety would
recommend him to *Jupiter* more than any
other Qualification. It went into the o-
ther World with People and they found
their Account in't both Living and *p.* 432.
Dead.

Upon the whole ; The *Plays* of *Æschylus* and *Sophocles* are formed upon Models
of Virtue : They joyn Innocence with
Pleasure,

Pleasure, and design the Improvement, of the *Audience.*

In *Euripides*'s *Bacchæ, Pentheus* is pull'd in pieces for using *Bacchus* with Disrespect. And the *Chorus* observes that God never fails to punish Impiety, and Contempt of Religion. *Polyphemus* blusters Atheistically, and pretends to be as great as *Jupiter* : But then his Eye is burnt out in the fifth Act. And the *Chorus* in *Heraclidæ* affirm it next to Madness not to worship the Gods. I grant he has some profane Passages stand uncorrected, and what wonder is it to see a *Pagan* Miscarry? *Seneca*, as he was inferiour in Judgment to the *Greeks*, so he is more frequent, and uncautious, in his Flights of extravagance. His Hero's and Heroines, are excessively bold with the Superior Beings. They rave to Distraction, and he does not often call them to an account for't. 'Tis true *Ajax Oileus* is made an Example for Blaspheming in a Storm. He is first struck with Thunder, and then carried to the Bottom: The Modern *Poets*, proceed upon the Liberties of *Seneca;* Their Madmen are very seldom reckon'd with. They are profane without Censure, and defie the *Living God* with success. Nay, in some respect they exceed even *Seneca* himself. He flies out only under Impatience; And never falls into these Fits without

Torture,

Act. 2.

p. 295.

Agam.
Act. 3.

Torture, and hard Ufage. But the *English Stage* are unprovok'd in their Irreligion, and Blaspheme for their Pleasure. But suppofing the *Theatres* of *Rome*, and *Athens* as bad as poffible, what Defence is all This ? Can we argue from *Heathenifm* to *Chriftianity* ? How can the *practife* be the fame, where the *Rule* is fo very different? Have we not a clearer Light to direct us, and greater Punifhments to make us afraid. Is there no Diftinction between Truth and Fiction, between Majefty and a Pageant ? Muft God be treated like an Idol, and the *Scriptures* banter'd like *Homers Elyfium*, and *Hefiods Theogonia?* Are thefe the Returns we make Him for his Supernatural Affiftance? For the more perfect Difcovery of Himfelf, the ftooping of his Greatnefs, and the Wonders of his Love. Can't we refufe the Happinefs without affronting the Offer ? Muft we add Contempt to Difobedience, and Out-rage to Ingratitude? Is there no Diverfion without Infulting the God that made us, the Goodnefs that would fave us, and the Power that can damn us ? Let us not flatter our felves, *Words* won't go for Nothing. Profanefs is a moft Provoking Contempt, and a Crime of the deepeft dye. To break through the Laws of a Kingdom is bad

enough;

enough; But to make *Ballads* upon the *Statute-Book*, and a Jest of Authority, is much worse. Atheists may fancy what they please, but God will *Arise and Maintain his own Cause*, and Vindicate his Honour in due time.

To conclude. Profaness tho' never so well corrected is not to be endured. It ought to be Banish'd without *Proviso*, or Limitation. No pretence of *Character* or Punishment, can excuse it; or any *Stage-Discipline* make it tolerable. 'Tis grating to *Christian* Ears, dishonourable to the Majesty of God, and dangerous in the Example. And in a Word, It tends to no point, unless it be to wear off the horrour of the Practise, to weaken the force of Conscience, and teach the Language of the Damn'd.

CHAP

C H A P. III.

The Clergy abused by the Stage.

THE Satyr of the *Stage* upon the *Clergy* is extreamly Particular. In other cafes, They level at a fingle Mark, and confine themfelves to Perfons. But here their Buffoonry takes an unufual Compafs ; They fhoot Chain'd-fhot, and ftrike at Univerfals. They play upon the *Character*, and endeavour to expofe not only the Men, but the Bufinefs. 'Tis true, the Clergy are no fmall Rub in the *Poets* way. 'Tis by their Miniftrations that Religion is perpetuated, the other World Refrefh'd, and the Intereft of Virtue kept up. Vice will never have an unlimited Range, nor Confcience be totally fubdued, as long as People are fo eafy as to be Prieft-ridden ! As long as thefe Men are look'd on as the Meffengers of Heaven, and the Supports of Government, and enjoy their old Pretentions in Credit and Authority ; as long as this Grievance continues, the *Stage* muft decline of Courfe, and Atheifm give Ground, and Lewdnefs lie under Cenfure,

H   and

and Discouragment. Therefore that Liberty may not be embarrass'd, nor Principles make Head against Pleasure, the *Clergy* must be attack'd, and rendred Ridiculous.

To represent a Person fairly and without disservice to his Reputation, two Things are to be observ'd. First He must not be ill used by others: Nor Secondly be made to Play the Fool Himself. This latter way of Abuse is rather the worst, because here a Man is a sort of *Felo de se*; and appears Ridiculous by his own fault. The Contradiction of both these Methods is practised by the *Stage*. To make sure work on't, they leave no stone unturn'd, The whole *Common place* of Rudeness is run through. They strain their Invention and their Malice: And overlook nothing in ill Nature, or ill Manners, to gain their point.

To give some Instances of their Civility! In the *Spanish Fryer*, *Dominick* is made a Pimp for *Lorenzo*; He is call'd *a parcel of Holy Guts and Garbage*, and said *to have room in his Belly for his Church steeple*.

Dominick has a great many of these Compliments bestow'd upon him. And to make the Railing more effectual, you have a general stroke or two upon the Profession: Would you know what are the
Infallible

18. 19. 20.

Infallible Church Remedies. Why 'tis to
Lie Impudently, and *Swear Devoutly.* A *p.* 37.
little before this *Dominick* Counterfits himfelf fick, retires, and leaves *Lorenzo* and
Elvira together; And then the Remark
upon the Intrigue follows. ' You fee *p.* 23.
' Madam (fays *Lorenzo*) 'tis Intereft go-
' verns all the World. He Preaches againft
' Sin, why? Becaufe he gets by't: He
' holds his Tongue, why? becaufe fo much
' more is bidden for his Silence. 'Tis but
' giving a Man his Price, and Principles
' of *Church* are bought off as eafily as
' they are in *State*: No man will be a
' Rogue for nothing; but Compenfation
' muft be made, fo much Gold for fo much
' Honefty; and then a Church-man will
' break the Rules of Chefs. For the Black
' Bifhop, will fkip into the White, and
' the White into the Black, without Con-
' fidering whether the remove be Law-
' ful.

At laft *Dominick* is difcover'd to the
Company, makes a difhonourable *Exit,* and
is pufh'd off the *Stage* by the Rabble. This
is great Juftice! The Poet takes care to
make him firft a Knave, and then an Example: But his hand is not even. For
Lewd *Lorenzo* comes off with *Flying Colours.*
'Tis not the Fault which is correćted but

the

the Priest. The Authors Discipline is seldom without a Biass. He commonly gives the *Laity* the Pleasure of an ill Action, and the *Clergy* the Punishment.

To proceed. *Horner* in his general Remarks upon Men, delivers it as a sort of Maxim, *that your Church-man is the greatest Atheist.* In this Play *Harcourt* puts on the Habit of a Divine. *Alithea* does not think him what he appears; but *Sparkish* who could not see so far, endeavours to divert her Suspicion. *I tell you (says he) this is Ned* Harcourt *of* Cambridge, *you see he has a sneaking Colledge look.* Afterwards his Character is sufficiently abused by *Sparkish* and *Lucy*; but not so much as by Himself. He tells you in an *Aside he must suit his Stile to his Coat.* Upon this wise Recollection, He talks like a servile, impertinent Fop,

In the *Orphan,* The Young Soldier *Chamont* calls the Chaplain Sr. *Gravity,* and treats him with the Language of *Thee,* and *Thou.* The Chaplain instead of returning the Contempt; Flatters *Chamont* in his Folly, and pays a Respect to his Pride. The Cavalier encouraged I suppose by this Sneaking, proceeds to all the Excesses of Rudeness,

Country Wife p. 6.

p. 35.

Ibid.

—— *is*

—— *is there not one*   p. 25.
Of all thy Tribe that's Honeſt in your School?
The Pride of your Superiours makes ye Slaves:
Ye all live Loathſome, Sneaking, Servile lives:
Not free enough to Practiſe generous Truth,
'Tho ye pretend to teach it to the World.

After a little Pauſe for Breath, the Railing improves.

If thou wouldſt have me not contemn thy Office,
And Character, think all thy Brethren Knaves,
Thy Trade a Cheat, and thou its worſt Pro-   p. 26.
     feſſour,
Inform me; for I tell thee Prieſt I'le know.

The Bottom of the Page is down-right Porters Rhetorick.

Art thou then
So far concern'd in't? ——
Curſe on that formal ſteady Villains Face!
Juſt ſo do all Bawds look; Nay Bawds they ſay;
Can Pray upon Occaſion; talk of Heaven;
Turn up their Gogling Eye-balls, rail at Vice;
Diſſemble, Lye, and Preach like any Prieſt,   *Ibid.*
Art thou a Bawd?

The *Old Batchelour* has a Throw at the *Diſſenting Miniſters.* The *Pimp Setter* pro-

vides their Habit for *Bellmour* to Debauch
Latitia. The Dialogue runs thus.

Bell. *And haſt thou Provided Neceſſaries?*
Setter. *All, all Sir, the large Sanctified Hat,
and the little preciſe Band, with a Swingeing
long Spiritual Cloak, to cover Carnal Knavery,* — *not forgetting the black Patch which*
Old Batch. *Tribulation* Spintext *wears as I'm inform'd*
p. 19. 20. *upon one Eye, as a penal Mourning for the*
— *Offences of his Youth* &c.

Barnaby calls another of that Character
Mr. *Prig*, and *Fondlewife* carrys on the
Humour lewdly in *Play-houſe Cant*; And
to hook the *Church* of *England* into the
Abuſe, he tacks a *Chaplain* to the End of
the Deſcription.

p. 27.

Lucy gives an other Proof of the *Poets.*
p. 41. good Will, but all little Scurilities are not
worth repeating.

In the *Double Dealer* the diſcourſe between *Maskwell* and *Saygrace* is very notable. *Maskwell* had a deſign to cheat *Mellifont* of his Miſtreſs, and engages the Chaplain in the Intrigue: There muſt be a
Levite in the caſe; *For without one of them
have a finger in't, no Plot publick, or pri-*
p. 71. *vate, can expect to proſper.*

To go on in the order of the *Play*.

Maskwell calls out at *Sagraces* door, Mr.
Saygrace Mr. *Saygrace*.

The other anſwers, *Sweet ſir I will but*
pen

*pen the last line of an Acrostick, and be
with you in the twingling of an Ejaculation,
in the pronouncing of an* Amen. &c.

Mask. *Nay good Mr.* Saygrace *do not
prolong the time,* &c.

Saygrace. *You shall prevail, I would break
off in the middle of a Sermon to do you
Pleasure.*

Mask. *You could not do me a greater——
except—— the business in hand—— have you
provided a Habit for Mellifont?*

Saygr. *I have,* &c.

Mask. *have you stich'd the Gownsleeve,
that he may be puzled and wast time in
putting it on?*

Saygr. *I have ; the Gown will not be in-
dued without Perplexity.* There is a little
more profane, and abusive stuff behind,
but let that pass.

The Author of *Don Sebastian* strikes
at the *Bishops* through the sides of the
Mufti, and borrows the Name of the *Turk,*
to make the *Christian* ridiculous. He
knows the transition from one Religion
to the other is natural, the Application easy, and the Audience but too well prepar'd.
And should they be at a loss he has else-
where given them a *Key* to understand
him.

For Priests of all Religions are the same. *Absal. and*
H 4   However *Achi.*

However that the Sense may be perfectly intelligible, he makes the Invective General, changes the Language, and rails in the stile of Christendom.

Benducar speaks,

——*Churchmen tho' they itch to govern all,*
Are silly, woful, awkard Polititians,
They make lame Mischief tho' they mean it well.

So much the better, for 'tis a sign they are not beaten to the Trade. The next Lines are an Illustration taken from a *Taylor*.

r: 24. *Their Intrest is not finely drawn and hid,*
But seams are coarsly bungled up and seen.

This *Benducar* was a rare Spokesman for a first *Minister*; And would have fitted *John* of *Leyden* most exactly!

In the Fourth *Act* the Mufti is *Depos'd* and *Captain Tom* reads him a shrewd Lecture at parting. But let that pass.

To go on, *Mustapha* threatens his great Patriark to put him to the Rack. Now you shall hear what an answer of Fortitude and Discretion is made for the *Mufti*.

Mufti. *I hope you will not be so barbarous to torture me. We may Preach Suffering to others, but alass holy Flesh is too well pamper'd*

to

to endure Martyrdom. By the way, if flin- p. 96.
ching from *Suffering* is a proof of *Holy
Flesh*, the *Poet* is much a Saint in his Constitution, witness his *Dedication* of *King
Arthur.*

In *Cleomenes, Cassandra* rails against Religion at the Altar, and in the midst of a
publick Solemnity.

Accurs'd be thou Grass-eating fodderd God ! p. 32.
*Accurs'd thy Temple ! more accurs'd thy
    Priests !*

She goes on in a mighty Huff, and
charges the Gods and Priesthood with
Confederacy, and Imposture. This Rant
is very unlikely at *Alexandria.* No People are more bigotted in their Superstition than the *Ægyptians* ; Nor any more
resenting of such an Affront. This Satyr
then must be strangely out of Fashion, and
probability. No matter for that ; it may
work by way of Inference, and be serviceable at Home. And 'tis a handsom
Compliment to Libertines and Atheists.

We have much such another swagge-
ring against Priests in *Oedipus.*

*Why seek I Truth from thee ?
The smiles of Courtiers and the Harlots tears,
The Tradesmens Oaths, and Mourning of an
    Heir,   Are*

Are Truths to what Priests tell.
O why has Priesthood privilege to Lie,
And yet to be believ'd!

Oedip.
p. 38.

And since They are thus Lively, I have one word or two to say to the *Play*.

When *Ægeon* brought the News of King *Polybus*'s Death, *Oedipus* was wonderfully surpriz'd at the Relation.

p. 48.

O all ye Powers is't possible? what, Dead!

And why not? was the Man invulnerable or immortal? Nothing of that: He was only Fourscore and Ten years old, that was his main security. And if you will believe the Poet he

Ibid.

Fell like Autumn Fruit that mellow'd long,
Ev'n wondred at because he dropt no sooner.

And which is more, *Oedipus* must be acquainted with his Age, having spent the greatest part of his time with him at *Corinth.* So that in short, the pith of the Story lies in this Circumstance. A Prince of Ninety years was dead, and one who was wondred at for dying no sooner. And now why so much Exclamation upon this occasion? Why must all the *Powers* in Being be Summon'd in to make the News Cre-

Credible? This *Poſſe* of *Interjections* would
have been more ſeaſonably raiſed if the
Man had been alive; for that by the Poets
Confeſſion had been much the ſtranger
Thing. However *Oedipus* is almoſt out
of his Wits about the Matter, and is Ur-
gent for an account of Particulars.

That ſo the Tempeſt of my joys may riſe
By juſt degrees, and hit at laſt the Stars.   *Ibid.*

This is an empty ill proportion'd Rant,
and without warrant in Nature or Antiquity. *Sophocles* does not repreſent *Oedi-*
pus in ſuch Raptures of Extravagant ſurprize. In the next page there's another
Flight about *Polybus* his Death ſomewhat
like This. It begins with a *Noverint Uni-*
verſi. You would think *Oedipus* was going to make a *Bond.*

Know, be it known to the limits of the World;

This is ſcarce Sence, be it known.

Yet farther, let it paſs yon dazling roof
The Manſion of the Gods, and ſtrike them deaf
With Everlaſting peals of Thundring joy.

This Fuſtian puts me in mind of a *Cou-*
plet of *Taylors* the *Water* Poet, which for
the

the Beauty of the Thought are not very
unlike.

*What if a Humble Bee should chance to strike,
With the But-End of an Antarkick Pole.*

I grant Mr. *Dryden* clears himself of
this *Act* in his *Vindication* of the *Duke* of
Guise. But then why did he let these
crude Fancies pass uncorrected in his
Friend? Such fluttering ungovern'd Tran-
sports, are fitter for a Boys *Declamation*
then a *Tragedy.* But I shall trouble my
self no farther with this *Play.* To return
therefore to the Argument in Hand. In the
Provok'd Wife Sir *John Brute* puts on the
Habit of a Clergyman, counterfeits himself
drunk; quarrels with the *Constable*, and
is knock'd down and seiz'd. He rails,
swears, curses, is lewd and profane, to all
Provok'd the Heights of Madness and Debauchery:
Wife. The *Officers* and *Justice* break jests upon
P. 45, 46, him, and make him a sort of Representa-
51, 52. tive of his *Order.*

This is rare *Protestant* Diversion, and
very much for the Credit of the *Reformation!* The Church of *England*, I mean the
Men of Her, is the only Communion in
the World, that will endure such Inso-
lences as these: The *Relapse* is if possible
more singularly abusive. *Bull* the Chaplain
wishes

wishes the Married couple joy, in Lan- *Relapse.*
guage horribly Smutty and Profane. To *p.* 74
transcribe it would blot the Paper to much.
In the next *Page Young Fashion* defires
Bull to make haft to Sr. *Tun-belly.* He
answers very decently, *I fly my good Lord.* *p.* 75.
At the end of this *Act Bull* speaks to
the Cafe of *Bigamy,* and determines it thus.
I do confess to take two Husbands for the Satis-
faction of — is to commit the Sin of Exorbi-
tancy, but to do it for the peace of the Spirit,
is no more then to be Drunk by way of Phy-
fick ; befides to prevent a Parents wrath is to
avoid the Sin of Difobedience, for when the
Parent is Angry, the Child is froward : The
Conclufion is infolently Profane, and let
it lie : The fpirit of this Thought is
borrow'd from Ben *Johnfons Bartholomew-*
Fair, only the Profanefs is mightily improved, and the Abufe thrown off the
Meeting Houfe, upon the *Church.* The
Wit of the *Parents being angry,* and the
Child froward, is all his own. *Bull* has *p.* 86.
more of this Heavy ftuff upon his Hands.
He tells *Young Fafhion Your Worfhips good-*
nefs is unfpeakable, yet there is one thing
feems a point of Confcience ; And Confcience
is a tender Babe.&c. *p.* 97.

Thefe *Poets* I obferve when They grow
lazy, and are inclined to Nonfence, they
commonly get a Clergy-man to fpeak it.
Thus

Thus they pass their own Dulness for Humour, and gratifie their Ease, and their Malice at once. *Coupler* instructs *Young Fashion* which way *Bull* was to be managed. He tells him as *Chaplains go now, he must be brib'd high, he wants Money, Preferment, Wine, and a Whore. Let this be procured for him, and I'll warrant thee he speaks Truth like an Oracle.*

89.

A few Lines forward, the Rudeness is still more gross, and dash'd with Smut, the common *Play-house* Ingredient. 'Tis not long before *Coupler* falls into his old Civilities. He tells *Young Fashion, Last Night the Devil run away with the Parson of* Fatgoose *Living.* Afterwards *Bull* is plentifully rail'd on in down right *Billings-gate* : made to appear Silly, Servile, and Profane ; and treated both in Posture and Language, with the utmost Contempt.

p. 94.

p. 95, 97.
105.

I could cite more *Plays* to this purpose ; But these are sufficient to show the Temper of the *Stage,*

Thus we see how hearty these People are in their Ill Will! How they attack Religion under every Form, and pursue the Priesthood through all the Subdivisions of Opinion. Neither *Jews* nor *Heathens, Turks* nor *Christians, Rome* nor *Geneva, Church* nor *Conventicle,* can escape

scape them. They are afraid leaft Virtue
fhould have any Quarters undifturbed,
Confcience any Corner to retire to, or
God be Worfhip'd in any Place. 'Tis
true their Force feldom carries up to their
Malice: They are too eager in the Combat to be happy in the Execution. The
Abufe is often both grofs and clumfey,
and the Wit as wretched as the Manners.
Nay Talking won't always fatisfy them.
They muft ridicule the *Habit* as well as
the Funtion, of the Clergy. 'Tis not
enough for them to play the Fool unlefs
they do it in *Pontificalibus*. The Farce
muft be play'd in a Religious Figure, and
under the Diftinctions of their Office!
Thus the Abufe ftrikes ftronger upon the
fenfe ; The contempt is better fpread, and
the little *Idea* is apt to return upon the
fame Appearance.

And now does this Rudenefs go upon
any Authorities ? Was the Priefthood
alwaies thought thus infignificant, and do
the Antient Poets palt it in this Manner ?
This Point fhall be tried, I fhall run
through the moft confiderable Authors
that the Reader may fee how they treat
the Argument. *Homer* ftands higheft
upon the Roll, and is the firft Poet both
in Time, and Quality ; I fhall therefore
begin with him. Tis true he wrote no
Plays ;

Plays ; but for Decency, Practise, and general Opinion, his Judgment may well be taken, Let us see then how the *Priests* are treated in his *Poem*, and what sort of Rank they hold.

Chryses Apollo's Priest appears at a Council of War with his Crown and guilt Scepter. He offers a valuable Ransom for his Daughter, and presses his Relation to *Apollo*. All the Army excepting. *Agamemnon* are willing to consider his Character, and comply with his Proposals. But this *General* refuses to part with the Lady, and sends away her Father with disrespect. *Apollo* thought himself affronted with this Usage, and revenges the Indignity in a Plague.

Hom. *Il.*
a. p. 3.
& dein.
Ed. Screvel.

Ουνεκα τον χρυσην ητιμασ᾽ αρητηρα
Ατρειδης.

Adrastus and *Amphius* the Sons of *Merops* a Prophet, commanded a considerable extent of Country in *Troas*, and brought a Body of Men to King *Priam's* Assistance.

Il. B. p. 91.

Ibid. p. 92. And *Ennomus* the Augur commanded the Troops of *Mysia* for the Besieged.

Phegeus and *Idæus* were the Sons of *Dares* the Priest of *Vulcan*. They appear in an Equipage of Quality, and charge *Diomedes* the third Hero in the *Grecian* Army.

Il. E p.
154. 155.

Army. *Idæus* after the Misfortune of the
Combat, is brought off by *Vulcan*. *Dolo-*
pion was *Prieſt* to *Scamander*, and regarded
like the God he *Belong'd* to, | Il. E. p.
154,155.

Θεὸς δ' ὣς τίετο δήμῳ. | Ibid. p.
158.

Uliſſes in his return from *Troy*, took
Iſmarus by Storm, and makes Prize of the
whole Town, excepting *Maron*, and his
Family. This *Maron* was *Apollo's Prieſt*,
and preſerv'd out of reſpect to his Function: He preſents *Uliſſes* nobly in Gold,
Plate, and Wine ; And this Hero makes
an honourable Mention of him, both as
to his Quality, and way of Living. | Odyſſ. I. p.
174. 181.

These are all the *Prieſts* I find Mentioned in *Homer* ; And we ſee how fairly
the Poet treats them, and what ſort of
Figure they made in the World.

To the Teſtimony of *Homer*, I ſhall
joyn that of *Virgil*, who tho' He follows
at a great diſtance of Time, was an Author of the firſt Rank, and wrote the
ſame kind of Poetry with the other. Now
Virgil tho' he is very extraordinary in
his Genius, in the Compaſs of his Learning, in the Muſick and Majeſty of his
Stile ; yet the exactneſs of his Judgment
ſeems to be his peculiar, and moſt diſtinguiſhing Talent. He had the trueſt

I   Reliſh

Relish imaginable, and always described Things according to *Nature*, *Custom*, and *Decency*. He wrote with the greatest Command of *Temper*, and *Superiority* of good *Sense*. He is never lost in smoak and Rapture, nor overborn with Poetick Fury ; but keeps his Fancy warm and his Reason Cool at the same time. Now this great Master of Propriety never Mentions any *Priests* without some *Marks* of *Advantage*. To give some Instances as they lie in Order.

When the *Trojans* were consulting what was to be done with the *Wooden-Horse*, and some were for lodging it within the Walls ; *Laocoon* appears against this Opinion at the Head of a numerous Party, harangues with a great deal of Sense, and Resolution, and examines the *Machine* with his Lance. In fine, He advised so well, and went so far in the Discovery of the Stratagem ; that if the *Trojans* had not been ungovernable, and as it were stupified by Fate and Folly, he had saved *Ænid. 2.* the Town.

Trojaque nunc stares Priamique arx alta maneres.

This *Laocoon* was *Neptunes* Priest, and either Son to *Priam*, or Brother to *Anchises*, *chifes*, who was of the Royal Family. *Ruaus. in* The next we meet with is *Pantheys* *Loc.* *Apollo's* Prieft. He is call'd *Pantheus O-triades*, which is an argument his Father was well known. His acquaintance with *Æneas* to whofe Houfe he was carrying his little Grandfon, argues him to be a Perfon of Condition. *Pantheus* after a *Æneid 2.* fhort relation of the Pofture of Affairs, joyns *Æneas's* little Handful of Men, char-ges in with him when the Town was feiz'd, and fired, and at laft dies Handfomly *Ibid.* in the Action.

The next is *Anius* King of *Delos*, Prince and *Prieft* in one Perfon.

Rex Anius, rex idem hominum Phæbique *Æneid. 3.* *Sacerdos.*

When *Æneas* was outed at *Troy*, and in queft of a new Country, he came to an Anchor at *Delos*; *Anius* meets him in a Religious Habit, receives him civilly, *Ibid.* and obliges him with his *Oracle*. In the Book now Mention'd we have another of *Apollo's* Priefts, his name is *Helenus*, Son of *Priam* and King of *Chaonia*. He en-tertains *Æneas* with a great deal of Friend-fhip, and Magnificence, gives him many material Directions, and makes him a rich Prefent at parting. To this Prince if you

Please we may joyn a Princess of the same Profession; and that is *Rhea Silvia* Daughter to *Numitor* King of *Alba*, and Mother to *Romulus*, and *Remus*. This Lady

Æn.ead. 1st. *Virgil* calls —— *regina Sacerdos* a Royal Priestess. Farther. When *Æneas* made a Visit upon Business to the *shades Below*, He

Æn. 6. had for his Guide, the famous *Sibylla Cumæa*, who Belong'd to *Apollo*. When he came thither amongst the rest of his Acquantance he saw *Polybætes* a Priest of *Ceres*. This *Polybætes* is mention'd with the three Sons of *Antenor*, with *Glaucus*, and *Thersilochus*, who Commanded in Cheif in the *Trojan Auxiliaries* : So that you may know his Quality by his Company. When *Æneas* had passed on farther, he saw *Orpheus* in *Elysium* : The Poet calls him the *Thracian* Priest. There needs not be much said of *Orpheus*; He is famous for his skill in Musick, Poetry,

Ibid. and Religious Ceremonies, He was one of the Hero's of Antiquity, and a principal Adventurer in the Expedition for the *Golden-Fleece*.

In the Seventh *Æneid* the Poet gives in a List of the Princes, and General Officers who came into the Assistance of *Turnus*; Amongst the rest he tells you,

Quin

Quin & Marrubia venit de gente Sacerdos,
Archippi regis missu fortissimus Umbro.

This *Priest* he commends both for his
Courage and his skill in Physick, Natural
Magick, and Phlosophy. He understood
the Virtue of *Plants*, and could lay Passions and Poysons asleep. His death
was extreamly regretted by his Country,
who made a Pompous aud Solemn Mourning for him.

Te nemus Angitia vitrea te Fucinus unda   *Æneid. 7.*
Te liquidi flevere lacus.

The *Potitij*, and the *Pinarij* Mention'd   *Lib. 1.*
Æneid 8. were as *Livy* observes, chosen
out of the first Quality of the Country,
and had the *Priesthood* hereditary to their
Family. To go on, *Æmonides*, and *Chloreus* make a glistering Figure in the *Feild*,
and are very remarkable for the Curiosity
of their Armour, and Habit. *Æmonides*'s
Finery is passed over in general.

Totus collucens veste atque insignibus armis. *Æneid.*
                                         10.

But the Equipage of *Chloreus* is flourish'd out at Length, and as I remember
admired by *Macrobius* as one of the Master

peices of *Virgil* in Defcription.   In fhort;
Æneid.11. He is all Gold, Purple, Scarlet, and Em-
broydery ; and as rich as Nature, Art, and
Rhetorick can make him.   To thefe I
might add *Rhamnes, Afylas,* and *Tolum-*
Æneid. 9. *nius,* who were all Perfons of Condition,
10. 11. and had Confiderable Pofts in the
Army.

It may be thefe laft were not ftrictly
Priefts.   Their Function was rather *Pro-*
phetick.   They interpreted the Refoluti-
ons of the Gods, by the voice of Birds,
the Infpection of Sacrifices, and their Ob-
fervations of Thunder.   This made their
Character counted Sacred, and their Re-
Guther. de- lation to the Deity particular.   And there-
jure Veter fore the *Romans* ranged them in the *Or-*
pontif. *der* of the *Priefts.*

Thus we fee the admired *Homer,* and
Virgil, always treat the *Priefts* fairly,
and defcribe them in Circumftances of
Credit: If 'tis faid that the Inftances I
have given are moftly in Names of *Fiction,*
and in Perfons who had no Being, unlefs
in the Poets fancy.   I anfwer, I am not
concern'd in the Hiftory of the Relation.
Whether the Mufter is true or falfe, 'tis
all one to my purpofe.   This is certain,
had the *Priefts* been People of fuch flen-
der Confideration as our *Stage Poets* endeavour to make them ; they muft have
ap-

appear'd in a different Figure; or rather
have been left out as too little for that
fort of *Poem*. But *Homer* and *Virgil*, had
other Sentiments of Matters: They were
govern'd by the Reafon of Things, and
the common ufage of the World. They
knew the *Priefthood* a very reputable Employment, and always efteem'd as fuch.
To have ufed the *Priefts* ill, They muft
have call'd their own Difcretion in queftion: They muft have run into impropriety, and fallen foul upon Cuftom,
Manners, and Religion. Now 'twas not
their way to play the Knave and the Fool
together: They had more Senfe than to
do a filly Thing, only for the Satisfaction of doing an ill one.

I fhall now go on to enquire what the
Greek *Tragedians* will afford us upon the
prefent Subject. There are but two *Plays*
in *Æfchylus* where the *Minifters* of the
Gods are reprefented. The one is in his
Eumenides, and here *Apollo's Prieftefs* only
opens the *Play*, and appears no more. The
other is in his *Seige* of *Thebes*. In this
Tragedy the *Prophet Amphiaraus* is one of
the Seven Commanders againft the *Town*.
He has the Character of a Modeft, Brave
Officer, and of one who rather affected to
be great in Action, than Noife.

In *Sophocle*'s *Oedipus Tyrannus*. *Jupiter*'s
Priest has a short part. He appears at the
Head of an *Address*, and delivers the Harangue by the King's Order. *Oedipus* in
his Passion treats *Tiresias* ruggedly ; *Tiresias* replies with Spirit and Freedom, and
plainly tell him he was none of his *Servant* but *Apollo*'s.

*Oedip. Tyr.
p. 148.*

Ibid. 169.   'Ου γὰρ τί σοι ζῶ δοῦλΘ ἀλλά λοξία.

And here we may observe that all *Oedipus* his reproaches relate to *Tiresias*'s person, there is no such Thing as a general Imputation upon his Function : But the *English Oedipus* makes the *Priesthood* an Im-
posturous Profession ; and rails at the
whole Order. In the next Tragedy, *Creon*
charges *Tiresias* with subornation ; and
that he intended to make a Penny of his
Prince. The *Priest* holds up his Character, speaks to the ill Usage with an
Air of Gravity, calls the King *Son*, and
foretells him his Misfortune.

p. 38.

*Antig. p.
256, 258,*

To go on to *Euripides*, for *Sophocles* has
nothing more. This Poet in his *Phanissæ*
brings in *Tiresias* with a very unacceptable report from the *Oracle*. He tells *Creon*
that either his Son must die, or the City be
lost. *Creon* keeps himself within Temper,
and gives no ill Language. And even
                                    when

when *Mœnecius* had kill'd himself, he _{*Eurip.*} neither complains of the Gods, nor re- _{*Phæniß. p.* 158, 159.} proaches the *Prophet*.

In his *Bacchæ*, *Tiresias* is honourably used by *Cadmus* ; And *Pentheus* who _{*Bacch.*} threatned him, is afterwards punish'd for _{*Act. 1.*} his Impiety. In another *Play Apollo*'s _{*Act. 4. Jon. Act 5.*} *Priestess* comes in upon a creditable account, and is respectfully treated. *Iphige-* _{*Iphig. in*} *nia Agamemnon*'s Daughter is made *Priest-* _{*Aulid. & in Taur.*} *ess* to *Diana*; and her Father thought himself happy in her Employment. These are all the *Priests* I remember represented in *Euripides*. To conclude the antient *Tragedians* together : *Seneca* seems to follow the Conduct of *Euripides*, and secures *Tiresias* from being outraged. *Oedipus* carries it smoothly with him and only desires him to out with the Oracle, and declare the Guilty Person. This *Tiresias* ex- _{*Oedip.*} cuses, and afterwards the Heat of the expostulation falls upon *Creon*. *Calchas* if not strictly a *Priest*, was an *Auger*, and had a Religious Relation. Upon this account *Agamemnon* calls him *interpres Deorum*; The Reporter of Fate, and the God's _{*Troad. A.*} *Nuntio*; And gives him an honourable _{2. p. 193.} Character.

This Author is done ; I shall therefore pass on to the *Comedians*. And here, *Aristophanes* is so declared an Atheist, that

I

I think him not worth the citing. Besides, he has but little upon the Argument: And where he does engage it, the *Priests* have every jot as good Quarter as the Gods.

Plut. Ran.
Aves.

As for *Terence*, he neither represents any *Priests*, nor so much as mentions them. *Chrysalus* in *Plautus* describes *Theotimus*

Bacchid.
Act. 2. 5 3.

Diana's *Priest*, as a Person of Quality, and Figure. In his *Rudens* we have a *Priestess* upon the *Stage*, which is the only In-

Rud. A. 1.
5. A. 2. 3.

stance in this *Poet*. She entertains the two Women who were wrecked, and is commended for her hospitable Temper. The Procurer *Labrax* swaggers that he will force the Temple, and begins the Attack. *Demades* a Gentleman, is surprized at his Insolence, and threatens him with Revenge. The report of so bold an attempt made him

Act. 3.
S. 2. 5.

cry out. *Quis homo est tanta Confidentia; qui sacerdotem audeat Violare?* It seems in those Days 'twas very infamous to affront a *Holy Character*, and break in upon the *Guards* of Religion *!* Thus we see how the Antient Poets behaved themselves in the Argument. *Priests* seldom appear in their *Plays*. And when they come 'tis Business of Credit that brings them. They are treated like Persons of Condition. They Act up to their Relation; neither sneak, nor prevaricate, nor do any thing unbecoming their Office.

And

And now a word or two of the *Moderns.*

The famous *Corneille* and *Moliere,* bring no *Priests* of any kind upon the *Stage.* The former leaves out *Tiresias* in his *Oedipus:.* Tho' this Omission balks his Thought, and maims the *Fable.* What therefore but the regard to Religion could keep him from the use of this Liberty? As I am inform'd the same Reservedness is practis'd in *Spain,* and *Italy:* And that there is no Theatre in *Europe* excepting the *English,* that entertains the *Audience* with *Priests.*

This is certainly the right method, and best secures the Outworks of Piety. The Holy Function is much too Solemn to be play'd with. Christianity is for no Fooling, neither the *Place,* the *Occasion* nor the *Actors* are fit for such a Representation. To bring the *Church* into the *Playhouse,* is the way to bring the *Playhouse* into the *Church.* 'Tis apt to turn Religion into *Romance*; and make unthinking People conclude that all Serious Matters are nothing but *Farce, Fiction,* and *Design.* 'Tis true the *Tragedies* at *Athens* were a sort of *Homilies,* and design'd for the Instruction of the People. To this purpose they are all Clean, Solemn, and Sententious. *Plautus* likewise informs us that the *Comedians* used to teach the People Morality. The *Rud. A. 4.* case *S. 7.*

case standing thus 'tis less suprizing to find the *Priests* sometimes Appear. The Play had grave Argument, and Pagan Indulgence, to plead in its behalf. But our *Poets* steer by an other *Compass*. Their Aim is to *destroy* Religion, their *Preaching* is against *Sermons*; and their Business, but Diversion at the best. In short, Let the Character be never so well managed no Christian Priest (especially,) ought to come upon the *Stage*. For where the Business is an Abuse, and the place a Profanation; the demureness of the Manner, is but a poor excuse. Monsieur *Racine* is an Exception to what I have observ'd in *France*. In his *Athalia, Joida* the *High*-Priest has a large part. But then the Poet does him Justice in his Station; he makes him Honest and Brave, and gives him a shining Character throughout. *Mathan* is another *Priest* in the same Tragedy. He turns Renegado, and revolts from God to *Baal*. He is a very ill Man but makes a considerable Appearance, and is one of the Top of *Athaliahs* Faction. And as for the *Blemishes* of his Life, they all stick upon his own Honour, and reach no farther than his Person: In fine the *Play* is a very Religious Poem; 'Tis upon the Matter all *Sermon* and *Anthem*. And if it were not designed for the *Theatre*, I have nothing to object. Let

Let us now juſt look over our own Country-men till King *Charles* the Second. *Shakeſpear* takes the Freedom to repreſent the *Clergy* in ſeveral of his *Plays* : But for the moſt part he holds up the *Function*, and makes them neither Act, nor Suffer any thing unhandſom. In one Play or two He is much bolder with the *Order*. * Sr. *Hugh Evans* a *Prieſt* is too Comical and Secular in his Humour. However he underſtands his Poſt, and converſes with the Freedom of a Gentleman. I grant in *Loves Labour loſt* the *Curate* plays the Fool egregiouſly ; And ſo does the *Poet* too, for the whole *Play* is a very ſilly one. In the Hiſtory of Sr. *John Old-Caſtle*, Sr. *John*, *Parſon* of *Wrotham* Swears, Games, Wenches, Pads, Tilts, and Drinks : This is extreamly bad, and like the Author of the *Relapſe* &c. Only with this difference ; *Shakeſpears* Sr. *John* has ſome Advantage in his Character. He appears Loyal, and Stout ; He brings in Sr. *John Acton*, and other Rebels Priſoners. He is rewarded by the King, and the Judge uſes him Civilly and with Reſpect. In ſhort He is repreſented Lew'd, but not Little ; And the Diſgrace falls rather on the Perſon, then the Office. But the *Relapſers* buſineſs, is to ſink the Notion, and Murther the Character, and make the Function,

Meaſure for Meaſure.
Much a do about Nothing.
Twelf-Night.
Henry 4th pt. 1ſt
Hen, 6, pt. 3d.
Romeo and Juliet.
* *Merry Wives of Windſor.*

ction deſpicable : So that upon the whole, *Shakeſpear* is by much the gentiler Enemy.

Towards the End of the *Silent Woman*, *Ben Johnſon* brings in a *Clergy-man*, and a *Civilian* in their *Habits*. But then he premiſes a handſom Excuſe, acquaints the *Audience*, that the *Perſons* are but borrow'd, and throws in a *Salvo* for the Honour of either profeſſion. In the Third *Act*, we have another *Clergy-man* ; He is abuſed by *Cutberd*, and a little by *Moroſe*. But his Lady checks him for the ill Breeding of the Uſage. In his *Magnetick Lady*, *Tale of a Tub*, and *Sad Sheapherd*, there *Eſſay of* are *Prieſts* which manage but untowardly. *Dramat.* But theſe *Plays* were his *laſt Works*, which *&c.* Mr. *Dryden* calls *his Dotages*. This Author has no more *Prieſts*, and therefore we'll take Leave.

Beaumont and *Fletcher* in the *Faithful Shepheardeſs, The Falſe one, A Wife for a Month*, and the *Knight of Malta*, give, us both *Prieſts* and *Biſhops*, part Heathen and part Chriſtian : But all of them ſave their Reputation and make a creditable Appearance. The *Prieſts* in the *Scornful Lady*, and *Spaniſh Curate* are ill uſed. The firſt is made a Fool, and the other a Knave. Indeed they ſeem to be brought in on purpoſe to make ſport, and diſſerve
Religion

Religion. And so much for *Beaumont* and *Fletcher*.

Thus we see the English *Stage* has always been out of Order, but never to the Degree 'tis at present.

I shall now take Leave of the *Poets*, and touch a little upon History and Argument.

And here I shall briefly shew the Right the *Clergy* have to Regard, and fair Usage, upon these Three following Accounts.

I. *Because of their Relation to the Deity.*
II. *Because of the Importance of their Office.*
III. *They have prescription for their Privilege. Their Function has been in Possession of Esteem in all Ages, and Countries.*

I. *Upon the account of their Relation to the Deity.*

The Holy *Order* is appropriated to the Divine Worship: And a *Priest* has the peculiar Honour to *Belong* to nothing less then God Almighty. Now the Credit of the *Service* always rises in proportion to the Quality and Greatness of the Master. And for this Reason 'tis more Honourable to serve a Prince, than a private Person. To apply this. Christian *Priests* are the Principal Ministers of Gods Kingdom.
They

They Represent his Person, Publish his Laws, Pass his Pardons, and Preside in his Worship. To expose a *Priest* much more to burlesque his Function, is an Affront to the Diety. All indignities done to Ambassadors, are interpreted upon their Masters, and reveng'd as such. To outrage the *Ministers* of Religion, is in effect to deny the Being, or Providence of God ; And to treat the *Bible* like a *Romance*. As much as to say the Stories of an other World are nothing but a little *Priest-craft*, and therefore I am resolv'd to Lash the Profession. But to droll upon the Institutions of God ; To make his Ministers cheap, and his Authority contemptible ; To do this is little less than open defyance. Tis a sort of Challenge to awaken his Vengeance, to exert his Omnipotence ; and do Right to his Honour. If the Profession of a Courtier was unfashionable, a Princes Commission thought a Scandal, and the *Magistracy* laught at for their Business ; the Monarch had need look to himself in time ; He may conclude his Person is despis'd, his Authority but a Jest, and the People ready either to change their Master, or set up for themselves. Government and Religion, no less than *Trade* Subsist upon Reputation. 'Tis true God can't be Deposed, neither does his

his Happiness depend upon Homage. But since he does not Govern by Omnipotence, since he leaves Men to their Liberty, Acknowledgment muſt ſink, and Obedience decline, in proportion to the Leſſenings of Authority. How provoking an Indignity of this kind muſt be, is eaſy to imagine.

II. The Functions and Authorities of Religion have a great Influence on *Society*. The Intereſt of this Life lies very much in the Belief of another. So that if our Hopes were bounded with *Sight*, and *Senſe*, if *Eternity* was out of the Caſe, General Advantage, and Publick Reaſon, and Secular Policy, would oblige us to be juſt to the *Prieſthood*. For *Prieſts*, and Religion always ſtand and fall together; Now Religion is the Baſis of Government, and Man is a wretched Companion without it. When Conſcience takes its Leave, Good Faith, and Good Nature goes with it. *Atheiſm* is all Self, Mean and Mercenary. The *Atheiſt* has no *Hereafter*, and therefore will be ſure to make the moſt of this World. Intereſt, and Pleaſure, are the Gods he Worſhips, and to theſe he'll Sacrifice every Thing elſe.

III. The *Prieſt-hood* ought to be fairly treated, becauſe it has preſcription for this Privilege. This is ſo evident a
K Truth,

Truth, that there is hardly any Age or Country, but affords sufficient Proof. A just Discourse upon this Subject would be a large Book, but I shall just skim it over and pass on. and

1st. For the Jews. *Josephus* tells us the Line of *Aaron* made some of the best Pedigrees, and that the *Priests* were reckon'd among the Principal Nobility.

De Bell. Judaic.

By the Old *Testament* we are inform'd that the *High-Priest* was the Second Person in the Kingdom. The Body of that Order had Civil Jurisdiction. And the *Priests* continued Part of the Magistracy in the time of our Saviour. *Jehoiada* the *High-Priest* was thought an Alliance big enough for the Royal Family. He Married the Kings Daughter; His Interest and Authority was so great that he broke the Usurpation under *Athalia* ; and ·was at theHead of the Restauration.And lastly the *Assamonean* Race were both Kings and Priests.

Deut 17. 9. 10. 2 *Chron.* 19. 8.

Math. 27. *Act.* 4. *Vid seldon de Synedr.*

2. *Chron.* 22. 23.

Joseph.

To Proceed. The *Ægyptian* Monarchy was one of the most antient and best polish'd upon Record. Here Arts and Sciences, the Improvment·of Reason, and the Splendor of Life had its first Rise. Hither 'twas that *Plato* and most of the Celebrated Philosophers travel'd for their Learning. Now in this Kingdom the

Priests

Priests made no vulgar Figure. These with the Military Men were the Body of the Nobility, and Gentry. Besides the Business of Religion, the *Priests* were the Publick *Annalists* and kept the Records of *History*, and *Government.* They were many of them bred in Courts, formed the Education of their Princes, and assisted at their Councils. When *Joseph* was Viceroy of *Ægypt*, and in all the height of his Pomp, and Power, the King Married him to the Daughter of *Potipherah Priest* of *On*. The Text says *Pharaoh gave him her to Wife*. This shows the Match was deliberate Choice, and Royal Favour, no stooping of Quality, or Condescensions of Love, on *Joseph*'s Side. *Diod. Sic.*

Gen. 41.

To pass on. The *Persian Magi,* and the *Druids,* of *Gaul* were of a Religious Profession, and consign'd to the Service of the Gods. Now all these were at the upper End of the Government, and had a great share of Regard and Authority. The Body of the *Indians* as *Diodorus Siculus* reports is divided into Seven parts. The first is the *Clan* of the *Bramines*, the *Priests,* and Philosophers of that Country. ' This Division is the least in Num-
' ber, but the first in Degree. Their Pri-
' vileges are extraordinary. They are ex-
Porph. de Abstin. Lib. 4. Cæsar de Bell. Gall. Lib. 6.

empted

'empted from Taxes, and Live Indepen-
' dent of Authority. They are called to
' the Sacrifices, and take care of Funerals ;
' They are look'd on as the Favourites
' of the Gods, and thought skillful in the
' Doctrins of an other Life: And upon
' these accounts are largely consider'd in
' Presents, and Acknowledgment. The
Priestesses of *Argos* were so Considerable,
that *Time* is dated from them, and they
stand for a Reign in *Chronology.* The

Lib. 6.

Brave *Romans* are commended by *Polybius*
for their Devotion to the Gods; Indeed
they gave great Proof of their being in
earnest; For when thier Cheif Magistrates,
their Consuls themselves, met any of
the *Vestals*, they held down their *Fasces*,
and stoop'd their *Sword* and *Mace* to Re-
ion.

Sen, in Controv.

ligThe *Priest-hood* was for sometime con-
fin'd to the *Patrician* Order, that is to
the Upper Nobility. And afterwards the
Emperours were generally *High-Priests*
themselves. The Romans in distress endeavour'd to make Friends with *Coriolanus*
whom they had banish'd before. To
this purpose they furnish'd out several *Solemn* Embasayes. Now the Regulation of
the Ceremony, and the Remarks of the

Dion Ha-lic.

Historian ; plainly discover that the *Body*
of the *Priests* were thought not inferior

to

to any other. One Testimony from *Tully*
and I have done. 'Tis in his Harangue
to the College of the *Priests*. *Cum multa
divinitus, Pontifices, a majoribus nostris in-
venta atque instituta sunt; tum nihil pre-* ProDom ad Pontif.
*clarius qàum quòd vos eosdem et Religioni-
bus Deorum immortalium, & summæ Rei
publicæ præesse voluerunt.* &c. *i. e. Amongst*
the many laudable *Instances* of our *Ancestors*
Prudence, and Capacity, I know nothing better contrived then their placing your *Order*
at the Helm, and setting the same *Persons*
at the Head both of *Religion,* and *Government.* Thus we see what *Rank* the *Priest-
hood* held among the *Jews,* and how Nature taught the *Heathen* to regard it. And
is it not now possess'd of as fair pretences
as formerly? Is Christianity any disadvantage to the Holy Office. And does
the Dignity of a Religion lessen the Publick Administrations in't? The *Priests of
the most High God* and of *Idolatry,* can't be
compared without Injury. To argue for
the Preference is a Reflection upon the
Creed. 'Tis true the *Jewish Priest-hood*
was instituted by God: But every Thing
Divine is not of Equal Consideration.
Realities are more valuable than *Types;*
And as the Apostle argues, the *Order*
of *Melchizedeck* is greater than that of
Aaron. The Author, (I mean the imme- Hebr. 7.

K 3   diate

diate one,) the Authorities, the Bufinefs, and the End, of the *Chriftian Prieft-hood*, are more Noble than thofe of the *Jewifh*. For is not *Chrift* greater than *Mofes*, *Heaven* better than the Land of *Canaan*, and the *Eucharift* to be prefer'd to all the *Sacrifices*, and *Expiations* of the *Law*? Thus the Right, and the Reafon of Things ftands. And as for *Fact*, the Chriftian World have not been backward in their Acknowledgments. Ever fince the firft Converfion of ˙Princes, the *Prieft-hood* has had no fmall fhare of Temporal Advantage. The *Codes*, *Novels*, and *Church Hiftory*, are Sufficient Evidence what Senfe *Conftantine* and his Succeffors had of thefe Matters. But I fhall not detain the *Reader* in remote Inftances.

To proceed then to Times and Countries more generally known. The People of *France* are branched into three Divifions, of thefe the *Clergy*, are the Firft. And in confequence of this Privilege, at the Affembly of the *States*, they are firft admitted to Harangue before the King.

In *Hungary* the *Bifhops* are very Confiderable, and fome of them great Officers of *State*. In *Poland* they are *Senators* that is part of the Upper *Noblefs*. In *Mufcovy* the *Bifhops* have an Honourable Station; and the Prefent *Czar* is defcended

from

Davila
Filmers
Freehold-
ers Grand
Inq.

Miræus De
Statu Re-
ligoChrift.
Mihæs
˙˙˙

from the *Patriarchal* Line. I suppose I
need say nothing of *Italy*. In *Spain* the *Sees*
generally are better endow'd than elswhere,
and Wealth alwaies draws Consideration. The *Bishops* hold their Lands by a
Military Noble *Tenure*, and are excused
from Personal Attendance. And to come
toward an end; They are Earls and Dukes
in *France*, and Soveraign Princes in *Ger-
many*. In *England* the *Bishops* are Lords
of Parliament: And the *Law* in plain words
distinguishes the *Upper House* into the *Spiritual* and *Temporal Nobility*. And several
Statutes call the Bishops *Nobles* by direct
Implication. To mention nothing more,
their *Heraldry* is regulated by *Garter*, and
Blazon'd by *Stones*, which none under the
Nobility can pretend to. In this Country
of ours, Persons of the First Quality have
been in *Orders* : To give an Instance of
some few. *Odo* Brother to *William* the
Conquerour was *Bishop* of *Baieux*, and Earl
of *Kent*. King *Stephens* Brother was *Bishop* of *Winchester*. *Nevill* Arch-Bishop
of *York* was Brother to the Great Earl
of *Warwick*, and *Cardinal Pool* was of the
Royal Family. To come a little lower,
and to our own Times. And here we
may reckon not a few Persons of Noble
Descent in Holy *Orders*. Witness the
Berklyes, *Comptons*, *Montagues*, *Crews*,

*Fletchers
Embassy.
Puffen-
derf In-
trodu-
ction.
à l' Hi-
stoire.*

*Heglins
Cosmogk.*

25 *Hen.*
8. *cap.*
22.
26, *Hen.*8.
cap. 2.
1. *Edw.*
6. *cap.*
12, &c.
Preamb.

K 4   and

and *Norths* ; The *Annesleys, Finches, Grayhams* &c. And as for the Gentry, there are not many good Familes in *England,* but either have, or have had a *Clergy-man* in them,

In short ; The *Priest-hood* is the profession of a Gentleman. A *Parson* notwithstanding the ignorant Pride of some People, is a Name of Credit, and Authority, both in Religion, and *Law.* The *Addition* of *Clerk* is at least equal to that of Gentleman. Were it otherwise the *Profession* would in many cases be a kind of Punishment. But the *Law* is far from being so singular as to make *Orders* a Disadvantage to *Degree.* No, The Honour of the Family continues, and the *Heraldry* is every jot as safe in the *Church,* as 'twas in the *State.* And yet when the *Laity* are taken leave of, not *Gentleman* but *Clerk* is usually. written. This Custom is an argument the Change is not made for the worse, that the Spiritual Distinction is as valuable as the other ; And to speak Modestly, that the first *Addition* is not lost, but Cover'd. Did the Subject require it, this Point might be farther made good. For the stile of a higher Secular Honour is continued as well with *Priest-hood* as without it. A Churchman who is either *Baronet,* or *Baron,* writes

writes himself so, notwithstanding His
Clerkship. Indeed we can't well imagine the Clergy degraded from Pater-
nal Honour without a strange Reflection on
the Country; without supposing *Julian* at
the Helm, the *Laws* Antichristian, and
Infidelity in the very *Constitution.* To
make the Ministers of Religion less upon
the score of their Function, would be a
Penalty on the *Gospel,* and a contempt
of the God of Christianity. 'Tis our Saviours reasoning ; *He that despises you, de-* S. Luke.
spises Me, and he that Despises Me, Despises 1c.
Him that sent me.

I hope what I have offer'd on this
Subject will not be misunderstood. There
is no Vanity in necessary Defence. To
wipe off Aspersions, and rescue Things
from Mistake, is but bare Justice : Besides,
where the Honour of God, and the Publick Interest are concern'd, a Man is bound
to speak. To argue from a resembling
Instance. He that has the Kings Commission ought to Maintain it. To let it
suffer under Rudeness is to betray it. To
be tame and silent in such cases, is not
Modesty but Meanness, Humility obliges
no Man to desert his Trust ; To throw
up his Privilege, and prove false to his
Character. And is our Saviours Authority inferiour to that of Princes ? Are
the Kingdoms of this World more Glorious

rious than that of the next? And can the Concerns of Time be greater than those of Eternity? If not, the reasoning above mention'd must hold in the Application.

And now by this time I conceive the ill Manners of the *Stage* may be in some measure apparent; And that the *Clergy* deserve none of that Coarse Usage which it puts upon them. I confess I know no *Profession* that has made a more creditable Figure, that has better Customs for their Privileges, and better Reasons to maintain them. And here setting aside the point of Conscience, where lies the Decency of falling foul upon this *Order*? What Propriety is there in Misrepresentation? In confounding Respects, disguising Features, and painting Things out of all Colour and Complexion? This crossing upon Nature and Reason, is great Ignorance, and out of Rule. And now what Pleasure is there in Misbehaviour and Abuse? Is it such an Entertainment to see Religion worryed by Atheism, and Things the most Solemn and Significant tumbled and tost by Buffoons? A Man may laugh at a Puppy's tearing a Wardrobe, but I think 'twere altogether as discreet to beat him off. Well! but the *Clergy* mismanage sometimes, and they must be told of their Faults. What then? Are the *Poets* their *Ordinaries*? Is the *Pulpit* under the Discipline

cipline of the *Stage*? And are those fit to correct the Church, that are not fit to come into it ? Besides, What makes them fly out upon the *Function* ; and rail by wholesale ? Is the *Priesthood* a crime, and the service of God a Disadvantage ? I grant Persons and Things are not always suited. A good *Post* may be ill kept, but then the Censure should keep close to the Fault, and the Office not suffer for the Manager. The *Clergy* may have their Failings sometimes like others, but what then ? The *Character* is still untarnish'd. The *Men* may be Little, but the *Priests* are not so. And therefore like other People, they ought to be treated by their best Distinction.

If 'tis Objected that the *Clergy* in *Plays* are commonly *Chaplains*, And that these *Belonging* to Persons of Quality they were obliged to represent them servile and submissive. To this I Answer

1*st*. In my former remark, that the *Stage* often outrages the whole *Order*, without regard to any particular Office. But were it not so in the

2*d*. Place, They quite overlook the Character, and mistake the Business of *Chaplains*. They are no *Servants*, neither *Moral* do they *Belong* to any *Body*, but God Al-*Essays*. mighty. This Point I have fully proved in another, *Treatise*, and thither I refer the *Reader*.

CHAP.

C H A P. IV.

The Stage-Poets make their Principal Per-
sons Vitious, and reward them at the
End of the Play.

THE Lines of Virtue and Vice are
Struck out by Nature in very Le-
gible Distinctions ; They tend to a different Point, and in the greater Instances the
Space between them is easily perceiv'd.
Nothing can be more unlike than the Original Forms of these Qualities : The First
has all the sweetness, Charms, and Graces imaginable ; The other has the Air of
a *Post* ill Carved into a *Monster*, and looks
both foolish and Frightful together. These
are the Native Appearances of good and
Evil : And they that endeavour to blot the
Distinctions, to rub out the Colours, or
change the Marks, are extreamly to blame.
'Tis confessed as long as the Mind is a-
wake, and Conscience goes true, there's
no fear of being imposed on. But when
Vice is varnish'd over with Pleasure, and
comes in the Shape of Convenience, the
case grows somewhat dangerous ; for then
the

the Fancy may be gain'd, and the Guards corrupted, and Reaſon ſuborn'd againſt it ſelf. And thus a *Diſguiſe* often paſſes when the Perſon would otherwiſe be ſtopt. To put *Lewdneſs* into a Thriving condition, to give it an Equipage of Quality; and to treat it with Ceremony and Reſpect, is the way to confound the Underſtanding, to fortifie the Charm, and to make the Miſchief invincible. Innocence is often owing to Fear, and Appetite is kept under by Shame; But when theſe Reſtraints are once taken off, when Profit and Liberty lie on the ſame ſide, and a Man can Debauch himſelf into Credit, what can be expected in ſuch a caſe, but that Pleaſure ſhould grow Abſolute, and Madneſs carry all before it ? The *Stage* ſeem eager to bring Matters to this Iſſue; They have made a conſiderable progreſs, and are ſtill puſhing their Point with all the Vigour imaginable. If this be not their Aim why is *Lewdneſs* ſo much conſider'd in Character and Succeſs ? Why are their Favourites Atheiſtical, and their fine Gentleman debauched ? To what purpoſe is *Vice* thus prefer'd, thus ornamented, and careſs'd, unleſs for Imitation ? That matter of Fact ſtands thus, I ſhall make good by ſeveral Inſtances: To begin then with their Men of Breeding and

Figure.

Figure. *Wild-blood* sets up for *Debauch-*

Moch A-
strol. p. 3.
&c.
ery, Ridicules Marriage, and Swears by
Mahomet. *Bellamy* makes sport with the

Mock A-
strol. p. 57,
59.
Devil, and *Lorenzo* is vitious and calls
his Father *Bawdy Magistrate*. *Horner* is

Spanish
Fryar. p.
61.
horridly Smutty, and *Harcourt* false to his
Friend who used him kindly. In the

Country
Wife. p.
25.
Plain Dealer Freeman talks coarsely, cheats
theWiddow,debauches her Son, and makes

Old Batch.
Double
Dealer. p.
34.
him undutiful. *Bellmour* is Lewd and
Profane, And *Mellefont* puts *Careless* in
the best way he can to debauch *Lady
Plyant*. These *Sparks* generally Marry
up the Top Ladys,and those that do not,are
brought to no Pennance, but go off with
the Character of Fine Gentlemen: In
Don-Sebastian, *Antonio* an Atheistical Bully
is rewarded with the Lady *Moraima*,
and half the *Muffty*'s Estate. *Valentine*

Love for
Love. p.
90.
in *Love for Love* is (if I may so call him)
the Hero of the *Play* ; This Spark the
Poet would pass for a Person of Virtue,
but he speaks to late. 'Tis true, He was
hearty in his Affection to *Angelica*. Now
without question, to be in Love with a
fine Lady of 30000 Pounds is a great
Virtue ! But then abating this single Commendation, *Valentine* is altogether com-

Love for
Love. p.
6, 7. 25.
61. 89.
91.
pounded of Vice. He is a prodigal Debauchee, unnatural, and Profane, Obscene,
Sawcy, and undutiful, And yet this Libertine

bertine is crown'd for the Man of Merit, has his Wishes thrown into his Lap, and makes the Happy *Exit*. I perceive we should have a rare set of *Virtues* if these *Poets* had the making of them! How they hug a Vitious Character, and how profuse are they in their Liberalities to Lewdness? In the *Provok'd Wife, Constant* Swears at Length, solicits Lady *Brute,* Confesses himself Lewd, and prefers Debauchery to Marriage. He handles the last Sybject very notably and worth the Hearing. *There is* (says he) *a poor sordid Slavery in Marriage, that turns the flowing Tide of Honour, and sinks it to the lowest ebb of Infamy. 'Tis a Corrupted Soil, Ill Nature, Avarice, Sloth, Cowardize, and Dirt, are all its Product.*——But then *Constancy*(*alias Whoring*) *is a Brave, Free, Haughty, Generous, Agent.* This is admirable stuff both for the Rhetorick and the Reason! The Character of *Young Fashion* in the *Relapse* p. 35. is of the same Staunchness, but this the *Reader* may have in another Place.

To sum up the Evidence. A fine Gentleman, is a fine Whoring, Swearing, Smutty, Atheistical Man. These Qualifications it seems compleat the *Idea* of Honour. They are the Top-Improvements of Fortune, and the distinguishing Glories of Birth and Breeding! This is

the

the *Stage-Test* for *Quality*, and those that can't stand it, ought to be *Disclaim'd*. The Restraints of Conscience and the Pedantry of Virtue, are unbecoming a Cavalier: Future Securities, and Reaching beyond Life, are vulgar Provisions: If he falls a Thinking at this rate, he forfeits his Honour ; For his Head was only made to run against a Post *!* Here you have a Man of Breeding and Figure that burlesques the *Bible*, Swears, and talks Smut to Ladies, speaks ill of his Friend behind his Back, and betraies his Interest. A fine Gentleman that has neither Honesty, nor Honour, Conscience, nor Manners, Good Nature, nor civil Hypocricy. Fine, only in the Insignificancy of Life, the Abuse of Religion and the Scandals of Conversation. These Worshipful Things are the *Poets* Favourites ; They appear at the Head of the *Fashion*; and shine in Character, and Equipage. If there is any Sense stirring, They must have it, tho' the rest of the *Stage* suffer never so much by the Partiality. And what can be the Meaning of this wretched Distribution of Honour ? Is it not to give Credit and Countenance to Vice, and to shame young People out of all pretences to Conscience, and Regularity ? They seem forc'd to turn Lewd in their own Defence : They can't other-

wise

wife juftifie themfelves to the Fafhion, nor keep up the Character of Gentlemen : Thus People not well furnifh'd with Thought, and Experience, are debauch'd both in Practife and Principle. And thus Religion grows uncreditable, and paffes for ill Education. The *Stage* feldom gives Quarter to any Thing that's ferviceable or Significant, but perfecutes Worth, and Goodnefs under every Appearance. He that would be fafe from their Satir muft take care to difguife himfelf in Vice, and hang out the *Colours* of Debauchery. How often is Learning, Induftry, and Frugality, ridiculed in Comedy ? The rich Citizens are often Mifers, and Cuckolds, and the *Univerfities*, Schools of Pedantry upon this fcore. In fhort ; Libertinifm and Profanefs, Dreffing, Idlenefs, and Gallantry, are the only valuable Qualities. As if People were not apt enough of themfelves to be Lazy, Lewd, and Extravagant, unlefs they were prick'd forward, and provok'd by Glory, and Reputation. Thus the Marks of Honour, and Infamy are mifapplyed, and the Idea's of Virtue and Vice confounded. Thus Monftroufnefs goes for Proportion, and the Blemifhes of Human Nature, make up the Beauties of it.

L

The

The fine Ladies are of the same Cut with the Gentlemen; *Moraima* is scandalously rude to her Father, helps him to a beating, and runs away with *Antonio*. *Angelica* talks sawcily to her Uncle, and *Belinda* confesses her Inclination for a Gallant. And as I have observ'd already, the Toping Ladies in the *Mock Astrologer, Spanish Fryar, Country Wife, Old Batchelour, Orphan, Double Dealer*, and *Love Triumphant*, are smutty, and sometimes Profane.

Don Sebast. Love for Love. p. 20 Provok'd Wife. p.64. Chap. 1. & 2.

And was Licentiousness and irreligion, alwaies a mark of Honour? No; I don't perceive but that the old *Poets* had an other Notion of Accomplishment, and bred their people of Condition a different way. *Philolaches* in *Plautus* laments his being debauch'd; and dilates upon the Advantages of Virtue, and Regularity. *Lusiteles* another Young Gentleman disputes handsomly by himself against Lewdness. And the discourse between him and *Philto* is Moral, and well managed. And afterwards he lashes Luxury and Debauching with a great deal of Warmth, and Satir. *Chremes* in *Terence* is a modest young Gentleman, he is afraid of being surpriz'd by *Thais*, and seems careful not to sully his Reputation. And *Pamphilus* in *Hecyra* resolves rather to be govern'd by Duty, than Inclination.

Mostel. A. 1. 2.

Trinum. A. 2. 1.

A. 2. 2.

Enuch. A. 3. 3.

Hecyr. A. 3. 4.

Plau-

Plautus's *Pinacium* tells her Friend *Panegyric* that they ought to acquit themselves fairly to their Husbands, tho' These should fail in their Regards towards them. For all good People will do justice tho' they don't receive it.   Lady *Brute* in the *Provok'd Wife* is govern'd by different maxims.   She is debauch'd with ill Usage, says *Virtue is an Ass, and a Gallant's worth forty on't.* *Pinacium* goes on to another Head of Duty, and declares that a Daughter can never respect her Father too much, and that Disobedience has a great deal of scandal, and Lewdness in't.   The Lady *Jacinta* as I remember does not treat her Father at this rate of Decency.   Let us hear a little of her Behaviour.   The *Mock Astrologer* makes the Men draw, and frights the Ladys with the Apprehension of a Quarrel.   Upon this; *Theodosia* crys *what will become of us!* *Jacinta* answers, *we'll die for Company: nothing vexes me but that I am not a Man, to have one thrust at that malicious old Father of mine, before I go.* Afterwards the old Gentleman *Alonzo* threatens his Daughters with a Nunnery. *Jacinta* spars again and says, *I would have thee to know thou graceless old Man, that I defy a Nunnery: name a Nunnery once more and I disown thee for my Father.*   I could carry on the Comparison between the old

Stich. A. I. I.

p. 3.

Stich. A. I. 2.

p. 60.

Ibid.

and Modern Poets somewhat farther. But this may suffice.

Thus we see what a fine time Lewd People have on the *English Stage.* No Censure, no mark of Infamy, no Mortification muſt touch them. They keep their Honour untarniſh'd, and carry off the Advantage of their Character. They are ſet up for the Standard of Behaviour, and the Maſters of Ceremony and Senſe. And at laſt that the Example may work the better, they generally make them rich, and happy, and reward them with their own Deſires.

Mr. *Dryden* in the *Preface* to his *Mock-Astrologer,* confeſſes himſelf blamed for this Practiſe. *For making debauch'd Perſons his* Protagoniſts, *or chief Perſons of the Drama ; And for making them happy in the Concluſion of the Play, againſt the Law of Comedy, which is to reward Virtue, and puniſh Vice.* To this Objection He makes a lame Defence. And anſwers

1ſt. *That he knows no ſuch Law conſtantly obſerv'd in Comedy by the Antient or Modern Poets.* What then? *Poets* are not always exactly in Rule. It may be a good Law tho' 'tis not conſtantly obſerv'd, ſome Laws are conſtantly broken, and yet ne're the worſe for all that. He goes on, and pleads the Authorities of *Plautus,* and *Terence.* I grant there are Inſtances of

Favour

Favour to vitious young People in those Authors, but to this I reply

1*st*. That those *Poets* had a greater compass of Liberty in their Religion. Debauchery did not lie under those Discouragements of Scandal, and penalty, with them as it does with us. Unless therefore He can prove *Heathenism*, and *Christianity* the same, his *precedents* will do him little service.

2*ly*. *Horace* who was as good a judge of the *Stage*, as either of those *Comedians*, seems to be of another Opinion. He condemns the obscenities of *Plautus*, and tells you Men of Fortune and Quality in his time; would not endure immodest Satir. He continues, that Poets were formerly admired for the great services they did. For teaching Matters relating to Religion, and Government; For refining the Manners, tempering the Passions, and improving the Understandings of Mankind: For making them more useful in Domestick Relations, and the publick Capacities of Life. This is a demonstration that Vice was not the Inclination of the Muses in those days; and that *Horace* beleiv'd the chief business of a *Poem* was, to Instruct the Audience. He adds farther that the *Chorus* ought to turn upon the Argument of the *Drama*, and support the Design of the *Acts*. That

De Art. Poet.

Ibid.

They ought to speak in Defence of Virtue, and Frugality, and show a Regard to Religion. Now from the Rule of the *Chorus*, we may conclude his Judgment for the *Play*. For as he observes, there must be a Uniformity between the *Chorus* and the *Acts* : They must have the same View, and be all of a Piece. From hence 'tis plain that *Horace* would have no immoral *Character* have either Countenance or good Fortune, upon the *Stage*. If 'tis said the very mention of the *Chorus* shews the Directions were intended for *Tragedy*. To this

I answer, that the Consequence is not good. For the use of a *Chorus* is not inconsistent with *Comedy*. The antient *Comedians* had it. *Aristophanes* is an Instance. I know 'tis said the *Chorus* was left out in that they call the *New Comedy*. But I can't see the conclusiveness of this Assertion. For *Aristophanes* his *Platus* is *New Comedy* with a *Chorus* in't. And *Aristotle* who lived after this Revolution of the *Stage*, mentions nothing of the Omission of the *Chorus*. He rather supposes its continuance by saying the *Chorus was added by the Government long after the Invention of Comedy.* 'Tis true *Plautus* and *Terence* have none, but those before them probably might. *Moliere* has now reviv'd them ;

Vid. Schol.

Libr. de Poet. cap. 5.

And

And *Horace* might be of his Opinion, for ought wee know to the contrary.

Laſtly. *Horace* having expreſly mentioned the beginning and progreſs of *Comedy*, diſcovers himſelf more fully: He adviſes a *Poet* to form his Work upon the Precepts of *Socrates* and *Plato*, and the Models of Moral Philoſophy. This was the way to preſerve Decency, and to aſſign a proper Fate and Behaviour to every *Character*. Now if *Horace* would have his *Poet* govern'd by the Maxims of Morality, he muſt oblige him to Sobriety of Conduct, and a juſt diſtribution of Rewards, and Puniſhments. *Ibid.*

Mr. *Dryden* makes Homewards, and endeavours to fortifie himſelf in Modern Authority. He lets us know that *Ben Johnſon after whom he may be proud to Err, gives him more than one example of this Conduct; That in the* Alchemiſt *is notorius,* where neither *Face* nor his *Maſter* are corrected according to their Demerits. *Fref Mock. Aſtrol.* But how Proud ſoever Mr. *Dryden* may be of an Errour, he has not ſo much of *Ben Jonſon's* company as he pretends. His Inſtance of *Face &c.* in the *Alchemiſt* is rather *notorious* againſt his Purpoſe then for it.

For *Face* did not Council his Maſter *Lovewit* to debauch the Widdow; neither

is it clear that the Matter went thus far.
He might gain her consent upon Terms
of Honour for ought appears to the contrary. 'Tis true *Face* who was one of
the Principal Cheats is Pardon'd and consider'd. But then his Master confesses
himself kind to a fault. He owns this
Indulgence was a Breach of Justice, and
unbecoming the Gravity of an old Man.
And then desires the Audience to excuse
him upon the Score of the Temptation.
But *Face continued in the Cousenage till the*
last without Repentance. Under favour I
conceive this is a Mistake. For does not
Face make an Apology before he leaves
the *Stage* ? Does he not set himself at the
Bar, arraign his own Practise, and cast
the Cause upon the Clemency of the Company ? And are not all these Signs of the
Dislike of what he had done ? Thus careful the *Poet* is to prevent the Ill Impressions of his *Play* ! He brings both Man
and Master to Confession. He dismisses
them like Malefactours ; And moves for
their Pardon before he gives them their
Discharge. But the *Mock-Astrologer* has a
gentler Hand : *Wild-Blood* and *Jacinta*
are more generously used : There is
no Acknowledgment exacted ; no Hardship put upon them : They are permitted to talk on in their Libertine way to
the

Ibid.

the Laſt: And take Leave without the
leaſt Appearance of Reformation. The
Mock-Aſtrologer urges *Ben Johnſon's Silent
Woman* as an other *Precedent* to his purpoſe. For *there* Dauphine *confeſſes himſelf in Love with all the Collegiate Lady's.
And yet this naughty* Dauphine *is Crowned
in the end with the Poſſeſſion of his Uncles
Eſtate, and with the hopes of all his Miſtreſſes.*
This Charge, as I take it, is ſomewhat
too ſevere. I grant *Dauphine* Profeſſes
himſelf in Love with the Collegiate Ladies
at firſt. But when they invited him to
a private Viſit, he makes them no Promiſe;
but rather appears tired, and willing to
diſengage. *Dauphine* therefore is not altogether ſo naughty as this Author repreſents him.

   Ben Johnſon's Fox is clearly againſt Mr.
Dryden. And here I have his own Confeſſion for proof. He declares the *Poets
end in this Play was the Puniſhment of Vice,
and the Reward of Virtue. Ben* was forced
to ſtrain for this piece of Juſtice, and
break through the *Unity of Deſign.* This
Mr. *Dryden* remarks upon him : How
ever he is pleaſed to commend the Performance, and calls it an excellent *Fifth
Act.*

   Ben Johnſon ſhall ſpeak for himſelf afterwards in the Character of a Critick ;

Ibid.

*Eſſay of
Drama-
tick Po-
etry.
p. 28.*

In

In the mean time I shall take a Testimony or two from *Shakespear*. And here we may observe the admir'd *Falstaffe* goes off in Disappointment. He is thrown out of Favour as being a *Rake*, and dies like a Rat behind the Hangings. The Pleasure he had given, would not excuse him. The *Poet* was not so partial, as to let his Humour compound for his Lewdness. If 'tis objected that this remark is wide of the Point, because *Falstaffe* is represented in Tragedy, where the Laws of Justice are more strickly observ'd. To this I answer, that you may call *Henry* the Fourth and Fifth, Tragedies if you please. But for all that, *Falstaffe* wears no *Buskins,* his Character is perfectly Comical from end to end.

The next Instance shall be in *Flowerdale* the *Prodigal.* This Spark notwithstanding his Extravagance, makes a lucky Hand on't at last, and marries up a rich Lady. But then the Poet qualifies him for his good Fortune, and mends his Manners with his Circumstances. He makes him repent, and leave off his Intemperance, Swearing &c. And when his Father warn'd him against a Relapse, He answers very soberly,

Heaven helping me I'le hate the Course of Hell.

The London Prodigal.

I

I could give some Instances of this kind
out of *Beaumount* and *Fletcher*, But there's
no need of any farther Quotation ; For
Mr. *Dryden* is not satisfied with his Apology
from Authority : He does as good as own
that this may be construed no better than
defending one ill practise by another. To
prevent this very reasonable objection he
endeavours to vindicate his *Precedents* from
the Reason of the Thing. To this purpose he *makes a wide difference between the
Rules of Tragedy and Comedy. That Vice
must be impartially prosecuted in the first, because the Persons are Great &c.*

It seems then *Executions* are only for
Greatness, and *Quality. Justice* is not
to strike much *lower* than a *Prince. Private People* may do what they *please.*
They are too *few* for *Mischief*, and too
Little for *Punishment!* This would be
admirable Doctrine for *Newgate*, and give
us a general *Goal-Delivery* without more
ado. But in *Tragedy* (says the *Mock
Astrologer.*) *the Crimes are likewise Horrid*, so that there is a necessity for
Severity and Example. And how stands
the matter in *Comedy* ? Quite otherwise.
There the *Faults are but the sallies of Youth,
and the Frailties of Human Nature.* For   *Ibid.*
Instance. There is nothing but a little
Whoring, Pimping. Gaming, Profaness
&c, And who could be so hard hearted
to

to give a Man any Trouble for This?
Such Rigours would be strangely Inhu-
mane! A *Poet* is a better natur'd Thing
I can assure you. These little Miscar-
rages *move Pity and Commiseration, and are*
not such as must of necessity be Punish'd.
This is comfortable Casuistry! But to be
Serious. Is Dissolution of Manners such a
Peccadillo? Does a Profligate Conscience
deserve nothing but Commiseration? And
are People damn'd only for *Humane Frail-*
ties? I perceive the Laws of Religion and
those of the *Stage* differ extreamly! The
strength of his Defence lies in this choice
Maxim, that the *Cheif End of Comedy is*
Delight. He questions *whether Instruction*
has any thing to do in Comedy; If it has, he
is sure *'tis no more then its secondary end*;
For the business of the Poet is to make you
laugh. Granting the Truth of this Principle, I somewhat question the servicea-
bleness of it. For is there no Diversion
to be had unless Vice appears prosperous,
and rides at the Head of Success. One
would think such a preposterous, distribution of Rewards, should rather
shock the Reason, and raise the Indignation
of the *Audience*. To laugh without reason is the Pleasure of Fools, and against
it, of something worse. The exposing of
Knavery, and making *Lewdness* ridiculous,
is a much better occasion for Laughter.

And

Ibid.

Ibid.

And this with submission I take to be the
End of *Comedy*. And therefore it does
not differ from *Tragedy* in the End, but
in the *Means*. Instruction is the principal Design of both. The one works by
Terror, the other by Infamy. 'Tis true,
they don't move in the same Line, but
they meet in the same point at last. For
this Opinion I have good Authority, besides what has been cited already.

1*st*. Monsieur *Rapin* affirms ' That De-
' light is the End that Poetry aims at, but
' not the Principal one. For Poetry being
' an Art, ought to be profitable by the qua-
' lity of it's own nature, and by the Essen-
' tial Subordination that all Arts should
' have to Polity, whose End in General is *Rapin Re-
' the publick Good. This is the Judg-*flect. &c.
' ment of *Aristotle* and of *Horace* his chief *p. 10.*
' Interpreter. *Ben Johnson* in his Dedicatory Epistle of his *Fox* has somewhat considerable upon this Argument; And declaims with a great deal of zeal, spirit, and
good Sense, against the Licentiousness of
the *Stage*. He lays it down for a Principle, ' That 'tis impossible to be a good *Poet*
' without being a good *Man*. That he
' (a good Poet) is said to be able to inform
' Young Men to all good Discipline, and
' enflame grown Men to all great Virtues
' &c.—— That the general complaint was
' that the *Writers* of those days had no-
'thing

'thing remaining in them of the Dignity
'of a *Poet*, but the abused Name. That
'now, especially in Stage Poetry, nothing
'but Ribaldry, Profanation, *Blasphemy*, all
'Licence of Offence to God and Man, is
'practised. He confesses a great part of
'this Charge is over-true, and is sorry he
'dares not deny it. But then he hopes all
'are not embark'd in this bold Adventure
'for Hell. For my part (says he) I can,
'and from a most clear Conscience affirm;
'That I have ever trembled to think to-
'wards the least Profaness, and loath'd the
'Use of such foul, and unwash'd Bawdry,
'as is now made the Food of the *Scene*.——
'The encrease of which Lust in Liberty,
'what Learned or Liberal Soul does not
'abhor? In whole *Enterludes* nothing but
'the Filth of the Time is utter'd——with
'Brothelry able to violate the Ear of a *Pa-*
'*gan*, and Blasphemy, to turn the Blood of
'a Christian to Water. He continues,
'that the Insolence of these Men had
'brought the *Muses* into Disgrace, and made
'*Poetry* the lowest scorn of the Age. He
'appeals to his Patrons the *Universities*,
'that his Labour has been heretofore, and
'mostly in this his latest Work, to reduce
'not only the antient Forms, but Manners
'of the *Scene*, the Innocence and the Doc-
'trine, which is the Principal End of Poesy,
'to

' to inform Men in the beſt Reaſon of Li-
' ving. Laſtly he adds, that ' he has imi-
' tated the Conduct of the Antients in this
' *Play*, The goings out (or Concluſions)
' of whoſe *Comedies*, were not always joy-
' ful but oft-times the Bawds, the Slaves,
' the Rivals, yea and the Maſters are mul-
' ted, and fitly, it being the Office of a
' *Comick Poet* (mark that !) to imitate Ju-
' ſtice, and Inſtruct to Life *&c.* Say you ſo !
Why then if *Ben Johnſon* knew any thing
of the Matter, Divertiſment and Laughing is not as Mr. *Dryden* affirms, the *Chief
End* of *Comedy*. This Teſtimony is ſo very full and clear, that it needs no explaining, nor any enforcement from Reaſoning, and Conſequence.

And becauſe Laughing and Pleaſure
has ſuch an unlimited Prerogative upon
the *Stage*, I ſhall add a Citation or two
from *Ariſtotle* concerning this Matter.
Now this great Man ' calls thoſe Buffoons,
' and Impertinents, who rally without any
' regard to Perſons or Things, to Decency,
' or good Manners. That there is a great
' difference between Ribaldry, and handſom
' Rallying. He that would perform ex-
' actly, muſt keep within the Character of
' Virtue, and Breeding. He goes on, and
' tells us that the old Comedians enter-
' tain'd the Audience with Smut, but the
'   ' Modern

'Modern ones avoided that Liberty, and
'grew more referv'd. This latter way he
'fays was much more proper and Gentile
'then the other. That in his Opinion
'Rallying, no lefs than Railing, ought to
'be under the Difcipline of Law; That
'he who is ridden by his *Jefts*, and minds
'nothing but the bufinefs of *Laughing*, is
'himfelf Ridiculous. And that a Man of
Libr. 4. de. 'Education and Senfe, is fo far from going
Morib. 'thefe Lengths that he wont fo much as
cap. 14. 'endure the hearing fome fort of Buf-
'foonry.

And as to the point of Delight in ge-
neral, the fame Author affirms, 'that fcan-
'dalous Satisfactions are not properly
'Pleafures. 'Tis only Diftemper, and falfe
'Appetite which makes them palatable.
'And a Man that is fick, feldom has his
'Taft true. Befides, fuppofing we throw
'Capacity out of the Queftion, and make
'Experiment and Senfation the Judge ;
'Granting this, we ought not to chop
'at every Bait, nor Fly out at every
'Thing that ftrikes the Fancy. The meer
'Agreeablenefs muft not overbear us, with-
'out diftinguifhing upon the Quality, and
'the Means. Pleafure how charming fo-
'ever, muft not be fetched out of Vice.
'An Eftate is a pretty thing, but if we
'purchafe by Falfhood, and Knavery,

we

'Knavery, we pay too much for't. Some
'Pleasures, are Childish and others abo-
'minable; And upon the whole, Pleasure,
'absolutely speaking, is no good Thing.
And so much for the Philosopher. And
because *Ribaldry* is used for Sport, a passage or two from *Quintilian*, may not be
unseasonable. This Orator does not only
Condemn the grosser Instances, but cuts
off all the *Double-Entendre's* at a Blow.
He comes up to the Regularity of Thought,
and tells us 'that the Meaning, as well as the
'Words of Discourse must be unsullied:
And in the same *Chapter* he adds that ' A
'Man of Probity has always a Reserve
'in his Freedoms, and Converses within
'the Rules of Modesty, and Character.
'And that Mirth at the expence of Virtue, is an Over-purchase, *Nimium enim
risus pretium est si probitatis impendio con-
stat.*

*De Mor.
Lib.* 10.
cap. 2.

*Instiut:
Lib.* 6:
c. 3.

Thus we see how these great *Masters*
qualify Diversion, and tie it up to *Pro-
visoes*, and Conditions. Indeed to make
Delight the main business of *Comedy* is an
unreasonable and dangerous Principle. It
opens the way to all Licentiousness, and
Confounds the distinction between Mirth,
and Madness. For if Diversion is the
Chief End, it must be had at any Price,
No serviceable Expedient must be refused,

tho' never so scandalous. And thus the worst Things are said, and the best abus'd; Religion is insulted, and the most serious Matters turn'd into Ridicule! As if the Blindside of an Audience ought to be caress'd, and their Folly and Atheism entertain'd in the first Place. Yes, if the Palate is pleas'd, no matter tho' the Body is Poyson'd! For can one die of an easier Disease than Diversion? But Raillery apart, certainly Mirth and Laughing, without respect to the Cause, are not such supreme Satisfactions! A man has sometimes Pleasure in losing his Wits. Frensy, and *Possession*, will shake the Lungs, and brighten the Face; and yet I suppose they are not much to be coveted. However, now we know the Reason of the Profaness, and Obscenity of the *Stage*, of their Hellish Cursing, and Swearing, and in short of their great Industry to make God, and Goodness Contemptible: 'Tis all to Satisfie the Company, and make People Laugh! A most admirable justification! What can be more engaging to an *Audience*, then to see a *Poet* thus Atheistically brave? To see him charge up to the Canons Mouth, and defy the Vengeance of Heaven to serve them? Besides, there may be somewhat of Convenience in the Case. To fetch Diversion out of In-

Innocence is no such easy matter. There's
no succeeding it may be in this method,
without Sweat, and Drudging. Clean
Wit, inoffensive Humour, and handsom
Contrivance, require Time, and Thought.
And who would be at this Expence, when
the Purchase is so cheap another way?
'Tis possible a *Poet* may not alwaies have
Sense enough by him for such an Occasion. And since we are upon supposals,
it may be the *Audience* is not to be gain'd
without straining a Point, and giving a
Loose to Conscience: And when People
are sick, are they not to be Humour'd?
In fine, We must make them Laugh, right
or wrong, for *Delight* is the *Cheif End of
Comedy.* *Delight* ! He should have said
Debauchery : That's the English of the
Word, and the Consequence of the Practise. But the Original Design of *Comedy*
was otherwise: And granting 'twas not
so, what then? If the *Ends* of Things
are naught, they must be mended. Mischief is the Chief end of Malice, would it
be then a Blemish in Ill Nature to change
Temper, and relent into Goodness? The
Chief *End* of a Madman it may be is to
Fire a House, must we not then bind
him in his Bed? To conclude. If *Delight* without Restraint, or Distinction,
without Conscience or Shame, is the Su-

pream

pream Law of *Comedy*, 'twere well if we
had lefs on't. Arbitrary Pleafure, is more
dangerous than Arbitrary Power. Nothing is more Brutal than to be aban-
don'd to Appetite; And nothing more
wretched than to ferve in fuch a Defign.
The *Mock-Aftrologer* to clear himfelf of
this Imputation, is glad to give up his
Principle at Laft. *Leaft any Man fhould
think* (fays He) *that I write this to make
Libertinifm amiable, or that I cared not to
debafe the end, and Inftitution of* Comedy.
(It feems then *Delight* is not the Chief
end.) *I muft farther declare that we make
not Vitious Perfons Happy, but only as Heaven makes Sinners fo.* &c. If this will hold,
all's well. But *Heaven* does not forgive
without Repentance. Let us fee then
what Satisfaction he requires from his
Wild-Blood, and what Difcipline he puts
him under. Why, He helps him to his
Miftrefs, he Marries him to a Lady of
Birth and Fortune. And now do you
think He has not made him an Example,
and punifh'd him to fome Purpofe! Thefe
are frightful Severities! Who would be
vitious when fuch Terrors hang over his
Head? And does *Heaven make Sinners
happy* upon thefe Conditions? Sure fome
People have a good Opinion of Vice, or
a very ill one of Marriage, otherwife they
would

would have Charged the Penance a little more. But I have nothing farther with the *Mock-Aftrologer*.

And now for the Conclufion of a *Chapter*, I fhall give fome Inftances of the *Manners* of the *Stage*, and that with refpect to Poetry, and Ceremony. *Manners* in the Language of Poetry, is a Propriety of Actions, and Perfons. To fucceed in this bufinefs, there muft always be a regard had to Age, Sex, and Condition: And nothing put into the Mouths of Perfons which difagrees with any of thefe Circumftances. 'Tis not enough to fay a witty Thing, unlefs it be fpoken by a likely Perfon, and upon a Proper occafion. But my Defign will lead me to this Subject afterwards, and therefore I fhall fay no more of it at prefent, but proceed to apply the Remark.

One Inftance of Impropriety in *Manners* both Poetical and Moral, is their making Women, and Women of Quality talk Smuttily. This I have proved upon them already, and could cite many more places to the fame Purpofe were it neceffary.

But I fhall go on, and give the *Reader* fome other examples of Decency, Judgment, and Probability. *Don-Sebaftian* will help us in fome meafure. Here

M 3   the

the *Mufti* makes a foolish Speech to the Rabble, and jests upon his own Religion. He tells them, *tho' your Tyrant is a Lawful Emperour, yet your Lawful Emperour is but a Tyrant,*——*That your Emperour is a Tyrant is most Manifest, for you were born to be Turks, but he has play'd the Turk with you.* And now is not this Man fit to Manage the *Alcoran,* and to be set up for on Oracle of State? *Captain Tom* should have had this Speech by right: But the *Poet* had a farther Design, and any thing is good enough for a *Mufti.*

p. 85.

Sebastian after all the violence of his Repentance, his grasping at self Murther, and Resolutions for the *Cell,* is strangely pleased with the Remembrance of his *Incest,* and wishes the Repetition of it: And *Almeida* out of her Princely Modesty, and singular Compunction, is of the same mind. This is somewhat surprising! *Oedipus* and *Jocasta* in *Sophocles* don't Repent at this rate. No: The horror of the first Discovery continues upon their Spirits: They never relapse into any fits of Intemperance, nor entertain themselves with a lewd Memory. This sort of Behaviour is not only more Instructive but more Natural too. It being very unlikely one should wish the Repeating a Crime, when He was almost Distracted

p. 129.

at

at the thoughts on't, At the thoughts
on't, tho' 'twas comitted under all the
Circumstances of excuse. Now when Ignorance and meer Mistake are so very
disquieting, 'tis very strange if a Man
should plague his Mind with the Aggrava-
tions of Knowledge; To carry Aversion, and
Desire, in their full strength upon the
same Object; To fly and pursue with so
much eagerness, is somewhat Unusual.

p. 32.

If we step to the *Spanish Fryar* He will
afford us a Flight worth the observing.
'Tis part of the Addresses of *Torrismond*
to *Leonora*.

You are so Beautiful
So wondrous Fair, you justifie Rebellion;
As if that faultless Face could make no Sin,
But Heaven by looking on it must forgive.

These are strange Compliments! *Torrismond* calls his Queen Rebel to her head,
when he was both her General and her
Lover. This is powerful Rhetorick to
Court a Queen with! Enough one would
think to have made the Affair desperate.
But he has a Remedy at hand. The
Poets Nostrum of Profaness cures all. He
does as good as tell Her, she may Sin as
much as she has a mind to. Her Face
is a Protection to her Conscience. For

Heaven

Heaven is under a necessity to forgive a Handsom Woman. To say all this ought to be pass'd over in *Torrismond* on the score of his Passion, is to make the Excuse more scandalous than the Fault, if possible. Such Raptures are fit only for *Bedlam,* or a place which I shan't name. *Love Triumphant* will furnish another Rant not altogether inconsiderable. Here *Celadea* a Maiden Lady when she was afraid her Spark would be married to another, calls out presently for a *Chaos.* She is for pulling the World about her ears, tumbling all the Elements together, and expostulates with Heaven for making Humane Nature otherwise than it should have been.

p 52.

> *Great Nature break thy chain that links to-*
>   *gether*
> *The Fabrick of this Globe, and make a Chaos,*
> *Like that within my Soul.* ——

Now to my fancy, if she had call'd for a *Chair* instead of a *Chaos,* trip'd off, and kept her folly to her self, the Woman had been much wiser. And since we have shown our Skill in vaulting on the High Ropes, a little *Tumbling* on the *Stage,* may not do amiss for variety.

Spanish Fryar. p. 38.

Now then for a jest or two. *Don Gomez* shall begin : And here he'le give us

a

a Gingle upon the double meaning of a word.

I think, says *Dominick* the Fryar, *it was my good Angel that sent me hither so opportunely.* *Gomez* suspects him brib'd for no creditable business and answers.

Gom. *Ay, whose good Angels sent you hither, that you know best Father.*

These *Spaniards* will entertain us with more of this fine Raillery. Colonel *Sancho* in *Love Triumphant* has a great stroak at it. He says his Bride *Dalinda* is no more *Dalinda*, but *Dalilah* the *Philistine*. _{p 70.} This Colonel as great a Soldier as he is, is quite puzzled at a *Herald*. He *thinks they call him* Herod, *or some such Jewish Name.* Here you have a good Officer _{p 61.} spoil'd for a miserable jest. And yet after all, this *Sancho* tho' he can't pronounce *Herald*, knows what 'tis to be *Laconick*, which is somewhat more out of his way. *Thraso* in *Terence* was a man of the same _{Enuch.} size in Sense, but for all that he does not quibble. *Albanact* Captain of the Guards, _{King Arth.} is much about as witty as *Sancho*. It _{p. 2.} seems *Emmeline* Heiress to the Duke of *Cornwal* was Blind. *Albanact* takes the rise of his Thought from hence ; And observes *that as Blind as she is, Coswald would have no blind Bargain of her.* *Carlos* tells *Sancho* he is sure of his Mistress, _{Love Trium. p. 26.}

and

and *has no more to do but to take out a License.*

Sancho replies, *Indeed I have her License for it.* *Carlos* is somewhat angry at this Gingle, and cries, *what quibling too in your Prosperity?* Adversity it seems is the only time for *punning.* Truly I think so too. For 'tis a sign a Man is much Distress'd when he flies to such an Expedient. However, *Carlos* needed not to have been so touchy: For He can stoop as low himself upon occasion. · We must know then that *Sancho* had made Himself a Hunch'd Back, to counterfeit the *Conde Alonzo.* The two Colonels being in the same Disguise, were just upon the edg of a Quarrel. After some Preliminaries in Railing, *Sancho* cries, *Don't provoke me*; *I am mischeivously bent.*

Carlos replies, *Nay, you are* Bent *enough in Conscience, but I have a* Bent Fist *for Boxing.* Here you have a brace of Quibbles started in a Line and a half. And which is worst of all, they come from *Carlos,* from a *Character* of Sense; And therefore the Poet, not the *Soldier,* must answer for them.

I shall now give the *Reader* a few Instances of the Courtship of the *Stage,* and how decently they treat the Women, and *Quality* of both *Sexes.* The *Women* who

are

are secured from Affronts by Custom, and have a Privilege for Respect, are sometimes but roughly saluted by these Men of Address. And to bar the Defence, this Coarseness does not alwaies come from Clowns, and Women-haters ; but from *Persons* of Figure, neither singular, nor ill Bred. And which is still worse, The Satir falls on blindly without Distinction, and strikes at the whole *Sex.*

Enter *Raymond* a Noble-man in the *Spanish Fryar.* p. 47.

O Vertue ! Vertue ! What art thou become ?
That men should leave thee for that Toy a woman,
Made from the dross and refuse of a Man ;
Heaven took him sleeping when he made her too,
Had Man been waking he had nee'r consented.

I did not know before that a Man's Dross lay in his *Ribs* ; I believe sometimes it lies Higher. But the Philosophy, the Religion, and the Ceremony of these Lines, are too tender to be touched. *Creon* a Prince in *Oedipus,* railes in General at the *Sex,* and at the same time is violently in Love with *Euridice.* This upon the Matter, is just as natural, as 'tis Civil. If any one would understand what the *Curse of all tender hearted Women is, Belmour* will inform him. What is it then? *Oedip.* p. 3.

'Tis

Old Batch.
P. 41.
'Tis the *Pox*. If this be true, the Women had need lay in a ftock of ill Nature betimes. It feems 'tis their only prefervative. It guards their Virtue, and their Health, and is all they have to truft to. *Sharper* another Man of Senfe in this *Play*, talks much at the fame rate. *Belinda* would know of him *where he got that excellent Talent of Railing?*

Sharp. *Madam the Talent was Born with me.*──*I confefs I have taken care to improve it, to qualifie me for the Society of Ladies.* Horner, a Topping *Character* in the *Country Wife*, is advifed to *avoid Women, and hate them as they do him.* He *Anfwers.*

P. 35.

Becaufe I do hate them, and would hate them yet more, I'll frequent e'm ; you may fee by Marriage, nothing makes a Man hate a Woman more than her Conftant Converfation. There is ftill fomething more Coarfe upon the *Sex* fpoken by *Dorax* but it is a privileged Expreffion, and as fuch I muft leave it. The *Relapfe* mends the Contrivance of the Satir, refines upon the Manner, and to make the Difcourfe the more probable, obliges the Ladies to abufe themfelves. And becaufe I fhould be loath to tire the *Reader*, *Berinthia* fhall clofe the Argument. This Lady having undertook

P. 22.

Don Sebaft.
P. 5.

took the Employment of a *Procurefs,* makes this remark upon it to her felf.

Berinth. So here is fine work ! But there was no avoiding it. ——*Befides, I begin to Fancy there may be as much Pleafure in carrying on another Bodies Intrigue, as ones own. This is at leaft certain, It exercifes almoft all the Entertaining Faculties of a Woman. For there is Employment for Hypocrifie, Invention, Deceit, Flattery, Mifchief, and Lying.*

Let us now fee what Quarter the *Stage* gives to *Quality.* And here we fhall find them extreamly free, and familiar. They drefs up the *Lords* in Nick Names, and expofe them in *Characters* of Contempt. *Double* Lord Froth is explain'd a *Solemn Coxcomb* ; *Dealer.* And *Lord Rake*, and *Lord Foplington* give *Perfon.* you their Talent in their Title. Lord *Relapfe.* *Plaufible* in the *Plain Dealer* Acts a ri- *Provuk'd* diculous Part, but is with all very civil. *Wife.* He tells *Manly he never attempted to abufe any Perfon,* The other anfwers ; *What?* *p. 4:* *you were afraid? Manly* goes on and declares *He would call a Rafcal by no other Title, tho' his Father had left him a Dukes.* That *p. 2.* is, he would call a Duke a Rafcal. This I confefs is very much *Plain Dealing.* Such Freedoms would appear but odly in Life, efpecially without Provocation. I muft own the *Poet* to be an Author of

good

good Senfe ; But under favour, thefe jefts,
if we may call them fo, are fomewhat
high Seafon'd, the Humour feems over-
ftrain'd, and the *Character* pufh'd too far.
To proceed. *Muftapha* was felling *Don
Alvarez* for a Slave. The Merchant asks
Don Sebaft. what *Virtues he has.* *Muftapha* replies.
p. 16. *Virtues quoth ah* ! *He is of a great Family
and Rich, what other Virtues would'ft thou
have in a Nobleman?* Don *Carlos* in *Love
Triumphant* ftands for a Gentleman, and
a Man of Senfe, and out-throws. *Muftapha* a Bars Length. He tells us *Nature
has given* Sancho *an empty Noddle, but
p. 17. Fortune in revenge has fill'd his Pockets :
juft a Lords Eftate in Land and Wit.* This
is a handfom Compliment to the Nobility ! And my Lord *Salisbury* had no doubt
Don Quix. of it a good Bargain of the *Dedication.*
part. 2. *Terefa's* general Defcription of a Countefs
p. 37. is confiderable in its Kind: But only 'tis
in no Condition to appear. In the *Relapfe,* Sir *Tunbelly* who had Miftaken Young
Fafhion for Lord *Foplington,* was afterwards undeceiv'd ; and before the fur-
prize was quite over, puts the Queftion,
*is it then poffible that this fhould be the true
Lord* Foplington *at laft ?* The Nobleman
removes the fcruple with great Civility
and Difcretion! *Lord* Fopl. *Why what
do you fee in his Face to make you doubt of
it ?*

it? Sir without presuming to have an ex-
traordinary Opinion of my Figure, give me
leave to tell you, if you had seen as many
Lords as I have done, you would not think
it Impossible a Person of a worse Taille then Relapse.
mine might be a Modern Man of Quality. p. 84.

I'm forry to hear *Modern Quality* de-
generates so much. But by the way, these
Liberties are altogether new. They are
unpractised by the Latin *Comedians*, and
by the *English* too till very lately, as the p. 24.
Plain Dealer observes. And as for *Moliere*
in *France*, he pretends to fly his Satir no
higher than a Marquis. L' Ombre

And has our *Stage* a particular Privi- de Moliere
lege? Is their *Charter* inlarg'd, and are
they on the same Foot of Freedom with
the *Slaves* in the *Saturnalia*? Must all
Men be handled alike? Must their
Roughness be needs play'd upon Title?
And can't they lash the Vice without
pointing upon the *Quality*? If as Mr.
Dryden rightly defines it, a *Play ought*
to be a just Image of Humane Nature; EssayDram
Why are not the Decencies of Life, and *Poet.*
the Respects of Conversation observ'd? p. 5.
Why must the Customes of Countries
be Cross'd upon, and the Regards of Honour overlook'd? What necessity is there
to kick the *Coronets* about the *Stage*, and
to make a Man a Lord, only in order to
make

make him a Coxcomb. I hope the *Poets* don't intend to revive the old Project of Levelling, and *Vote* down the House of *Peers*. In earnest, the *Play-house* is an admirable School of Behaviour *!* This is their way of managing Ceremony, distinguishing Degree, and Entertaining the *Boxes* ! But I shall leave them at present to the Enjoyment of their Talent, and proceed to another Argument.

C H A P.

CHAP. V.

Remarks upon Amphytrion, King Arthur, Don Quixote, *and the* Relapse.

SECTION I.

THE following *Plays*, excepting the Laſt, will fall under the ſame Heads of Commendation with the Former. However, ſince the *Poets* have here been prodigal in their Expence, and dreſs'd themſelves with more Curioſity then ordinary, they deſerve a proportionable Regard. So much Finery muſt not be Crowded. I ſhall therefore make Elbow-Room for their Figure, and allow them the Compaſs of a diſtinct *Chapter*.

To begin with *Amphytrion*. In this *Play* Mr. *Dryden* repreſents *Jupiter* with the Attributes of the ſupream Being: He furniſhes him with Omnipotence, makes him the Creator of Nature, and the Arbiter of Fate, puts all the Functions of Providence in his Hand, and deſcribes him with the Majeſty of the true God. And when he has put Him in this glorious

Amphit.
P. 1, 2,
3, 8, 9.

N   Equi-

Equipage, he brings him out for Diversion. He makes him express himself in
p. 8. 17. the most intemperate Raptures: He is
willing to *Renounce* his *Heaven* for his
Brutality, and employ a whole *Eternity* in
Lewdness. He draws his Debauch at its
full Length, with all the Art, and Height-
ings, and Foulness of Idea immaginable.
This *Jupiter* is not contented with his success against *Amphitrion*, unless he brings
Alcmena into the Confederacy, and makes
her a Party *ex post Facto*. He would not
have her think of her *Husband*, but her
Lover, that is, her *Whoremaster*. 'Tis not
the success, but the manner of gaining it
which is all in all. 'Tis the Vice which
is the charming Circumstance. Innocence
and Regularity, are dangerous Compani-
ons ; They spoil Satisfaction, and make
every Thing insipid ! Unless People take
care to discharge their Virtue, and clear
off their Conscience, their Senses will va-
p. 18. nish immediately ! For *Jupiter*, says he,
would *owe nothing to a Name so dull as*
Husband. And in the next Page.

That very name of Wife and Marriage,
19. *Is poyson to the dearest sweets of Love.*

I would give the *Reader* some more
of these fine Sentences, but that they are
too

too much out of Order to appear. The
truth is, Our *Stage-Poets* seem to fence a-
gainst Censure by the excess of Lewdness;
And to make the overgrown size of a
Crime, a Ground for Impunity. As if
a Malefactor should project his Escape by
appearing too scandalous for Publick Try-
al. However, This is their Armour of
Proof, this is the Strength they retreat to.
They are fortified in Smut, and almost
impregnable in Stench, so that where they
deserve most, there's no coming at them.
To proceed. I desire to know what Authority Mr. *Dryden* has for this extraordinary Representation? His Original *Plautus,*
is no President. Indeed *Plautus* is the only bold Heathen that ever made *Jupiter*
tread the *Stage.* But then he stops far
short of the Liberties of the *English Amphitrion.* *Jupiter* at *Rome,* and *London,*
have the same unaccountable Design; but
the Methods of pursuit are very different.
The First, does not solicit in scandalous
Language, nor flourish upon his Lewdness, nor endeavours to set it up for the
Fashion. *Plautus* had some regard to the
Height of the Character, and the Opinion of his Country, and the Restraints of
Modesty. The Sallies of *Aristophanes* do
not come up to the case; And if they
did, I have cut off the Succours from that

Quarter already. *Terence's Chærea* is the next bold Man: However, here the Fable of *Jupiter* and *Danae* are just glanced at, and the Expression is clean; and He that tells the Story, a Young Libertine. These are all circumstances of extenuation, and give quite another Complexion to the Thing. As for the *Greek Tragedians* and *Seneca*, there's no Prescription can be drawn from them. They mention *Jupiter* in Terms of Magnificence and Respect, and make his Actions, and his Nature of a piece. But it may be the Celebrated *Homer*, and *Virgil* may give Mr. *Dryden* some Countenance. Not at all. *Virgil's Jupiter* is alwaies great, and solemn, and keeps up the port of a Deity. 'Tis true, *Homer* does not guard the Idea with that exactness, but then He never sinks the Character into Obscenity. The most exceptionable passage is that where *Jupiter* relates his Love Adventures to *Juno*. Here this pretended Deity is charm'd with *Venus's* Girdle, is in the height of his Courtship, and under the Ascendant of his Passion. This 'tis confess'd was a slippery Place, and yet the Poet makes a shift to keep his Feet. His *Jupiter* is Little, but not nauseous; The Story, tho' improper, will bear the telling, and look Conversation in the Face. However; These Free-

doms

doms of *Homer* were counted intolerable.: I shall not insist on the Censures of *Justin Martyr*, or *Clemens Alexandrinus* : Even the Heathen could not endure them. The Poets are lashed by *Plato* upon this Score; For planting Vice in Heaven, and making their Gods infectious; If Mr. *Dryden* answers that *Jupiter* can do us no Harm. He is known to be an Idol of Lewd Memory, and therefore his Example can have no Force : Under Favour this is a mistake : For won't Pitch daub when a dirty Hand throws it; or can't a Toad spit Poyson because she's ugly ? Ribaldry is dangerous under any Circumstances of Representation. And as *Menander* and St. *Paul* express it, *Evil Communications corrupt good Manners*. I mention them both, because if the *Apostle* should be dislik'd, the *Comedian* may pass. But after all, Mr. *Dryden* has not so much as a Heathen President for his Singularities. What then made him fall into them ? Was it the Decency of the Thing, and the Propriety of *Character*, and Behaviour ? By no means. For as I have observ'd before, Nature and Operations, ought to be proportion'd, and Behaviour suited to the Dignity of Being. To draw a Monkey in Royal Robes, and a Prince in *Antick*, would be Farce upon

Euseb. præpar. Evarg.

Colours, entertain like a Monſter, and pleaſe only upon the ſcore of Deformity. Why then does Mr. *Dryden* croſs upon Nature and Authority, and go off as he Confeſſes, from the Plan of *Plautus*, and *Moliere*? Tho' by the way, the Engliſh *Amphitryon* has borrow'd moſt of the Libertine Thoughts of *Moliere*, and improv'd them. But to the former queſtion. Why muſt the beaten Road be left? He tells us, T*hat the difference of our* Stage *from the Roman and the French did ſo re-* *quire it.* That is, our *Stage* muſt be much more Licentious. For you are to obſerve that Mr. *Dryden*, and his Fraternity, have help'd to debauch the *Town*, and Poyſon their Pleaſures to an unuſal Degree: And therefore the Diet muſt be dreſs'd to the Palate of the *Company*. And ſince they are made *Scepticks*, they muſt be entertain'd as ſuch. That the Engliſh *Amphitryon* was contriv'd with this View is too plain to be better interpreted. To what purpoſe elſe does *Jupiter* appear in the ſhape of *Jehovah*? Why are the incommunicable *Attributes* burleſqu'd, and Omnipotence applyed to Acts of Infamy? To what end can ſuch Horrible ſtuff as this ſerve, unleſs to expoſe the Notion, and extinguiſh the Belief of a Deity? The Perfections of God, are Himſelf. To

Ep. Ded.

ridicule

ridicule his Attributes and his Being, are
but two words for the same Thing. These
Attributes are bestow'd on *Jupiter* with
great Prodigality, and afterwards execra-
bly outrag'd. The Case being thus, the
Cover of an Idol, is to thin a pretence
to Screen the Blasphemy. Nothing but
Mr. *Dryden's Absolom* and *Achitophel* can
out-do This. Here I confess the Motion
of his Pen is bolder, and the Strokes more
Black'd. Here we have Blasphemy on
the top of the Letter, without any trouble of Inference, or Construction. This
Poem runs all upon Scripture Names, Upon Suppositions of the true Religion, and
the right Object of Worship. Here Profaness is shut out from Defence, and lies
open without Colour or Evasion. Here
are no Pagan Divinities in the Scheme, so
that all the Atheistick Raillery must point
upon the true God. In the beginning
we are told that *Absalom* was *David's* Natural Son: So then there's a blot in his
Scutcheon, and a Blemish upon his Birth.
The *Poet* will make admirable use of this
remark presently! This *Absalom* it seems
was very extraordinary in his Person and
Performances. Mr. *Dryden* does not certainly know how this came about, and
therefore enquires of himself in the first
place,

Whe-

p. 1. *Whether inspired with a diviner Lust,*
His Father got him——

    This is down right Defiance of the
Living God! Here you have the very
Essence and Spirit of Blasphemy, and the
Holy Ghost brought in upon the most
hideous Occasion. I question whether
the Torments and Despair of the Damn'd,
dare venture at such Flights as these.
They are beyond Description, I Pray
God they may not be beyond Pardon too.
I can't forbear saying, that the next bad
Thing to the writing these Impieties, is
to Suffer them. To return to *Amphitryon*.
Phœbus and *Mercury* have *Manners* assign'd
very disagreeable to their Condition.
The later abating Propriety of Language,
talks more like a *Water-man* than a Deity.
They rail against the Gods, and call *Mars*
and *Vulcan* the *two Fools of Heaven*. *Mer-*
cury is pert upon his Father *Jupiter*, makes
jests upon his Pleasures, and his Greatness, and is horribly smutty and profane.

p. 3. 16. &c. And all this Misbehaviour comes from
him in his own shape, and in the sub-
limity of his Character. Had He run
Riot in the Disguise of *Sosia*, the Discourse
and the Person had been better adjusted,
and the Extravagance more Pardonable.
                        But

But here the Decorum is quite loſt. To
ſee the *Immortals* play ſuch Gambols, and
the biggeſt Beings do the leaſt Actions,
is ſtrangely unnatural. An Emperour in
the Grimaces of an Ape, or the Diver-
ſions of a Kitten, would not be half ſo ridiculous. Now as Monſieur *Rapin* obſerves, without Decorum there can be
no *probability*, nor without Probability any
true Beauty. Nature muſt be minded,
otherwiſe Things will look forced, tawdry, and chimerical. Mr. *Dryden* diſcour-
ſes very handſomly on this occaſion in
his *Preface* to *Albion* and *Albanius*. He p. 1.
informs us, *That Wit has been truly defin'd
a propriety of Words and Thoughts.* ——
*That Propriety of Thought is that Fancy
which ariſes naturally from the Subject.* Why
then without doubt, the Quality, of Characters ſhould be taken care of, and great
Perſons appear like themſelves. Yes, yes,
all this is granted by implication, and Mr.
Dryden comes ſtill nearer to the preſent
caſe. He tells us, that *Propriety is to be
obſerved, even in Machines* ; *And that the
Gods are all to manage their Peculiar Pro-
vinces.* He inſtances in ſome of their re-
ſpective Employments; but I don't find that
any of them were to talk Lewdly. No.
He plainly ſuppoſes the contrary. For
as he goes on, *If they were to ſpeak upon*
the

the *Stage* it would follow of necessity, that the *Expressions* should be Lofty, *Figurative, and Majestical*. It seems then their Behaviour should be agreeable to their Greatness. Why then are not these Rules observ'd, in the *Machines* of *Amphitrion*? And as I take it, Obscenity has not the Air of Majesty, nor any Alliance with the *Sublime*. And as for the *Figurative* Part, 'tis generally of the same Cut with the *Lofty*: The Smut shines clear, and strong, through the Metaphor, and is no better screen'd than the Sun by a Glass Window. To use *Mercury* thus ill, and make the God of Eloquence speak so unlike himself, is somewhat strange! But tho' the *Antients* knew nothing of it, there are Considerations above those of *Decency*. And when this happens, *A Rule must rather be trespass'd on, than a Beauty left out*. 'Tis Mr. *Dryden's* opinion in his *Cleomenes*, where he breaks the *Unity of Time*, to describe the *Beauty* of a Famine. *Pref.* Now Beauty is an arbitrary Advantage, and depends upon Custom and Fancy. With some People the Blackest Complexions are the handsomest. 'Tis to these *African* Criticks that Mr. *Dryden* seems to make his Appeal. And without doubt he bespeaks their Favour, and strikes their Imagination luckily enough. For to lodge Divinity and Scandal together; To make

the

the Gods throw *Stars*, like *Snow-balls* at one another, but especially to Court in Smut, and rally in Blasphemy, is most admirably entertaining! This is much better than all the Niceties of *Decorum*. 'Tis handsomly contriv'd to slur the Notion of a Superiour Nature, to disarm the Terrors of Religion, and make the Court Above as Romantick as that of the *Fairies*. A Libertine when his Conscience is thus reliev'd, and Atheism sits easie upon his Spirits, can't help being grateful upon the Occasion. Meer Interest will oblige him to cry up the Performance, and solicit for the *Poets* Reputation! Before I take leave of these *Machines*, it may not be amiss to enquire why the Gods are brought into the *Spiritual Court*. Now I suppose the *p. 1.* Creditableness of the Business, and the *Poets* Kindness to those *Places*, are the principal Reasons of their coming. However, He might have a farther Design in his Head, and that is, to bring *Thebes* to *London*, and to show the Antiquity of *Doctors Commons*. For if you will believe *Mercury*, this Conference between him and *Phæbus* was held three thousand years *19.* ago. Thus *Shakespear* makes *Hector* talk *Troil. and Cressid.* about *Aristotles* Philosophy, and calls Sr. *John Old Castle*, *Protestant*. I had not *The Hist. of Sr. John Old Castle.* mention'd this Discovery in Chronology,

but

but that Mr. *Dryden* falls upon *Ben Johnson*, for making *Cataline give Fire at the Face of a Cloud*, before Guns were invented.

By the Pattern of these pretended *Deities*, we may guess what sort of *Mortals* we are likely to meet with. Neither are we mistaken. For *Phædra* is bad enough in all Conscience, but *Bromia* is a meer Original. Indeed when Mr. *Dryden* makes *Jupiter*, and *Jupiter* makes the Women, little less can be expected. So much for *Amphitrion*.

King Arthur. I shall pass on to *King Arthur* for a word or two. Now here is a strange jumble and Hotch potch of Matters, if you mind it. Here we have *Genii*, and *Angels, Cupids, Syrens,* and *Devils* ; *Venus* and St. *George, Pan* and the *Parson*, the Hell of Heathenism, and the Hell of *Revelation* ; A fit of Smut, and then a Jest about Original Sin. And why are Truth and Fiction, Heathenism and Christianity, the most Serious and the most Trifling Things blended together, and thrown into one Form of Diversion? Why is all this done unless it be to ridicule the whole, and make one as incredible as the other? His *Airy* and *Earthy Spirits* discourse of the first state of Devils, of their *Chief* of their Revolt, their Punishment, and Impostures.

postures. This Mr. *Dryden* very Religiously calls a *Fairy way of Writing, which depends only on the Force of Imagination.* Ep. Ded. What then is the Fall of the Angels a Romance? Has it no basis of Truth, nothing to support it, but strength of Fancy, and Poetick Invention? After He had mention'd Hell, Devils, &c. and given us a sort of *Bible* description of these formidable Things; I say after he had formed his Poem in this manner, I am surprized to hear him call it a *Fairy kind of Writing.* Is the History of *Tophet* no better prov'd than that of *Styx*? Is the Lake of *Brimstone* and that of *Phlegeton* alike dreadful? And have we as much Reason to believe the Torments of *Titius* and *Prometheus,* as those of the Devils and Damn'd? These are lamentable Consequences! And yet I can't well see how the *Poet* can avoid them. But setting aside this miserable Gloss in the *Dedication,* the Representation it self is scandalously irreligious. To droll upon the Vengeance of Heaven, and the Miseries of the Damn'd, is a sad Instance of Christianity! Those that bring Devils upon the *Stage,* can hardly believe them any where else. Besides, the Effects of such an Entertainment must needs be admirable! To see Hell thus play'd with is a mighty Refreshment to a lewd Conscience,

science, and a byass'd Understanding. It
heartens the Young Libertine, and con-
firms the well-wishers to Atheism, and
makes Vice bold, and enterprizing. Such
Diversions serve to dispel the Gloom, and
guild the Horrors of the *Shades below*, and
are a sort of Ensurance against Damnation.
One would think these *Poets* went upon
absolute Certainty, and could demonstrate
a Scheme of Infidelity. If they could,
They had much better keep the Secret.
The divulging it tends only to debauch
Mankind, and shake the Securities of Civil Life. However, if they have been in
the other World and find it empty, and un-
inhabited, and are acquainted with all the
Powers, and Places, in Being; If they can
show the Impostures of Religion, and the
Contradictions of Common Belief, they
have something to say for themselves.
Have they then infallible Proof and Ma-
thematick Evidence for these Discoveries?
No Man had ever the Confidence to say
This: And if He should, he would be but
laughed at for his Folly. No Conclusions can exceed the Evidence of their Principles; you may as well build a Castle in
the Air, as raise a Demonstration upon a
Bottom of Uncertainty. And is any Man
so vain as to pretend to know the Extent
of Nature, and the Stretch of Possibility,
and

and the Force of the Powers Invisible? So that notwithstanding the Boldness of this *Opera*, there may be such a Place as Hell; And if so, a Discourse about Devils, will be no *Fairy way of Writing*. For a *Fairy way of Writing*, is nothing but a *History of Fiction*; A subject of Imaginary Beings; such as never had any existence in Time, or Nature. And if as Monsieur *Rapin* observes, *Poetry* requires a mixture of Truth and *Fable*; Mr. *Dryden* may make his advantage, for his *Play* is much better founded on Reality than He was aware of.

It may not be improper to consider in a word or two, what a frightfull Idea the *Holy Scriptures* give us of Hell. 'Tis describ'd by all the Circumstance of Terror, by every Thing dreadful to Sense, and amazing to Thought. The Place, the Company, the Duration, are all Considerations of Astonishment. And why has God given us this solemn warning? Is it not to awaken our Fears, and guard our Happiness; To restrain the Disorders of Appetite, and to keep us within Reason, and Duty? And as for the *Apostate Angels*, the *Scriptures* inform us of their lost Condition, of their Malice and Power, of their active Industry and Experience; and all these Qualities Correspondent

dent to the Bulk of their Nature, the Antiquity of their Being, and the Mifery
of their State. In fhort, They are painted in all the formidable Appearances imaginable, to alarm our Caution, and put
us upon the utmoſt Defence.

Let us fee now how Mr. *Dryden* repre-
fents thefe unhappy Spirits, and their
Place of Abode. Why very entertain-
ingly! Thofe that have a true Taſt for
Atheiſm were never better regaled. One
would think by this *Play* the Devils were
meer Mormo's and Bugbears, fit only to
fright Children and Fools. They rally
upon Hell and Damnation, with a great
deal of Air and Pleafantry; and appear like
Robin Good-fellow, only to make the Company laugh. *Philidel*: Is call'd a *Puling
Sprite*. And why fo? For this pious reafon, becaufe

He trembles at the yawning Gulph of Hell,
Nor dares approach the Flames leaſt he ſhould
Singe
p. 6. *His gaudy filken Wings.*
He fighs when he ſhould plunge a Soul in
Sulphur,
As with Compaſſion touch'd of Foolifh Man.

The anfwer is, *What a half Devil's he.*
You

You see how admirably it runs all upon the Christian Scheme ! Sometimes they
are *Half-Devils*, and sometimes *Hopeful-
Devils*, and what you please to make sport
with. *Grimbald* is afraid of being, *whooped
through Hell at his return,* for miscarrying
in his Business. It seems there is great
Leisure for Diversion! There's *Whooping*
in Hell, instead of *Weeping* and *Wailing*!
One would fancy Mr. *Dryden* had Day-
light and Company, when these Lines
were written. I know his Courage is extraordinary ; But sure such Thoughts
could never bear up against Solitude and
a Candle !

And now since he has diverted himself with the *Terrors* of *Christianity*, I
dont wonder he should treat those that
Preach them with so much Civility ! enter *Poet* in the Habit of a *Peasant.*

*We ha' cheated the Parson we'el cheat him
   again,*
For why should a Blockhead have one in ten ?
For prating so long like a Booklearned Sot,
Till Pudding, and Dumpling burn to pot.

These are fine comprehensive stroaks !
Here you have the *Iliads* in a Nutshell !
Two or three courtly words take in the
whole Clergy : And what is wanting in
      O   Wit,

Wit, is made up in Abuſe, and that's as well. This is an admirable *Harveſt Catch*, and the poor Tith-ſtealers ſtand highly indebted. They might have been tired with Cheating in *Proſe*, had not they not been thus ſeaſonably releiv'd in Doggrell! But now there is Muſick in playing the Knave. A Countryman now may fill his Barn, and humour his ill Manners, and ſing his Conſcience aſleep, and all under one. I dont queſtion but theſe *four Lines* ſteal many a Pound in the year. Whether the *Muſe* ſtands indictable or not, the Law muſt determine. But after all, I muſt ſay the Deſign is notably laid. For Place and Perſon, for Reliſh and Convenience, nothing could have, been better. The Method is very ſhort clear, and Practicable. 'Tis a fine portable Infection, and coſts no more Carriage •than the Plague.

Well! the Clergy muſt be contented: It might poſſibly have been worſe for them if they had been in his favour: For he has ſometimes a very unlucky way of ſhowing his Kindneſs. He commends the *Earl of Leiceſter for conſidering the Friend, more than the Cauſe*; that is, for his Partiality; The Marqueſs of *Halifax* for *quitting the Helm, at the approach of a Storm*; As if Pilots were made only for fair Weather.

£p. Ded.
DonSebaſt.

Ded. King
Arthur.

\ ther.

ther. 'Tis Presum'd these Noble Persons are unconcern'd in this Character. However the *Poet* has shown his skill in Panegyrick, and 'tis only for that I mention it. He commends *Atticus* for his Trimming, and *Tully* for his Cowardize, and speaks meanly of the Bravery of *Cato*. Afterwards he professes his Zeal for the Publick welfare, and is pleas'd to *see the Nation so well secur'd from Foreign Attempts* &c. However he is in some pain about the Coming of the *Gauls*: 'Tis possible for fear they should invade the *Muses*, and carry the *Opera's* into Captivity, and deprive us of *the Ornaments of Peace*.

Sebast. K. Arth:

Ibid:

And now He has serv'd his Friends, he comes in the last place like a modest Man, to commend Himself. He tells us there were a great many *Beauties* in the Original Draught of this *Play*. But it seems Time has since tarnish'd their Complexion. And He gives *Heroick* Reasons for their not appearing. To speak Truth, (all Politicks apart,) there are strange Flights of Honour, and Consistencies of Pretention in this Dedication! But I shall forbear the Blazon of the *Atcheivment*, for fear I should commend as unluckily as Himself.

SECT. II.

Remarks upon Don Quixot, &c.

MR. *Durfey* being somewhat particular in his Genius and Civilities, I shall consider him in a word or two by himself. This Poet writes from the *Romance* of an ingenious Author: By this means his Sense, and *Characters* are cut out to his Hand. He has wisely planted himself upon the shoulders of a *Giant*; but whether his Discoveries answer the advantage of his standing, the Reader must judge.

What I have to object against Mr. *Durfey* shall most of it be ranged under these three Heads.

I. *His Profaness with respect to Religion and the* Holy Scriptures.
II. *His Abuse of the Clergy.*
III. *His want of Modesty and Regard to the Audience.*

I. *His Profaness, &c.*
And here my first Instance shall be in a bold *Song* against Providence.

Providence that formed the Fair
  In such a charming Skin,
Their Outside made his only care,
  And never look'd within.

Part 1st.
P. 20.

Here the *Poet* tells you Providence makes Mankind by halves, huddles up the Soul, and takes the least care of the better Moyety. This is direct blaspheming the Creation, and a Satir upon God Almighty. His next advance is to droll upon the Resurrection.

Sleep and indulge thy self with Rest,
Nor dream thou e're shalt rise again.

P. 20.

His Third Song makes a jest of the *Fall,* rails upon *Adam* and *Eve,* and burlesques the Conduct of *God Almighty* for not making Mankind over again.

When the World first knew Creation,
A Rogue was a Top-Profession,
When there was no more in all Nature but
    Four,
There were two of them in Transgression.

P. 37.

He that first to mend the Matter,
Made Laws to bind our Nature,
Should have found a way,

O 3   *To*

To make Wills obey,
And have Modell'd new the Creature.

In this and the following page, the *Redemption* of the World is treated with the same respect with the *Creation*. The word *Redeemer*, which among Christians is appropriated to our Blessed Saviour, and like the Jewish Tetragrammaton peculiarly reserv'd to the Deity; This adorable Name (*Redeemer and Dear Redeemer,*) is applyed to the ridiculous Don *Quixote.* These Insolencies are too big for the Correction of a Pen, and therefore I shall leave them. After this horrible abuse of the Works, and Attributes of God, he goes on to make sport with his Vengeance. He makes the Torments of Hell a very Comical Entertainment : As if they were only Flames in Painting, and Terrors in *Romance.* The *Stygian Frogs* in *Aristophanes* are not represented with more Levity, and Drolling. That the *Reader* may see I do him no wrong, I shall quote the places which is the main Reason why I have transcrib'd the rest of his Profaness.

Appear ye fat Feinds that in Limbo do groan,
That were when in Flesh the same souls with
his own :

You

You that always in Lucifers Kitchin reside,
'Mongst Sea-coal and Kettles, and Grease new-
    ly try'd :
That pamper'd each day with a Garbidge of
    Souls,
Broil Rashers of Fools for a Breakfast on
    Coals.

In the Epilogue you have the History of *Balaam*'s Ass exposed, and the Beast brought upon the *Stage* to laugh at the Miracle the better ;

And as 'tis said a parlous Ass once spoke,
When Crab-tree Cudgel did his rage provoke.
So if you are not civil, —— I fear
He'el speak again. ——

In the second *Part* the Devil is brought upon the *Stage.* He cries as *he hopes to be Saved.* And *Sancho warrants him a good Christian.* Truly I think he may have more of Christianity in him than the Poet. For he trembles at that God, with whom the other makes Diversion.

P. 18.

I shall omit the mention of several outrages of this Kind, besides his deep mouth'd swearing, which is frequent, and pass on to the Second Head, which is His Abuse of the Clergy. And since Reveal'd Religion has been thus horribly treated,

O 4

'tis

'tis no Wonder if the *Ministers* of it have the same Usage.

And here we are likely to meet with some passages extraordinary enough. For to give Mr. *Durfey* his due, when he meddles with Church men he lays about him like a Knight Errant : Here his Wit and his Malice, are generally in extreams, tho' not of the same Kind. To begin.

Part. 1. p. 13. He makes the Curate *Perez* assist at the ridiculous Ceremony of *Don Quixots* Knighting. Afterwards Squire *Sancho* confessing his mistake to *Quixote*, tells him, *Ah consider dear Sir no man is born wise.* And what if he was born wise ? He may be *Bred* a Fool, if he has not a care. But how does he prove this Memorable Sentence ? Because a *Bishop is no more than another man without Grace and Good Breeding.* I must needs say if the *Poet* had any share of either of these Qualities, he would be less bold with his Superiors ; and not give his Clowns the Liberty to droll thus heavily upon a solemn *Character.* This *Sancho* Mr. *Durfey* takes care to inform us is *a dry shrewd Country Fellow,* The reason of this Character is for the strength of it somewhat surprising. 'Tis *person. Dram.* because *he blunders out Proverbs upon all Occasions, tho' never so far from the purpose.* Now if blundring and talking nothing

to

to the purpose, is an argument of *Shrewd-ness*; some Peoples *Plays* are very shrewd Performances. To proceed. *Sancho* complains of his being married, because it hindred him from better offers. *Perez* the Curate is sorry for this Misfortune. *For as I remember* says he *'twas my luck to give* Teresa *and you the Blessing*. To this *Sancho* replies. *A Plague on your Blessing! I perceive I shall have reason to wish you hang'd for your Blessing* — *Good finisher of Fornication, good Conjunction Copulative*. For this irreverence and Profaness *Perez* threatens him with Excommunication. *Sancho* tells him, *I care not, I shall lose nothing by it but a nap in the Afternoon*. In his Second Part, *Jodolet* a Priest is call'd a *Holy Cormorant*, and made to dispatch *half a Turkey, and a Bottle of Malaga for his Breakfast*. Here one Country Girl chides another for her sawcyness. *D'ee* (says she)*make a Pimp of a Priest?* *Sancho* interposes with his usual shrewdness: *A Pimp of a Priest, why is that such a Miracle?* In the Second *Scene* the Poet Provides himself another Priest to abuse. *Mannel* the Steward calls *Bernardo* the Chaplain Mr. *Cuff-Cushion*, and tells him a *Whore is a Pulpit he loves*. —— In settling the Characters *Mannel* is given out for *a witty pleasant Fellow*. And now you see he comes up to Expectation. To the Blind all *Colours* are

p. 51.

p. 3.

p. 7.

p. 10.

are alike, and Rudeneſs, and Raillery are the ſame thing! Afterwards, *Bernardo* ſays *Grace* upon the *Stage*; and I ſuppoſe Prays to God to bleſs the Entertainment of the Devil. Before they riſe from Table, the *Poet* contrives a Quarrel between *Don Quixot* and *Bernardo*. The Prieſt railes on the Knight, and calls him *Don Coxcomb* &c. By this time you may imagine the Knight heartily Provok'd, ready to buckle on his *Baſon*, and draw out for the Combat, Let us hear his Reſentment.

Don Quix. *Oh thou old black Fox with a Fire brand in thy Tail, thou very Prieſt: Thou Kindler of all Miſcheifs in all Nations. De'e hear Homily: Did not the Reverence I bear theſe Nobles——I would ſo thrum your Caſſock you Church Vermin.*

p. 41.

p. 47.

At laſt he bids *Bernardo* adieu in Language too Profane and Scandalous to relate. In the Fourth *Act* His Song calls the Clergy *Black Cattle*, and ſays *no Body now minds what they ſay.* I could alledge more of his `Courtſhip` to the *Order*, but the *Reader* might poſſibly be tired, and therefore I ſhall proceed in the

Part. 1ſt. p. 7, 8. pt. 2d. p. 57.

Third, place to his want of Modeſty, and Regard to the Audience. As for Smut *Sancho* and *Tereſa* talk it broad, and ſingle ſens'd, for almoſt a page together. *Mary* the *Buxſom* has likewiſe her ſhare

of

of this Accomplifhment. The firſt Epilogue is Garniſh'd with a Couplet of it; *pt.* 2*d.* *p.* 60. *Marcella* the Maiden Shepherdeſs raves in Raptures of Indecency: And ſometimes you have it mixt up with Profaneſs, to *pt.* 1*ſt.* *p.* 38. *pt.* 2*d.* *p.* 14. make the Compoſition the ſtronger. But this entertainment being no Novelty, I ſhall paſs it over; And the rather becauſe there are ſome other Rarities which are not to be met with elſe where.

Here he diverts the Ladies with the Charming Rhetorick of *Snotty-Noſe, filthy Vermin in the Beard, Nitty Jerkin, and Louſe Snapper, with the Letter in the Chamber-pot, and natural Evacuation*; with an abuſive deſcription of a Counteſs, and a rude ſtory of a certain Lady, and with ſome other varieties of this Kind, too coarſe to be named. *pt.* 1*ſt.* *p.* 7, 8. *pt.* 2*d.* *p.* 52. *pt.* 2*d.* *p.* 36. 49. *pt.* 2*d.* *p.* 37. 44. This is rare ſtuff for Ladies, and Quality! There is more of *Phyſick,* than *Comedy* in ſuch Sentences as theſe. *Crocus Metallorum* will ſcarſe turn the Stomack more effectually. 'Tis poſſible Mr. *Durfey* might deſign it for a *Receipt.* And being Conſcious the *Play* was too dear, threw a Vomit into the Bargain. I wonder Mr. *Durfey* ſhould have no more regard to the *Boxes* and *Pitt!* That a Man who has *ſtudied the* *Preſ. pt.* 3*d.* *Scenes of Decency and Good Manners with ſo much Zeal,* ſhould practiſe with ſo little Addreſs! Certainly *indefatigable Diligence,*

Care

Ibid. *Care and Pains*, was never more unfortunate! In his *third Part*, *Buxsome* swears faster, and is more scandalous, and impertinent, than in the other two. At these Liberties, and some in *Sancho*, the Ladies took Check. This Censure Mr. *Durfey* seems heartily sorry for. He is *extreamly concern'd that the Ladies, that* *Pref.* *Essential part of the Audience*, should think his Performance *nauseous and undecent.* That is, he is very sorry they brought their Wits, or their Modesty along with them. However Mr. *Durfey* is not so Céremonious as to submit: He is resolved to keep the Field against the Ladies; And endeavours to defend himself by saying, *I know no other way in Nature to do the Characters right, but to make a Romp,* *Ibid.* *speak like a Romp, and a clownish Boor blunder* &c.

By his favour, all Imitations tho' never so well Counterfeited are not proper for the *Stage*. To present Nature under every Appearance would be an odd undertaking. A Midnight *Cart*, or a *Dunghil* would be no Ornamental *Scene*. Nastyness, and dirty Conversation are of the same kind. For *Words* are a Picture to the Ear, as Colours and *Surface* are to the Eye. Such Discourses are like dilating upon Ulcers, and Leprosies: The more

Na-

Natural, the worfe; for the Difguft always rifes with the Life of the Defcription. Offenfive Language like offenfive Smells, does but make a Man's Senfes a burthen, and affords him nothing but Loathing and Averfion. Beaftlinefs in Behaviour, gives a difparaging Idea of Humane Nature, and almoft makes us forry we are of the fame Kind. For thefe reafons 'tis a Maxime in Good Breeding never to fhock the Senfes, or Imagination. This Rule holds ftrongeft before *Women*, and efpecially when they come to be entertain'd. The Diverfion ought to be fuited to the Audience; For nothing pleafes which is difproportion'd to Capacity, and Guft. The Rudeneffes and broad Jefts of Beggars, are juft as acceptable to Ladies as their Rags, and Cleanlinefs. To treat Perfons of Condition like the *Mob*, is to degrade their Birth, and affront their Breeding. It levells them with the loweft Education. For the fize of a Man's Senfe, and Improvement, is difcovered by his Pleafures, as much as by any thing elfe.

But to remove from *Scenes* of *Decency*, to *Scenes* of Wit. And here *Mannel* and *Sancho*, two *pleafant fharp Fellows*, will divert us extreamly. *Mannel* in the Difguife of a Lady addreffes the Dutchefs in this manner.

Perfon.
Dram

manner. *Illustrious Beauty* ——. *I must desire to know whether the most purisidiferous Don* Quixote *of the Manchissima, and his squireiferous* Panca, *be in this Company or no.* This is the Ladies speech! Now comes *Sancho. Why look you Forsooth, without any more Flourishes, the Governour* Panca *is here, and Don* Quixotissimo *too; therefore most afflictedissimous Matronissima, speak what you willissimus, for we are all ready to be your Servitorissimus.*

pt. 2d.
P. 31.

I dare not go on, for fear of overlaying the *Reader.* He may cloy himself at his Leisure. The *Scene* between the *Taylor* and *Gardiner,* lies much in the same Latitude of Understanding.

p. 51.

The Third *Part* presents a set of *Poppets,* which is a Thought good enough; for this Play is only fit to move upon *Wires.* 'Tis pity these little *Machines* appear'd no sooner, for then the Sense, and the *Actors* had been well adjusted. In explaining the *Persons,* He acquaints us that *Carasco is a Witty Man:* I can't tell what the Gentleman might be in other Places, but I'm Satisfied he is a Fool in his *Play.* But some *Poets* are as great Judges of Wit, as they are an Instance; And have the Theory and the Practise just alike.

Mr. *Durfeys Epistles Dedicatory* are to the full as diverting as his *Comedies.* A little of them may not be amiss.   In

In his firſt, He thus addreſſes the *Dutches of Ormond*. *'Tis Madam from your Graces Proſperous Influence that I date my Good Fortune.* To *Date* from time and Place, is vulgar and ordinary, and many a *Letter* has miſcarried with it: But to do it from an *Influence*, is Aſtrological, and ſurprizing, and agrees extreamly with the *Hemiſphere of the Play-houſe.* Theſe Flights one would eaſily imagine were the *Poor Off-ſpring* of Mr. *Durfey*'s *Brain*, as he very judiciouſly phraſes it.

Pref. pt. 1ſt.

Ibid.

One Paragraph in his Dedication to Mr. *Montague* is perfect *Quixotiſm* ; One would almoſt think him enchanted. I'll give the Reader a Taſt.

Had your Eyes ſhot the haughty Auſterity upon me of a right Courtier,——— your valued minutes had never been diſturb'd with dilatory Trifles of this Nature, but my Heart on dull Conſideration of your Merit, had ſupinely wiſh'd you proſperity at a Diſtance. I'm afraid the *Poet* was under ſome Apprehenſions of the Temper he complains of. For to my thinking, there is a great deal of *Supineſs*, and *dull Conſideration* in theſe Periods. He tells his Patron *his Smiles have embolden'd him.* I confeſs I can't ſee how He could forbear ſmiling at ſuch Entertainment. However Mr. *Durfey* takes Things by the beſt Handle, and is reſolv'd

pt. 3d.

to

to be happy in his Interpretation. But to be serious. Were I the Author, I would discharge my Muse unless she prov'd kinder. His way is rather to cultivate his Lungs, and Sing to other Peoples Sense: For to finish him in a word, he is *Vox, & præterea nihil*. I speak this only on Supposition that the rest of his Performances are like These. Which because I have not perused I can judge of no farther than by the Rule of *ex pede Herculem*. I shall conclude with Monsieur *Boileau*'s *Art* of *Poetry*. This citation may possibly be of some service to Mr. *Durfey*; For if not concern'd in the Application, he may at least be precaution'd by the Advice.

The Translation runs thus.

p. 53.

I like an Author that Reforms the Age;
And keeps the right Decorum of the Stage:
That always pleases by just Reasons Rule:
But for a tedious Droll a Quibbling Fool,
Who with low nauseous Baudry fills his Plays;
Let him be gone and on two Tressells raise
Some Smithfield *Stage, where he may act his*
　　Pranks,
And make Jack-puddings *speak to Mounte-*
　banks.

SECT.

SECT. III.

Remarks upon the Relapse.

THE *Relapse* shall follow *Don Quixot,* upon the account of some Alliance between them. And because this *Author* swaggers so much in his *Preface,* and seems to look big upon his Performance, I shall spend a few more thoughts than ordinary upon his *Play,* and examine it briefly in the *Fable,* the *Moral,* the *Characters, &c.* The Fable I take to be as follows.

Fashion *a Lewd, Prodigal, younger Brother, is reduced to extremity: Upon his arrival from his Travels, he meets with* Couplet, *an old sharping Match-maker; This Man puts him upon a project of cheating his Elder Brother* Lord Foplington, *of a rich Fortune. Toung* Fashion *being refused a Summ of Money by his Brother, goes into* Couplers *Plot, bubbles Sir* Tunbelly *of his Daughter, and makes himself Master of a fair Estate.*

From the Form and Constitution of the *Fable,* I observe

1*st.* That there is a *Misnommer* in the Title. The *Play* should not have been call'd the *Relapse, or Virtue in Danger:*

P   Lovelace,

Lovelace, and *Amanda,* from whose *Characters* these Names are drawn, are Persons of Inferiour Consideration. *Lovelace* sinks in the middle of the *Fourth* Act, and we hear no more of him till towards the End of the *Fifth,* where he enters once more, but then 'tis as *Cato* did the Senate house, only to go out again. And as for *Amanda* she has nothing to do but to stand a shock of Courtship, and carry off her Virtue. This I confess is a great task in the *Play-house,* but no main matter in the *Play.*

The *Intrigue,* and the *Discovery,* the great Revolution and success, turns upon *Young Fashion.* He without Competition, is the Principal Person in the *Comedy.* And therefore the *Younger Brother,* or the *Fortunate Cheat,* had been much a more proper Name. Now when a *Poet* can't rig out a *Title Page,* 'tis but a bad sign of his holding out to the *Epilogue.*

2*ly.* I observe the *Moral* is vitious: It points the wrong way, and puts the *Prize* into the wrong Hand. It seems to make *Lewdness* the reason of *Desert,* and gives *Young Fashion* a second Fortune, only for Debauching away his First. A short view of his *Character,* will make good this Reflection. To begin with him: He confesses himself a *Rake,* swears, and

Blasphemes,

Blaſphemes, Curſes, and Challenges his Elder Brother, cheats him of his Miſtreſs, and gets him laid by the Heels in a Dog-Kennel. And what was the ground of all this unnatural quarrelling and outrage? Why the main of it was only becauſe Lord *Foplington* refuſed to ſupply his Luxury, and make good his Extravagance. This *Young Faſhion* after all, is the *Poets* Man of Merit. He provides, a *Plot* and a Fortune, on purpoſe for him. To ſpeak freely, A Lewd Character ſeldom wants good Luck in *Comedy.* So that when ever you ſee a thorough Libertine, you may almoſt ſwear he is in a riſing way, and that the *Poet* intends to make him a great Man. In ſhort; This *Play* perverts the End of *Comedy*: Which as Monſieur *Rapin* obſerves ought to regard Reformation, and publick Improvement. But the *Relapſer* had a more faſhionable Fancy in his Head. His *Moral* holds forth this notable Inſtruction.

Reflect, &c. p.131.

1*ſt.* That all *Younger Brothers* ſhould be careful to run out their Circumſtances as Faſt, and as Ill as they can. And when they have put their Affairs in this poſture of Advantage, they may conclude themſelves in the high Road to Wealth, and Succeſs. For as *Faſhion* Blaſphemouſly applies it, *Providence takes care of Men of Merit.*

R. lapſe. p. 19.

P 2   2*dly*

2*ly.* That when a Man is pres'd, his busineſs is not to be govern'd by Scruples, or formalize upon Conſcience and Honeſty. The quickeſt Expedients are the beſt; For in ſuch caſes the Occaſion juſtifies the Means, and a Knight of the *Poſt*, is as good as one of the *Garter.* In the

3*d.* Place it may not be improper to look a little into the *Plot.* Here the *Poet* ought to play the Politician if ever. This part ſhould have ſome ſtroaks, of Conduct, and ſtrains of Invention more then ordinary. There ſhould be ſomething that is admirable, and unexpected to ſurprize the Audience. And all this Fineſs muſt work by gentle degrees, by a due

Reflect. preparation of *Incidents,* and by Inſtru-
p. 133. ments which are probable. 'Tis Mr. *Rapins* remark, that without probability *every Thing is lame and Faulty.* Where there is no pretence to *Miracle* and *Machine,* matters muſt not exceed the force of Beleif. To produce effects without proportion; and likelyhood in the Cauſe, is Farce, and Magick, and looks more like Conjuring than Conduct. Let us examine the *Relapſer* by theſe Rules. To diſcover his *Plot,* we muſt lay open ſomewhat more of the *Fable.*

‘ Lord *Foplington* a Town Beau, had
‘ agreed to Marry the Daughter of Sir.
‘ *Tun-*

' *Tun-belly Clumsey* a Country Gentleman,
' who lived Fifty miles from *London*.
' Notwithstanding this small distance, the
' Lord had never seen his Mistress, nor
' the Knight his Son in Law. Both par-
' ties out of their great Wisdom, leave
' the treating the Match to *Coupler*. When
' all the preliminaries of Settlement were
' adjusted, and Lord *Foplington* expected
' by Sir *Tun-belly* in a few days, *Coupler*
' betrays his Trust to *Young Fashion*. He
' advises him to go down before his Bro-
' ther : To Counterfeit his Person, and
' pretend that the strength of his Inclina-
' tions brought him thither before his time,
' and without his Retinue. And to make
' him pass upon Sir *Tun-belly*, *Coupler* gives
' him his *Letter*, which was to be Lord
' *Foplingtons* Credential. *Young Fashion*
' thus provided, posts down to Sir *Tun-
' belly*, is received for Lord *Foplington*, and
' by the help of a little Folly and Knavery
' in the Family, Marries the young Lady
' without her Fathers Knowledge, and a
' week before the Appointment.

This is the Main of the Contrivance.
The Counterturn in Lord *Foplingtons* appearing afterwards, and the Support of
the main *Plot*, by *Bulls*, and *Nurses* at-
testing the Marriage, contain's little of
Moment. And here we may observe that

Lord *Foplington* has an unlucky Disagreement in his *Character*; This Misfortune sits hard upon the credibility of the Design. 'Tis true he was Formal and Fantastick, Smitten with Dress, and Equipage, and it may be vapour'd by his Perfumes; But his Behaviour is far from that of an Ideot. This being granted, 'tis very unlikely this Lord with his five Thousand pounds *per annum*, should leave the choise of his Mistress to *Coupler*, and take her Person and Fortune upon *Content*. To court thus blindfold, and by *Proxy*, does not agree with the Method of an Estate, nor the Niceness of a *Beau*. However the *Poet* makes him engage Hand over Head, without so much as the sight of her Picture. His going down to Sir *Tunbelly* was as extraordinary as his Courtship. He had never seen this Gentleman. He must know him to be beyond Measure suspicious, and that there was no Admittance without *Couplers* Letter. This *Letter* which was, the Key to the Castle, he forgot to take with him, and tells you *'twas stolen by his Brother Tam*. And for his part he neither had the Discretion to get another, nor yet to produce that written by him to Sir *Tun-belly*. Had common Sense been consulted upon this Occasion, the *Plot* had been at an End, and the *Play* had sunk

in

p. 27.

p. 79.

Ibid.

in the Fourth *Act.* The Remainder fub-
fifts purely upon the ftrength of *Folly,*
and of Folly altogether improbable, and
out of *Character.* The *Salvo* of Sir *John*
Friendly's appearing at laft, and vouching
for Lord *Foplington,* won't mend the matter. For as the *Story* informs us, Lord
Foplington never depended on this Referve: *p.* 81.
He knew nothing of this Gentleman be-
ing in the Country, nor where he Lived.
The truth is, Sir *John* was left in *Town,*
and the Lord had neither concerted his
journey with him, nor engaged his Affiftance. *p.* 83.

Let us now fee how Sir. *Tun-belly* hangs
together. This Gentleman the *Poet* makes
a *Juftice* of *Peace,* and a *Deputy Lieutenant,*
and feats him fifty Miles from *London :*
But by his Character you would take him
for one of *Hercules's* Monfters, or fome
Gyant in *Guy* of *Warwick.* His Behaviour is altogether *Romance,* and has nothing
agreeable to Time, or Country. When
Fafhion, and *Lory,* went down, they find
the Bridge drawn up, the Gates barr'd,
and the Blunderbufs cock'd at the firft
civil Queftion. And when Sir *Tun-belly*
had notice of this formidable Appearance,
he Sallies out with the *Poffe* of the Family,
and marches againft a Couple of Strangers
with a *Life Gaurd* of Halberds, Sythes,

and

and Pitchforks. And to make sure work, Young *Hoyden* is lock'd up at the first approach of the Enemy. Here you have prudence and wariness to the excess of Fable, and Frensy. And yet this mighty man of suspition, trusts *Coupler* with the Disposal of his only Daughter, and his Estate into the Bargain. · And what was this *Coupler*? Why, a sharper by *Character*, and little better by Profession. Farther. Lord *Foplington* and the Knight, are but a days Journey asunder, and yet by their treating by Proxy, and Commission, one would Fancy a dozen Degrees of *Latitude* betwixt them. And as for Young *Fashion*, excepting *Couplers* Letter, he has all imaginable Marks of Imposture upon him. He comes before his Time, and without the Retinue expected, and has nothing of the Air of Lord *Foplington's* Conversation. When Sir *Tun-belly* ask'd him, *pray where are your Coaches and Servants my Lord?* He makes a trifling excuse. *Sir, that I might give you and your Fair Daughter a proof how impatient I am to be nearer akin to you, I left my Equipage to follow me, and came away Post, with only one Servant.* To be in such a Hurry of Inclination for a Person he never saw, is somewhat strange! Besides, 'tis very unlikely Lord *Foplington* should hazard his

Com-

p. 59.

The Relapse.

Complexion on Horseback, out ride his Figure, and appear a Bridegroom in *Deshabille*. You may as soon perswade a Peacock out of his Train, as a *Beau* out of his Equipage; especially upon such an Occasion. Lord *Foplington* would scarsely speak to his Brother just come a *Shore*, till the Grand Committee of *Taylors, Seamtresses, &c.* was dispatch'd. Pomp, and Curiosity were this Lords Inclination; why then should he mortifie without necessity, make his first Approaches thus out of Form, and present himself to his Mistress at such Disadvantage? And as this is the Character of Lord *Foplington*, so 'tis reasonable to suppose Sir *Tunbelly* acquainted with it. An enquiry into the Humour and management of a Son in Law, is very natural and Customary. So that we can't without Violence to Sense, suppose Sir *Tunbelly* a Stranger to Lord *Foplington's* Singularities. These Reasons were enough in all Conscience to make Sir *Tunbelly* suspect a Juggle, and that *Fashion* was no better then a Counterfeit. Why then was the *Credential* swallow'd without chewing, why was not *Hoyden* lock'd up, and a pause made for farther Enquiry? Did this *Justice* never hear of such a Thing as Knavery, or had he ever greater reason to guard against it? More wary steps might

p. II.

might well have been expected from Sir
Tunbelly. To run from one extream of
Caution, to another of Credulity, is highly improbable. In short, either Lord
Foplington and Sir *Tunbelly* are Fools, or
they are not. If they are, where lies the
Cunning in over-reaching them? What
Conquest can there be without Opposition?
If they are not Fools, why does the *Poet*
make them so? Why is their Conduct so
grofs, so particolour'd, and inconsistent?
Take them either way, and the *Plot* mis-
carries. The first supposition makes it
dull, and the later, incredible. So much
for the *Plot.* I shall now in the

4*th.* Place touch briefly upon the *Manners.*

The *Manners* in the Language of the
Stage have a signification somewhat particular. *Aristotle* and *Rapin* call them the
Causes and Principles of Action. They
are formed upon the Diversities of Age,
and Sex, of Fortune, Capacity, and Education. The propriety of *Manners* con-
sifts in a Conformity of Practise, and Principle; of Nature, and Behaviour. For
the purpose. An old Man must not appear with the Profuseness and Levity of
Youth; A Gentleman must not talk like a
Clown, nor a Country Girl like a Town
Jilt. And when the *Characters* are feign'd
'tis

'tis *Horace*'s Rule to keep them Uniform, and confiftent, and agreeable to their firft fetting out. The *Poet* muft be careful to hold his *Perfons* tight to their *Calling* and pretentions. He muft not fhift, and fhuffle their Underftandings ; Let them skip from Wits to Blockheads, nor from Courtiers to Pedants. On the other hand. If their bufinefs is playing the Fool, keep them ftrictly to their Duty, and never indulge them in fine Sentences. To manage otherwife, is to defert *Nature*, and makes the *Play* appear monftrous, and Chimerical. So that inftead of an *Image of Life*, 'tis rather an Image of Impoffibility. To apply fome of thefe remarks to the *Relapfer*.

The fine *Berinthia*, one of the Top-Characters, is impudent and Profane. *Lovelace* would engage her Secrecy, and bids her Swear. She anfwers *I do.*

Lov. By what ?

Berinth. *By Woman.*

Lov. *That's Swearing by my Deity, do it by your own, or I fhan't believe you.*

Berinth. *By Man then.* p. 47.

This Lady promifes *Worthy* her Endeavours to corrupt *Amanda* ; and then They make a Profane jeft upon the Office. p. 51. In the progrefs of the *Play* after a great deal of Lewd Difcourfe with *Lovelace*,

Ber-

P. 74.
Berinthia is carried off into a Closet, and Lodged in a *Scene* of Debauch. Here is Decency, and Reservedness, to a great exactness! Monsieur *Rapin* blames *Ariosto*, and *Tasso*, for representing two of their Reflect. P. 40. Women over free, and airy. These *Poets* says he, *rob Women of their Character, which is Modesty.* Mr. *Rymer* is of the same Opinion: His words are these. *Nature knows no-* *Tragedies of the last Age consi- der'd, &c. P. 113, 114.* *thing in the Manners which so properly, and particularly distinguish a Woman, as her Modesty.*——*An impudent Woman is fit only to be kicked, and expos'd in Comedy.*

Now *Berinthia* appears in *Comedy* 'tis true; but neither to be *kick'd*, nor *expos'd*. She makes a Considerable Figure, has good Usage, keeps the best Company, and goes off without Censure, or Disadvantage. Let us now take a Turn or two with Sir *Tun-belly's* Heiress of 1500 pounds a year. This Young Lady swears, talks smut, and is upon the matter just as rag-manner'd as *Mary the Buxsome*. 'Tis plain the *Relapser* copyed Mr. *Durfey's* Original, which is a sign he was somewhat Pinch'd. Now this *Character* was no great Beauty in *Buxsome*; But it becomes the Knights Daughter much worse. *Buxsome* was a poor Pesant, which made her Rudeness more natural, and expected. But *Deputy Lieutenants* Children don't use

use to appear with the Behaviour of Beggars. To breed all People alike, and
make no distinction between a *Seat*, and a
Cottage, is not over artful, nor very cere-
monious to the Country Gentlemen. The
Relapser gives *Miss* a pretty Soliloquy,
I'll transcribe it for the *Reader*.

She swears by her Maker, *'tis well I
have a Husband a coming, or I'de Marry* p. 58.
*the Baker I would so. No body can knock
at the Gate, but presently I must be lock'd
up, and here's the Young Gray-hound——can
run loose about the House all day long, she
can, 'tis very well!* Afterwards her Language is too Lewd to be quoted. Here
is a Compound of Ill Manners, and Contradiction! Is this a good Resemblance of
Quality, a Description of a great Heiress,
and the effect of a Cautious Education?
By her Coarsness you would think her
Bred upon a Common, and by her Confidence, in the Nursery of the *Play-house*. I
suppose the *Relapser* Fancies the calling her
Miss Hoyden is enough to justifie her Ill
Manners. By his favour, this is a Mistake.
To represent her thus unhewn, he should
have suited her Condition to her Name,
a little better. For there is no Charm in
Words as to matters of Breeding, An un-
fashionable Name won't make a Man a
Clown. Education is not form'd upon
                                    Sounds,

Sounds, and Syllables, but upon Circumftances, and Quality. So that if he was
refolv'd to have fhown her thus unpolifh'd,
he fhould have made her keep *Sheep,* or
brought her up at the *Wafh-Boul.*

p. 61. Sir *Tun-belly* accofts Young *Fafhion* much
at the fame rate of Accomplifhment. My
Lord,——*I humbly crave leave to bid you
Welcome in Cup of Sack-wine.* One would
imagine the *Poet* was overdozed before
he gave the *Juftice* a Glafs. For *Sack-
wine* is too low for a *Petty Conftable.* This
peafantly expreffion agrees neither with
the Gentlemans Figure, nor with the reft
of his Behaviour. I find we fhould have
a Creditable *Magiftracy,* if the *Relapfer* had
the Making them. Here the *Characters*
are pinch'd in Senfe, and ftinted to fhort
Allowance. At an other time they are
over-indulged, and treated above Expectation.

For the purpofe. Vanity and Forma-
lizing is Lord *Foplingtons* part. To let
him fpeak without Aukwardnefs, and
Affectation, is to put him out of his Element. There muft be Gumm and ftif-
fening in his Difcourfe to make it natural.
However, the *Relapfer* has taken a fancy
to his Perfon, and given him fome of the
moft Gentile raillery in the whole *Play.*
To give an Inftance or two. This Lord
in

in Difcourfe with *Fafhion* forgets his Name,
flies out into Senfe, and fmooth expreffion, out talks his Brother, and abating
the ftarch'd Similitude of a *Watch*, dif-
covers nothing of Affectation, for almoft *p. 42.*
a *Page* together. He relapfes into the fame
Intemperance of good Senfe, in an other
Dialogue between him and his Brother.
I fhall cite a little of it.

Y. Fafh. *Vnlefs you are fo kind to affift
me in redeeming my Annuity, I know no
Remedy, but to go take a Purfe.*

L. Fopl. *Why Faith Tam* ———*to give* *p. 43.*
*you my Senfe of the Thing, I do think taking
a Purfe the beft Remedy in the World, for
if you fucceed, you are releiv'd that way, if
you are taken* ———*you are reliev'd to'ther.*

Fafhion being difappointed of a fupply
quarrels his Elder Brother, and calls him *p. 44.*
the Prince of Coxcombs.

L. Fopl. *Sir I am proud of being at the
Head of fo prevailing a party.*

Y. Fafh. *Will nothing then provoke thee?
draw Coward.*

L. Fopl. *Look you Tam, your poverty
makes your Life fo burdenfome to you, you
would provoke me to a Quarrel, in hopes
either to flip through my Lungs into my Eftate,
or elfe to get your felf run through the Guts, to
put an end to your Pain. But I fhall difap-
point you in both.* &c.

This

This Drolling has too much Spirit, the Air of it is too free, and too handsomly turn'd for Lord *Foplingtons* Character. I grant the *Relapser* could not aford to lose these Sentences. The Scene would have suffer'd by the Omission. But then he should have contriv'd the matter so, as that they might, have been spoken by Young *Fashion* in *Asides*, or by some other more proper Person. To go on. Miss *Hoyden* sparkles too much in Conversation. The *Poet* must needs give her a shining Line or two, which serves only to make the rest of her dullness the more remarkable. Sir. *Tun-belly* falls into the same Misfortune of a Wit, and rallies above the force of his Capacity. But the place having a mixture of Profaness, I shall forbear to cite it. Now to what purpose should a Fools Coat be embroider'd ? Finery in the wrong place is but expensive Ridiculousness. Besides, I don't perceive the *Relapser* was in any Condition to be thus liberal. And when a *Poet* is not overstock'd, to squander away his Wit among his *Block-heads*, is meer Distraction. His men of Sense will smart for this prodigality. *Lovelace* in his discourse of *Friendship*, shall be the first Instance. *Friendship* (says he) *is said to be a plant of tedious growth , its Root composed of tender* Fibers,

p. 64.
At 10p.

p. 85.

nice

nice in their Taſt, &c. By this Deſcription the Palate of a *Fiber*, ſhould be ſomewhat more *nice* and diſtinguiſhing, then
the *Poets* Judgment. Let us examin ſome
more of his Witty People. Young *Faſhion*
fancies by *Miſſes* forward Behaviour, ſhe
would have a whole *Kennel* of *Beaux* after her at *London*. And then *Hey to the*   *p.* 64.
Park, and the Play, and the Church, and the
Devil. Here I conceive the ranging of
the Period is amiſs. For if he had put the
Play, and the *Devil* together, the Order of
Nature, and the Air of Probability had been
much better obſerv'd.

   Afterwards *Coupler* being out of Breath
in coming up ſtairs to *Faſhion*, asks him
why the —— *canſt thou not lodge upon the* *p.* 94.
Ground-floor ?

   Y. Faſh. *Becauſe I love to lye as near*
Heaven as I can. One would think a Spark
juſt come off his Travels, and had made
the *Tour* of *Italy* and *France*, might have
rallied with a better Grace ! However if
he lodg'd in a *Garret*, 'tis a good *Local*
jeſt. I had almoſt forgot one pretty remarkable Sentence of *Faſhion* to *Lory*. *I* *p.* 15.
ſhall ſhew thee (ſays he) *the exceſs of my*
Paſſion by being very calm. Now ſince
this *Gentleman* was in a vein of talking
Philoſophy to his Man, I'm ſorry he broke
of ſo quickly. Had he gone on and ſhown
          Q   him

him the *Excess* of a Storm and no Wind
stirring, the Topick had been spent, and
the Thought improv'd to the utmost.

Let us now pass on to *Worthy*, the *Re-
lapsers* fine Gentleman. This Spark sets
up for Sense, and Address, and is to have
nothing of Affectation or Conscience to
spoil his Character. However to say no
more of him, he grows Foppish in the last
Scene, and courts *Amanda* in Fustian, and
Pedantry. First, He gives his Periods a
turn of Versification, and talks *Prose* to
her in *Meeter*. Now this is just as agreeable as it would be to *Ride* with òne Leg,
and *Walk* with the other. But let him
speak for himself. His first business is to
bring *Amanda* to an Aversion for her Husband ; And therefore he perswades her to
*Rouse up that Spirit Women ought to bear ;
and slight your God if he neglects his Angel.*
He goes on with his Orisons. *With
Arms of Ice receive his Cold Embraces, and
keep your Fire for those that come in Flames.*
Fire and Flames, is Mettal upon Mettal ;
'Tis false Heraldry. *Extend the Arms
of Mercy to his Aid. His zeal may give
him Title to your Pity, altho' his Merit cannot claim your Love.* Here you have *Arms*
brought in again by Head and shoulders.
I suppose the design was to keep up the
Situation of the *Allegory.* But the latter

part

p. 99.

Ibid.

part of the Speech is very Pithy. He would have her refign her Vertue out of Civility, and abufe her Husband on Principles of good Nature. *Worthy* purfues his point, and Rifes in his Addrefs. He falls into a Fit of Diffection, and hopes to gain his Miftrefs by Cutting his Throat. He is for *Ripping up his Faithful Breaft,* to prove the Reality of his Paffion. Now when a Man Courts with his Heart in his Hand, it muft be great Cruelty to refufe him! No Butcher could have Thought of a more moving Expedient! However, *Amanda* continues obftinate, and is not in the ufual Humour of the *Stage.* Upon this, like a well bred Lover he feizes her by Force, and threatens to Kill her. *Nay struggle not for all's in vain, or Death, or Victory, I am determin'd.* In this rencounter the Lady proves too nimble, and flips through his Fingers. Upon this difappointment, he cries, *there's Divinity about her, and fhe has difpenc'd fome Portion on't to me.* His Paffion is Metamorphos'd in the Turn of a hand: He is refin'd into a *Platonick* Admirer, and goes off as like a *Town Spark* as you would wifh. And fo much for the *Poets* fine Gentleman.

p. 100.

I fhould now examine the *Relapfer's Thoughts and Expreffions,* which are two other Things of Confideration in a *Play.*

The

The *Thoughts* or *Sentiments are the Expressions of the Manners, as Words are of the Thoughts*. But the view of the *Characters* has in some measure prevented this Enquiry. Leaving this Argument therefore, I shall consider his *Play* with respect to the

Three Unities of Time, Place, and Action.

And here the *Reader* may please to take notice, that the Design of these Rules, is to conceal the Fiction of the *Stage*, to make the *Play* appear Natural, and to give it an Air of Reality, and *Conversation*.

The largest compass for the first *Unity* is Twenty Four Hours: But a lesser proportion is more regular. To be exact, the Time of the History, or *Fable*, should not exceed that of the *Representation*: Or in other words, the whole Business of the *Play*, should not be much longer than the Time it takes up in *Playing*.

The Second *Unity* is that of *Place*. To observe it, the *Scene* must not wander from one Town, or Country to another. It must continue in the same House, Street, or at farthest in the same City, where it was first laid. The Reason of this Rule depends upon the *First*. Now the Compass of *Time* being strait, that of *Space* must bear a Correspondent Proportion.

Long

Long journeys in *Plays* are impracticable.
The Diſtances of *Place* muſt be ſuited to
Leiſure, and Poſſibility, otherwiſe the ſup-
poſition will appear unnatural and abſurd.
The

Third *Unity* is that of *Action*; It con-
ſiſts in contriving the chief Buſineſs of
the *Play* ſingle, and making the concerns
of one Perſon diſtinguiſhably great above
the reſt. All the Forces of the *Stage* muſt
as it were ſerve Under one *General*: And
the leſſer Intrigues or Underplots, have
ſome Relation to the Main. The very
Oppoſitions muſt be uſeful, and appear only to be Conquer'd, and Countermin'd.
To repreſent Two conſiderable Actions
independent of each other, Deſtroys the
beauty of Subordination, weakens the
Contrivance, and dilutes the pleaſure. It
ſplits the *Play*, and makes the *Poem* double.
He that would ſee more upon this ſubject *Diſcourſe*
may conſult *Corneille*. To bring theſe Re- *des Trois*
marks to the Caſe in hand. And here we *Unitez.*
may obſerve how the *Relapſer* fails in all *pt. 3d.*
the *Rules* above mention'd.

1ſt. His *Play* by modeſt Computation
takes up a weeks Work, but five days you
muſt allow it at the loweſt. One day muſt
be ſpent in the Firſt, Second, and part of
the Third *Act*, before Lord *Foplington* ſets
forward to Sir *Tun-belly*. Now the Length

of the Diſtance, the Pomp of the Retinue, and the Niceneſs of the Perſon being
conſider'd; the journey down, and up a-
gain, cannot be laid under four days. To
put this out of doubt, Lord, *Foplington* is
particularly careful to tell *Coupler*, how
concern'd he was not to overdrive, *for fear
of diſordering his Coach-Horſes.* The Laws
of *Place*, are no better obſerv'd than thoſe
of *Time*. In the Third *Act* the *Play* is in
Town, in the Fourth *Act* 'tis ſtroll'd Fifty
Miles off, and in the Fifth *Act* in *London*
again. Here *Pegaſus* ſtretches it to purpoſe! This *Poet* is fit to ride a Match with
Witches. *Juliana Cox* never Switched a
Broom ſtock with more Expedition! This
is exactly

Titus at *Walton Town*, and *Titus* at *Iſling-*
ton.

One would think by the probability of
matters, the *Plot* had been ſtolen from
Dr. *O——s.*

The *Poet*'s Succeſs in the laſt *Unity* of
Action is much the ſame with the former.
Lovelace, *Amanda*, and *Berinthia*, have no
ſhare in the main Buſineſs. Theſe Second
rate *Characters* are a detached Body:
Their Intereſt is perfectly Foreign, and
they are neither Friends, nor Enemies to
the

p. 88.

the *Plot*. *Young* Fa*fh*ion does not *fo* much
as *fee* them till the Clo*fe* of the Fifth *Act*,
and then they meet only to fill the *Stage* :
And yet the*fe* *Per*f*ons* are in the *Poets* account very con*fi*derable ; In*fo*much that
he has mi*fn*amed his *Play* from the Figure
of two of them. This *ft*rangne*fs* of *Per-*
f*ons*, di*ftinct* Company, and inconnexion
of Affairs, de*ft*roys the Unity of the *Poem*.
The contrivance is *juft* as wi*fe* as it would
be to cut a Diamond in two. There is
a lo*fs* of Lu*ft*re in the Divi*fi*on. Increa-
*fi*ng the Number, abates the Value, and
by making it more, you make it le*fs*.

Thus far I have examin'd the *Dramatick*
Merits of the *Play*. And upon enquiry,
it appears *à* Heap of Irregularities. There
is neither Propriety in the *Name*, nor Contrivance in the *Plot*, nor Decorum in the
Characters. 'Tis a thorough Contradi*c*-
tion to Nature, and impo*ffi*ble in *Time*,
and *Place*. Its *Shining Graces* as the Au- *Pref.*
thor calls them, are *Bla*f*phemy* and *Baudy*,
together with a mixture of *Oaths*, and
*Cur*f*ing*. Upon the whole ; The *Relap-*
f*er's* Judgment, and his Morals, are pretty
well adj*uft*ed. The *Poet*, is not much bet-
ter than the *Man*. As for the *Profane* ^{fee Chap.}
part, 'tis hideous and *fu*perlative. But ^{2d.}
this I have con*fi*der'd el*fe*where. All that
I *fh*all ob*fe*rve here is, that the Author was

*fen*sible

senfible of this Objection. His Defence in his *Preface* is moſt wretched : He pretends to know nothing of the Matter, and that *'tis all Printed* ; Which only proves his Confidence equal to the reſt of his Virtues. To out-face Evidence in this manner, is next to the affirming there's no ſuch Sin as *Blaſphemy*, which is the greateſt Blaſphemy of all. His Apology confiſts in railing at the *Clergy* ; a certain ſign of ill Principles, and ill Manners. This He does at an unuſual rate of Rudeneſs and Spite. He calls them the Saints with Screw'd *Faces, and wry Mouths.* And after a great deal of ſcurrilous Abuſe too groſs to be mention'd, he adds ; *If any Man happens to be offended at a ſtory of a Cock and a Bull, and a Prieſt and a Bull-dog, I beg his Pardon,* &c. This is brave *Bear-Garden* Language ! The *Relapſer* would do well to tranſport his Muſe to *Samouroan* * There 'tis likely he might find Leiſure to lick his *Abortive Brat* into ſhape ; And meet with proper Buſineſs for his Temper, and encouragement for his Talent.

Pref.

An Academy in Lithua nia, for the Education of Bears.
Pere Au rill Voyage en Divers Etats, &c.
P. 240.

C H A P.

C H A P. VI.

The Opinion of Paganism, *of the* Church, *and* State, *concerning the* Stage.

HAving in the foregoing *Chapters* dif-cover'd fome part of the Diforders of the *Englifh Stage* ; I fhall in this Laft, prefent the *Reader* with a fhort View of the Senfe of *Antiquity,* To which I fhall add fome *Modern* Authorities ; From all which it will appear that *Plays* have ge-nerally been look'd on as the *Nurferies of Vice,* the *Corrupters* of *Youth,* and the *Grievance* of the *Country* where they are fuffer'd.

This proof from *Teftimony* fhall be ranged under thefe three Heads.

Under the *Firft,* I fhall cite fome of the moft celebrated *Heathen Philofophers,* Orators, and Hiftorians ; Men of the big-geft Confideration, for Senfe, Learning, and Figure. The

Second, Shall confift of the *Laws* and *Conftitutions* of *Princes, &c.* The

Third, Will be drawn from *Church- Re-cords,* from F*athers,* and *Councils* of unex-ceptionable

ceptionable Authority, both as to Persons,
and Time.

1*st*. I shall produce some of the most
celebrated Heathen Philosophers &c. To
begin with *Plato*. 'This Philosopher tells us
Plat. de ' that *Plays* raise the Passions, and per-
Repub. Lib. ' vert the use of them, and by consequence
10. *Euseb.* ' are dangerous to Morality. For this
Præpar. ' Reason he banishes these Diversions his
Evarg. ' *Common-Wealth.*

Xenophon who was both a Man of *Let-*
ters and a great *General*, commends the
Cyropæd. *Persians* for the Discipline of their Edu-
P. 34. cation. 'They won't (says he) so much
' as suffer their Youth to hear any thing
' that's Amorous or Tawdry. They
were afraid want of Ballast might make
them miscarry, and that 'twas dangerous
to add weight to the Byass of Nature.

Aristotle lays it down for a Rule ' that
' the Law ought to forbid Young People
Polit. Lib. ' the seeing of *Comedies*. Such permissions
7. *cap.* 17. ' not being safe till Age and Discipline
' had confirm'd them in sobriety, forti-
' fied their Virtue, and made them as it
' were proof against Debauchery. This
Philosopher who had look'd as far into
Polit. Humane Nature as any Man, observes
Lib. 8. farther. 'That the force of Musick and
' *Action* is very affecting. It commands
' the Audience and changes the Passions to
' a

' a Resemblance of the Matter before them.
So that where the Representation is foul,
the Thoughts of the Company must
suffer.

Tully crys out upon ' Licentious *Plays* *Tusc. Quest.*
' and *Poems,* as the bane of Sobriety, and *Lib.* 4.
' wise Thinking : That *Comedy* subsists *De Leg.* *Lib.* 1.
' upon Lewdness, and that Pleasure is the
' Root of all Evil.

Livy, reports the Original of *Plays* a-
mong the *Romans.* ' He tells us they
' were brought in upon the score of Re-
' ligion, to pacifie the Gods, and remove a
' *Mortality.* But then He adds that the
' Motives are sometimes good, when the
' Means are stark naught : That the Re- *Dec.* 1.
' medy in this case was worse than the *Lib.* 7.
' Disease, and the Atonement more Infec-
' tious then the Plague.

Valerius Maximus, Contemporary with
Livy, gives much the same Account of
the rise of *Theatres* at *Rome.* 'Twas De-
' votion which built them. And as for
' the Performances of those Places, which
' Mr. *Dryden* calls the *Ornaments,* this Au-
' thor censures as the Blemishes of *Peace.*
And which is more, He affirms ' They
' were the Occasions of Civil Distractions ;
' And that the *State* first Blush'd, and
' then Bled, for the Entertainment. He *Lib.* 2.
' concludes the consequences of *Plays* in- *cap.* 4.
' tolerable ;

'tolerable; And that the *Massilienses* did well
'in clearing the Country of them. *Seneca*
'complains heartily of the Extravagance
'and Debauchery of the Age: And how
'forward People were to improve in that
'which was naught. That scarce any Body
'would apply themselves to the Study of
'Nature and Morality, unless when the
'*Play-House* was shut, or the Weather
'foul. That there was no body to teach
'*Philosophy*, because there was no body
'to Learn it : But that the *Stage* had *Nur-*
'*series*, and Company enough. This Mis-
'application of time and Fancy, made
'Knowledge in so ill a Condition. This
'was the Cause the Hints of Antiquity
'were no better pursued ; that some In-
'ventions were sunk, and that Humane
'Reason grew Downwards rather than
'otherwise. And elswhere he avers that
'there is nothing more destructive to Good
'Manners then to run Idling to see *Sights*.
'For there Vice makes an insensible Ap-
'proach, and steals upon us in the Dis-
'guise of pleasure.

Natural
Quest. Lib.
7. cap. 32.

Epist. 7.

'*Tacitus* relating how *Nero* hired de-
'cay'd Gentlemen for the *Stage*, com-
'plains of the Mismanagement ; And lets
'us know 'twas the part of a Prince to re-
'leive their Necessity, and not to Tempt
'it. And that his Bounty should rather
'have

Annal.
lib. 14.
cap. 14.

' have set them above an ill practise, than
' driven them apon't.

And in another place, He informs us
that ' the German Women were Guard-
' ed against danger, and kept their Honour *De Mor.*
' out of Harms way, by having no *Play- German !*
' Houses amongst them. *cap. 19.*

Plays, in the Opinion of the Judicious *Sympoſiac.*
Plutark are dangerous to corrupt Young *Lib. 7.*
People; And therefore *Stage* Poetry when *De Audi-*
it grows too hardy, and Licentious, *p. 15.*
ought to be checkt. This was the Opi- *Ed. par.*
nion of these Celebrated *Authors* with
respect to *Theatres* : They Charge them
with the Corruption of Principles, and
Manners, and lay in all imaginable Caution against them. And yet these Men
had seldom any thing but this World in
their Scheme ; and form'd their Judgments only upon Natural Light, and Common Experience. We see then to what sort
of Conduct we are oblig'd. The case is
plain ; Unless we are little enough to renounce our Reason, and fall short of Philosophy, and live *under* the Pitch of *Heathenism.*

To these Testimonies I shall add a
Couple of *Poets,* who both seem good
Judges of the Affair in Hand.

The first is *Ovid,* who in his Book
De Arte Amandi, gives his *Reader* to understand

stand that the *Play-House* was the most
likely Place for him to Forage in. Here
would be choice of all sorts : Nothing being more common than to see Beauty surpriz'd, Women debauch'd, and Wenches
Pick'd up at these Diversions.

·Lib. 1·

Sed tu præcique curvis venare Theatris,
Hæc loca sunt voto fertiliora tuo.
—— *ruit ad celebres cultissima Fæmina*
   Ludos ;
Copia judicium sæpe morata meum est.
Spectatum veniunt, veniunt Spectentur ut
   ipsæ ;
Ille locus casti damna pudoris habet.

And afterwards relating the imperfect
beginning of *Plays* at the Rape of the *Sa-*
bine Virgins, he adds,

Silicit exillo solennia more Theatra
Nunc quoque formosis insidiosa manent.

This *Author* some time after wrote the
Remedy of *Love*. Here he pretends to Pre-
scribe for Prudence, if not for Sobriety.
And to this purpose, He forbids the seeing of *Plays*, and the reading of *Poets*,
especially some of them. Such Recreations
being apt to feed the *Distemper*, and make
the *Patient* relapse.

At

At tanti tibi sit non indulgere Theatris
Dum bene de vacuo Pectore cedat amor.
Enervant animos Citharæ, Cantusque, lyra-
que
Et vox, & numeris brachia mota suis. Remed.
Illic assidue ficti saltantur amantes, Amor.
Quid caveas, actor, quid juvet, arte docet.

In his *De Tristibus*, He endeavours to
make some Amends for his scandalous
Poems, and gives *Augustus* a sort of *Plan*
for a Publick *Reformation*. Amongst other
Things, he advises the suppressing of *Plays*,
as being the promoters of Lewdness, and
Dissolution of Manners.

Ut tamen hoc fatear ludi quoque semina Lib. 2.
præbent
Nequitiæ, tolli tota Theatra jube.

To the Testimony of *Ovid*, I could
add *Plautus*, *Propertius*, and *Juvenal*, but
being not willing to overburthen the *Rea-*
der, I shall content my self with the *Plain-*
Dealer as one better known at *Home*.
This *Poet* in his *Dedication* to *Lady B,*
some Emiment *Procuress*, pleads the Merits of his Function, and insists on being
Billeted upon *free Quarter*. *Madam* (says
he) *I think a Poet ought to be as free of*
your

*your Houses, as of the Play-Houses: since
he contributes to the support of both, and
is as necessary to such as you, as the Ballad-
singer to the Pick-purse, in Convening the
Cullies at the Theatres to be pick'd up, and*

Ep. Ded. *Carried to a supper, and Bed, at your Houses.*
This is franck Evidence, and ne're the
less true, for the Air of a Jest.

I shall now in the Second
Place proceed to the *Censures* of the
State; And show in a few Words how
much the *Stage* stands discouraged by the
Laws of other Countrys and our own.

*Plut. De
Glor. A-
theniens.*
To begin with the *Athenians.* This
People tho' none of the worst Freinds to
the *Play-House* 'thought a *Comedy* so un-
'reputable a Performance, that they made
'a Law that no Judge of the *Ariopagus*
'should make one.

*Plut. La-
con Insti-
tut.*
The *Lacedemonians*, who were remarkable for the Wisdom of their *Laws*, the
Sobriety of their *Manners*, and their Breeding of brave Men. This *Government*
would not endure the *Stage* in any Form,
nor under any Regulation.

*Cic. de Re-
pub. Lib.
4. cited by,
St. Augu-
stine. Libr.
2. de ci.
dei. cap.
13.*
To pass on to the *Romans. Tully* in-
'forms us that their *Predecessours* counted
'all *Stage-Plays* uncreditable and Scanda-
'lous. In so much that any *Roman* who
'turn'd *Actor* was not only to be Degraded,
'but likewise as it were disincorporated,
and

' and unnaturalized by the *Order* of the
' *Censors.*

St. *Augustine* in the same Book, commends the *Romans* for refusing the *Jus Ci-*
vitatis to *Players*, for seizing their Freedoms,
and making them perfectly Foreign to
their *Government.* *L. 2. cap.* *29.*

We read in *Livy* that the Young Peo- *Dec. 1.*
ple in *Rome* kept the *Fabulæ Attellanæ* to *Libr. 7.*
themselves. ' They would not suffer this
' Diversion to be blemish'd by the *Stage.*
' For this reason, as the Historian observes, *Ab Hiſtri-*
' the *Actors* of the *Fabulæ Atellanæ* were *onibus Pol-*
' neither expell'd their *Tribe*, nor refused to *lui.*
' serve in *Arms*; Both which Penalties it ap-
' pears the *Common Players* lay under.

In the *Theodoſian Code, Players* are call'd *xv. Cod.*
Perſonæ inhoneſtæ; that is, to *Translate* it *Theod. Tit.*
softly, Persons Maim'd, and Blemish'd in *vii. p. 375.*
their Reputation. Their *Pictures* might
be seen at the *Play-House*, but were not
permitted to hang in any creditable Place * *in loco Ho-*
of the *Town*, Upon this *Text Gothofred* *neſto.*
tells us the Function of *Players* was counted
scandalous * by the *Civil Law.* L. 4. And *turpe mu-*
that those who came upon the *Stage* to di- *nus.*
vert the people, had a mark of Infamy set
upon them. *Famoſi ſunt ex Edicto.* *L. 1. §. 6.*
de his qui
I shall now come down to our own *notantur*
Constitution. And I find by 39. *Eliz.* *infamia.*
cap. 4. 1. *Jac. cap.* 7. That *Gothofred.*
Ibid. p.
R *376.*

all Bearwards, Common Players of Enterludes, Counterfeit Egyptians &c. shall be taken, adjudged and deem'd Rogues, Vagabonds, and sturdy beggars, and shall sustain all pain and Punishment, as by this Act is in that behalf appointed.

The *Penalties* are infamous to the last degree, and *Capital* too, unless they give over. 'Tis true, the first *Act* excepts those *Players* which belong to a Baron or other Personage of higher Degree, and are authorized to Play under the hand and Seal of Armes of such Baron, or Personage. But by the later *Statute* this Privilege of *Licensing* is taken away: And all of them are expresly brought under the Penalty without Distinction.

About the Year 1580, there was a Petition made to Queen *Elizabeth* for suppressing of *Play-Houses*. 'Tis somewhat remarkable, and therefore I shall transcribe some part of the Relation.

Many Godly Citizens, and other well disposed Gentlemen of London, *considering that* Play-Houses *and* Dicing-Houses, *were Traps for Young Gentlemen and others, and perceiving the many Inconveniencies and great damage that would ensue upon the long suffering of the same, not only to particular Persons but to the whole City; And that it would also be a great disparagement to the Governours, and a dishonour to the Government of this Honourable City, if they should*

any

any longer continue, acquainted some Pious Magistrates therewith, desiring them to take some Course for the suppression of Common Play-Houses, &c. within the City of London *and Liberties thereof ; who thereupon made humble suit to Queen* Elizabeth *and her Privy Council, and obtain'd leave of her Majesty to thrust the Players out of the City, and to pull down all Play-Houses, and Dicing-Houses within their Liberties, which accordingly was effected. And the Play-Houses in* Grace-Church-street *&c. were quite put down and suppress'd.*

Rawlidge his Monster, lately found out, &c. p. 2, 3, 4.

I shall give a Modern Instance or two from *France,* and so conclude these Authorities.

Gazett Roterdam. Dec. 20. Paris.

In the Year 1696. we are inform'd by a Dutch *Print,* M. *L' Archevéque appuyé* &c. That the Lord Arch-Bishop 'support'd by the interest of some Reli-'gious Persons at Court, has done his ut-'most to suppress the *Publick Theatres* by 'degrees ; or at least to clear them of 'Profaness.

And last Summer the *Gazetts* in the *Paris Article* affirm. That the King has 'order'd the *Italian Players* to retire out 'of *France* because they did not observe 'his *Majesties Orders,* but represented im-'modest *Pieces,* and did not correct their 'Obscenities, and indecent *Gestures.*

French Amsterdam Harlem Gazetts. Paris, May. 17. 1697.

R 2   The

The same *Intelligence* the next week after, acquaints us 'that some Persons of 'the first *Quality* at Court, who were 'the Protectors of these *Comedians*, had so-'licited the French King to recal his *Or-*'*der* against them, but their Request had 'no success.

And here to put an end to the Modern Authorities, I shall subjoyn a sort of *Pastoral Letter* publish'd about two years since by the Bishop of *Arras* in *Flanders*. The *Reader* shall have as much of it as concerns him in both Languages.

MAN-

MANDEMENT
DE MONSEIGNEUR
L' Illuſtriſſime Et Reverendiſſime
EVE QUE D' ARRAS
CONTRE LA COMEDIE.

GUY DE SEVE DE ROCHE CHOUART
par la grace de *Dieu & du Saint Siége Apo-*
ſtolique *Eveque d' Arras*, A tous fideles dela *Ville d'*
Arras Salut & Benediction. Il faut ignorer ſa Religion pour ne pas connoître l' horreur qu'elle a mar-
quée dans tous les temps des Spectacles, & de la
Comedie en particulier. Les ſaints Peres la con-
damnent dans leurs écrits ; Ils la regardent comme un reſte du paganiſme, & Comme une école d'
impureté. L' Egliſe l' a toûjours regardée avec abo-
mination, & ſi elle n'a pas abſolument rejetté de
ſon ſein ceux qui exercent ce métier infame &
ſcandaleux, elle les prive publiquement des Sacremens, & n' oublie rien pour marquer en toutes ren-
countres ſon averſion pour cét état & pour l' inſpirer
a ſes Enfans. Des Rituels de Diocéſes tres reglés
les mettent au nombre des perſonnes que les Curés
ſont obligés de traiter comme excommunies ; Celui
de *Paris* les joint aux Sorciers, & aux Magiciens,
& les regarde comme manifeſtement infames ; Le
Eveques les plus ſaints leur font refuſer publiquement,
les Sacremens ; Nous avons veu un des premiers
Eveques de *France* ne vouloir pas par cette raiſon recevoir au mariage un homme de cet état ; un autre
ne vouloir pas leur accorder la terre Sainte ; Et dans

les Statuts d' un prelat bien plus illustre per son me-
rite, par sa Pieté, & par l' austerité de sa vié que
par la pourpre dont il est revestu, on les trouve avec
les concubinaires, les Usuriers, les Blasphemateurs,
les Femmes debauchées, les excommuniés denoncés,
les Infames, les Simoniaque's, & autres personnes
scandaleuses mis au nombre de ceux a qui on doit re-
fuser publiquement la Communion.

Il est donc impossible de justifyer la Comedie sans
vouloir condamner l' Eglise, les saints peres, les plus
saint Prelats, mais il ne l' est pas moins de justifier
ceux qui par leur assistance a ces spectacles non seule-
ment prennent part au mal qui s'y fait, mais contri-
buent en même temps á retenir ces malheureux mini-
stres de Satan dans une profession, qui les separant
des Sâcremens de l' Eglise les met dans un état per-
petuel de peché & hors de salut s'ils ne l' abandon-
nent. ——

Et á egard des Comediens & Commediennes, Nous
defendons trés expressement à nos pasteurs & á nos
Confesseurs des les recevoir aux Sacremens si cé n'est
qu' ils aient fait Penitence de leur peché, donné des
preuves d'amendment, renoncé á leur Etat, & re-
pare pat une satisfaction publique telle que nous juge-
rons á propos de leur ordonner, le Scandale public
qu'ils ont donné. Fait & ordonné á Arras le qua-
triéme jour de Decembre mil six cent quatre-vingt
quinze.

Trois Let-
tres Pasto-
rales De
Monseig-
neur L'
Eveque
D' Arras
&c.
A Delf.
1697.

Guy Evêque d' Arras
Et plus bas
Par Monseigneur

CARON.

In

In English thus,

An Order of the most Illustrious and most Reverend Lord Bishop of Arras *against* Plays.

'GUY DE SEVE DE ROCHE
'CHOUART by the grace of God,
'&c. Bishop of *Arras*. To all the Faithful in
'the Town of *Arras* Health and Bene-
'diction. A man must be very ignorant
'of his Religion, not to know the great
'disgust it has always declar'd, for *Pub-*
'*lick Sights*, and for *Plays* in particular.
'The Holy *Fathers* condemn them in
'their writings; They look upon them
'as reliques of Heathenism, and Schools of
'Debauchery. They have been always
'abominated by the Church; And not-
'withstanding those who are concern'd
'in this Scandalous Profession; are not
'absolutely expell'd by a Formal Excom-
'munication, yet She publickly refuses
'them the Sacraments, and omits nothing
'upon all occasions, to show her aversion
'for this Employment, and to transfuse

R 4   'the

'the same sentiments into her Children.
' The *Rituals* of the best govern'd Dioceses,
' have ranged the *Players* among those
' whom the Parish Priests are oblig'd to
' treat as Excommunicated Persons. The
' *Ritual* of *Paris* joyns them with Sorce-
' rers, and Magicians, and looks upon them
' as notoriously infamous; The most emi-
' nent Bishops for Piety, have publickly
' denied them the Sacraments: For this
' reason, we our selves have known one
' of the most considerable Bishops in *France*,
' turn back a *Player* that came to be
' Married; And an other of the same order,
' refused to bury them in Consecrated
' Ground: And by the *Orders* of a Bishop,
' who is much more illustrious for his
' worth, for his Piety, and the Strictness
' of his Life, than for the *Purple* in his
' Habit; They are thrown amongst For-
' nicators, Usurers, Blasphemers, Lewd
' Women, and declar'd Excommunicates,
' amongst the Infamous, and Simoniacal,
' and other Scandalous Persons who are
' in the List of those who ought publick-
' ly to be barr'd Communion.

' Unless therfore we have a mind to
' condemn the Church, the Holy Fathers,
' and the most holy Bishops, 'tis impossi-
' ble to justifie *Plays*; neither is the De-
' fence of those less impracticable, who
' by

' by their Countenance of thefe Diverfions,
' not only have their fhare of the Mif-
' chief there done, but contribute at the
' fame time to fix thefe unhappy Minifters
' of Satan in a Profeffion, which by de-
' priving them of the Sacraments of the
' Church, leaves them under a conftant
' neceffity of Sinning, and out of all hopes
' of being faved, unlefs they give it
' over.——

From the general Unlawfulnefs of
Plays, the Bifhop proceeds to argue more
ftrongly againft feeing them at times
which are more particularly devoted to
Piety, and Humiliation : And therefore he
ftrickly forbids his Diocefs the *Play-Houfe*
in *Advent*, *Lent*, or under any publick
Calamity. And at laft concludes in this
Manner.

' As for the Cafe of *Players* both Men,
' and Women, we exprefly forbid all our
' Rectors, Paftors, and Confeffours, to ad-
' mit them to the Sacraments, unlefs they
' fhall repent them of their Crime, make
' proof of their Reformation, renounce
' their *Bufinefs*, and retrieve the Scandal
' they have given, by fuch publick Satis-
' faction as we fhall think proper to in-
' joyn them. Made and Decreed at *Arras*
' the fourth day of *December* 1695.

Guy Bifhop of *Arras*. &c.

I

I shall now in the Third

Place, give a short account of the sense of the *Primitive* Church concerning the *Stage*: And first I shall instance in her *Councils*.

Ann. 305.
Can. 67.

The Council of *Illiberis*, or *Collioure* in *Spain*, decrees,

'That it shall not be lawful for any
'Woman who is either in full Communion
'or a probationer for Baptism, to Marry,
'or Entertain any *Comedians* or *Actors*; who-
'ever takes this Liberty shall be Excommunicated.

Ann. 314.
Can. 5.

The First Council of *Arles*, runs thus,

'Concerning *Players*, we have thought
'fit to Excommunicate them as long as they
'continue to *Act*.

Ann. 452.

The Second Council of *Arles* made their 20*th* Canon to the same purpose, and al-most in the same words.

Ann. 397.
Can. 11.

The Third Council of *Carthage*, of which St. *Augustine* was a Member, ordains,

'That the Sons of Bishops, or other
'Clergy-men should not be permitted to
* Secula- 'furnish out Publick *Shews*, or *Plays* * or
ria specta-
cula, which 'be present at them: Such sort of Pagan
manifestly 'Entertainments being forbidden all the
compre-
hends the 'Laity. It being always unlawful for all
Stage. 'Christians to come amongst *Blasphe-*
'*mers.*

This

This last branch shews the *Canon* was Principally level'd against the *Play-House*: And the reason of the Prohibition, holds every jot as strong against the *English*, as against the *Roman Stage*.

By the 35th *Canon* of this *Council* 'tis decreed,

' That *Actors* or others belonging to the
' *Stage*, who are either *Converts*, or *Peni-*
' *tents* upon a Relapse, shall not be denied
' *Admission* into the Church. This is farther proof, that *Players* as long as they
kept to their Employment were bar'd
Communion.

Another *African Council* declares,

' That the Testimony of People of ill *Ann. 424.*
' Reputation, of *Players*, and others of such *Can. 96.*
' scandalous Employments, shall not be ad-
' mitted against any Person.

The Second *Council* of *Chaalon* sets *Concil.*
forth,   *Cabilon.*
                                            Ann. 813.
' That Clergy men ought to abstain *Can. 9.*
' from all over-engaging Entertainments
' in Musick or *Show*. (*oculorum auriumque*
' *illecebris*.) And as for the smutty, and Li-
' centious Insolence of *Players*, and Buf-
' foons, let them not only decline the Hear-
' ing it themselves, but likewise conclude
' the *Laity* oblig'd to the same Conduct.

I could cite many more Authorities of this Kind, but being conscious of the Nice-
nefs

ness of the *Age*, I shall forbear, and proceed to the Testimony of the *Fathers*.

To begin with *Theophilus* Bishop of *Antioch*, who lived in the Second *Century*.

Libr. 3. *ad Antol.*

' 'Tis not lawful (says he) for us to be
' present at the *Prizes* of your *Gladiators*,
' least by this means we should be *Accessa-*
' *ries* to the Murthers there committed.
' Neither dare we presume upon the Liber-

* *Specta-cula.*

' ty of your other *Shews*, * least our Sen-
' ses should be tinctur'd, and disoblig'd,
' with Indecency, and Profaness. The
' Tragical Distractions of *Tereus* and *Thy-*
' *estes*, are Nonsense to us. We are for
' seeing no Representations of Lewdness.
' The Stage-Adulteries of the *Gods*, and
' *Hero's* , are unwarrantable Entertain-
' ments : And so much the worse, be-
' cause the Mercenary *Players* set them off
' with all the Charms and Advantages of
' Speaking. God forbid that *Christians*
' who are remarkable for Modesty, and
' Reserv'dness ; who are obliged to Disci-
' pline, and train'd up in Virtue, God for-
' bid I say, that we should dishonour our
' Thoughts, much less our Practise, with
' such Wickedness as This !

Tertullian who liv'd at the latter end
of this Century is copious upon this
subject ; I shall translate but some Part of
it.

it. In his Apologetick. He thus addresses
the Heathens.

‘ We keep off from your publick *Shews,*
‘ because we can't understand the War-
‘ rant of their Original. There's Super-
‘ stition and Idolatry in the Case: And
‘ we dislike the Entertainment because we
‘ dislike the reason of its Institution. Be-
‘ sides, We have nothing to do with the
‘ Frensies of the *Race-Ground,* the Lewd-
‘ ness of the *Play-House,* or the Barbari-
‘ ties of the *Bear-Garden.* The *Epicureans*
‘ had the Liberty to state the Notion,
‘ and determine the Object of Pleasure.
‘ Why can't we have the same Privilege?
‘ What Offence is it then if we differ from
‘ you in the Idea of Satisfaction? If we
‘ won't understand to brighten our Hu-
‘ mour, and live pleasantly, where's the
‘ harm? If any body has the worst on't,
‘ 'tis only our selves.

His Book *de Spectaculis* was wrote on
purpose to diswade the Christians, from the
publick Diversions of the *Heathens,* of
which the *Play-House* was one. In his
first Chapter He gives them to understand, ‘ That the Tenour of their Faith,
‘ the Reason of Principle, and the Order
‘ of Discipline, had bar'd them the Enter-
‘ tainments of the *Town.* And therefore
‘ He exhorts them to refresh their Me-
                              ‘ mories,

'mories, to run up to their Baptism,
'and recollect their first Engagements.
'For without care, Pleasure is a strange
'bewitching Thing. When it gets the
'Ascendant, 'twill keep on Ignorance for
'an Excuse of Liberty, make a man's Con-
'science wink, and suborn his Reason a-
'gainst himself.

Chap. 3.   'But as he goes on, some peoples Faith
'is either too full of Scruples, or too bar-
'ren of Sense. Nothing will serve to set-
'tle them but a plain Text of *Scripture.*
'They hover in uncertainty because 'tis
'not said as expresly thou shalt not go
'to the *Play-House*, as 'tis thou shalt not
'Kill. But this looks more like Fencing
'than Argument. For we have the Mea-
'ning of the prohibition tho' not the sound,
'in the first *Psalm. Blessed is the Man
that walks not in the Council of the Ungodly,
nor stands in the way of Sinners, nor sits in
the Seat of the Scornful.*

Ibid.   'The *Censors* whose business 'twas to
Cap. 10. 'take care of Regularity and Manners,
'look'd on these *Play-Houses* as no other
'than *Batteries* upon Virtue and Sobriety,
'and for this reason often pull'd them
'down before they were well built. so
'that here we can argue from the *Pre-
'cedents* of meer *Nature*, and plead the
'*Heathens* against themselves. Upon this
                                    'view

'view *Pompey* the Great, when he built
'his *Dramatick* Bawdy-House, clapp'd a
'*Chappel* a Top on't. He would not let it
'go under the Name of a Play-House, but
'conven'd the people to a Solemn Dedi-
'cation, and called it *Venus's* Temple ; Gi-
'ving them to understand at the same
'time that there were *Benches* under it for
'Diversion. He was afraid if he had not
'gone this way to work, The *Censors*
'might afterwards have razed the Monu-
'ment, and branded his Memory. Thus a
'Scandalous pile of Building was pro-
'tected : The Temple, cover'd the *Play-*
'*House*, and Discipline was baffled by
'*Superstition*. But the Design is notably
'suited to the Patronage of *Bacchus* * and
'*Venus*. These two Confederate Devils
'of Lust and Intemperance, do well toge-
'ther. The very Functions of the *Players*
'resemble their *Protectors*, and are in-
'stances of Service and Acknowledgment.
'Their Motion is effeminate, and their
'Gestures vitious and Significant : And
'thus they worship the Luxury of one
'*Idoll*, and the Lewdness of the other.

  ' And granting the Regards of Quality,
'the Advantages of Age, or Temper,
'may fortifie some People ; granting Mo-
'desty secur'd, and the Diversion as it
'were refin'd by this Means : Yet a Man
                                    'must

The Play-houses were dedicated to Bacchus.

Lid. cap. 15.

' must not expect to stand by perfectly un-
' moved, and impregnable. No body can
' be pleas'd without Sensible Impressions.
' Nor can such Perceptions be received
' without a Train of Passions attending
' them. These Consequences will be sure
' to work back upon their Causes, solicite
' the Fancy, and heighten the Original
' Pleasure. But if a Man pretends to be a
' *Stoick* at *Plays*, he falls under another
' Imputation. For where there is no Im-
' pression, there can be no Pleasure : And
' then the *Spectator* is very much Im-
' pertinent, in going where he gets no-
' thing for his Pains. And if this were
' all ; I suppose Christians have something

Ibid. cap. ' else to do than to ramble about to no pur-
22. ' pose.

' Even those very Magistrates who abet
' the *Stage*, discountenance the *Players*.
' They stigmatize their *Character*, and
' cramp their Freedoms. The whole
' Tribe of them is thrown out of all Ho-
' nour and Privilege. They are neither
' suffer'd to be Lords, nor Gentlemen :
' To come within the *Senate*, or harangue
' the People, or so much as to be Members
' of a *Common-Council*. Now what Caprice
' and Inconsistency is this ! To love what
' we punish, and lessen those whom we ad-
' mire ! To cry up the Mystery, and cen-
' sure

' sure the practise; For a Man to be as it
' were eclips'd upon the score of Merit is
' certainly an odd sort of Justice! True.
' But the Inference lies stronger another
' way. What a Confession then is this of
' an Ill Business; when the very Excellen-
' cy of it is not without Infamy?

' Since therefore Humane Prudence has
' thought fit to degrade the *Stage*, not-
' withstanding the Divertingness of it.
' Since Pleasure can't make them an Inte- *Ibid. cap.*
' rest Here, nor shelter them from Censure. 23.
' How will They be able to stand the shock
' of Divine Justice, and what *Reckoning*
' have they *Reason* to expect Hereafter?

' All things consider'd 'tis no wonder
' such People should fall under *Possession*.
' God knows we have had a sad Example
' of this already. A certain Woman went *Ibid. cap.*
' to the *Play-House*, and brought the Devil 26.
' Home with Her. And when the Un-
' clean Spirit was press'd in the *Exorcism*
' and a k'd how he durst attack a Christi-
' an. I have done nothing (says he) but
' what I can justify. For I seiz'd her up-
' on my own Ground. Indeed, how ma-
' ny Instances have we of others who have
' apostatiz'd from God, by Correspondence
' with the Devil? What *Communion has
Light with Darkness? No Man can serve*

two *Masters*, nor have Life and Death in
' him at the same time.

Ibid.
cap. 27.

' Will you not then avoid this Seat of
' Infection? The very Air suffers by their
' Impurities ; And they almost Pronounce
' the Plague.   What tho' the performance
' may be in some measure pretty and enter-
' taining? What tho' Innocence, yes and Vir-
' tue too, shines through some part of it ?
' 'Tis not the custom to prepare Poyson
' unpalatable, nor make up Ratzbane with
' Rhubarb and Sena.   No. To have the
' Mischief speed, they must oblige the
' Sense, and make the Dose pleasant.
' Thus the Devil throws in a Cordial
' Drop to make the Draught go down;
' And steals some few Ingredients from the
' *Dispensatory* of Heaven.   In short, look
' upon all the engaging Sentences of the
' Stage ; Their flights of Fortitude, and
' Philosophy, the Loftiness of their Stile,
' the   Musick   of   the   Cadence ,   and
' the Finess of the Conduct ; Look upon
' it only I say as Honey dropping from
' the Bowels of a Toad, or the Bag of a
' Spider : Let your Health over-rule your
' Pleasure, and don't die of a little *Li-*
' *quorishness.*

Ibid. cap.
28.

' In earnest Christian, our time for En-
' tertainment is not yet : you are two cra-
' ving and ill managed if you are so violent
' for

'for Delight. And let me tell you, no
'wiſer than you ſhould be, if you count
'ſuch Things Satisfaction. Some Philoſo-
'phers placed their Happineſs in bare
'Tranquillity. Eaſineſs of Thought, and
'Abſence of Pain, was all they aim'd at.
'But this it ſeems won't Satisfie Thee.
'Thou lieſt ſighing and hankering after
'the *Play-houſe.* Prethee recollect thy ſelf:
'Thou knoweſt Death ought to be our
'Pleaſure, And therefore I hope Life may
'be a little without it. Are not our De-
'ſires the ſame with the Apoſtles, *To be*
'*Diſſolv'd and to be with Chriſt.* Let us act
'up to our pretentions, and let Pleaſure be
'true to Inclination.

'But if you can't wait for Delight; if *Ibid. cap:*
'you muſt be put into preſent Poſſeſſion, 29.
'wee'l caſt the Cauſe upon that Iſſue.
'Now were you not unreaſonable, you
'would perceive the Liberalities of Provi-
'dence, and find your ſelf almoſt in the
'midſt of Satisfaction. For what can be
'more tranſporting than the Friendſhip of
'Heaven, and the Diſcovery of Truth, than
'the Senſe of our Miſtakes, and the Par-
'don of our Sins? What greater Pleaſure
'can there be, than to ſcorn being *Pleas'd?*
'To contemn the World? And to be a
'Slave to Nothing? 'Tis a mighty ſatis-
'faction I take it, to have a clear Conſcience;

S 2 'To

' To make Life no Burthen, nor Death
' any Terror ! To trample upon the
' *Pagan* Deities ; To batter *Principali-*
' *ties* and *Powers,* and force the Devils to

By Exor-cisms ' Refign ! * Thefe are the Delights, thefe
' are the noble Entertainments of Chrifti-
' ans: And befides the advantage of the
' Quality, they are always at hand, and
' coft us nothing.

Lib. 3. *Clemens Alexandrinus* affirms ' That the
Pædag.
Ann. 204. ' *Circus* and *Theatre* may not improperly
cap. 11. ' be call'd the *Chair* of *Peſtilence.* ———
' Away then with thefe Lewd, Ungodly
' Diverfions, and which are but Imperti-
' nence at the Beft. What part of Impu-
' dence either in words or practife, is omit-
' ted by the Stage ? Don't the Buffoons
' take almoft all manner of Liberties, and
' plunge through Thick and Thin, to make
' a jeft ? Now thofe who are affected with
' a vitious fatisfaction, will be haunted with
' the Idea, and fpread the Infection. But
' if a man is not entertain'd to what pur-
' pofe fhould he go Thither ? Why fhould
' he be fond where he finds nothing, and
' court that which fleeps upon the Senfe ?
' If 'tis faid thefe Diverfions are taken on-
' ly to unbend the Mind, and refresh Na-
' ture a little. To this I anfwer. That
' the fpaces between Bufinefs fhould not
' be

'be fill'd up with such Rubbish. A wise
'man has a Guard upon his Recreations,
'and always prefers, the Profitable to the
'Pleasant.

Minutius Felix delivers his Sense in _{Ann. 206.}
these Words:

'As for us, who rate our Degree by
'our Virtue, and value our selves more
'upon our Lives, than our Fortunes; we
'decline your Pompous *Shews*, and pub-
'lick Entertainments. And good Reason
'we have for our Aversion. These Things
'have their Rise from Idols, and are the
'Train of a false Religion. The Plea-
'sure is ill Descended, and likewise Viti-
'ous and ensnaring. For who can do less
'than abominate, the Clamorous Disor-
'ders of the *Race-Ground*, and the pro-
'fession of Murther at the *Prize*. And
'for the *Stage*, there you have more
'Lewdness, tho' not a jot less of Distra-
'ction. Sometimes your *Mimicks*, are so
'Scandalous and Expressing, that 'tis almost
'hard to distinguish between the *Fact* and
'the *Representation*. Sometimes a Lusci-
'ous *Actor* shall whine you into Love,
'and give the Disease that he Counterfeits.

St. *Cyprian* or the Author *de Spectaculis*,
will furnish us farther.

Here this Father argues against those
who thought the *Play-House* no unlawful

Diversion,

Diversion, because 'twas not Condemn'd
by express *Scripture*. 'Let meer Modesty
'(says he) supply the *Holy Text*: And
'let *Nature* govern where *Revelation*
'does not reach. Some Things are too
'black to lie upon *Paper*, and are more
'strongly forbidden, because unmention'd.
'The Divine Wisdom must have had a
'low Opinion of *Christians*, had it descen-
'ded to particulars in this Case. Silence
'is sometimes the best Method for Autho-
'rity. To Forbid often puts People in
'mind of what they should not do; And
'thus the force of the Precept is lost by
'naming the Crime. Besides, what need
'we any farther Instruction? Discipline
'and general Restraint makes up the
'Meaning of the Law; and common Rea-
'son will tell you what the Scripture has
'left unsaid. I would have every one
'examine his own Thoughts, and inquire
'at Home into the Duties of his Profes-
'sion. This is a good way to secure
'him from Indecency. For those Rules
'which a Man has work'd out for him-
'self, he commonly makes most use of. ——
And after having describ'd the infamous
Diversions of the *Play-house*; He expostulates in this Manner.

'What business has a Christian at such
'Places as these? A Christian who has not
'the

'the Liberty so much as to think of an
'ill Thing. Why does he entertain him-
'self with Lewd Representations? Has
'he a mind to discharge his Modesty,
'and be flesh'd for the *Practise*? Yes. this
'is the Consequence. By using to see these
'Things, hee'l learn to do them.——
'What need I mention the Levities, and
'Impertinence in *Comedies*, or the ranting
'Distractions of *Tragedy*? Were these
'Things unconcern'd with Idolatry, Chri-
'stians ought not to be at them. For
'were they not highly Criminal, the Fool-
'ery of them is egregious, and unbecom-
'ing the Gravity of *Beleivers*.——

'As I have often said these Foppish,
'these pernicious Diversions, must be a-
'voided. We must set a Guard upon
'our Senses, and keep the Sentinal always
'upon Duty. To make Vice familiar to
'the ear, is the way to recommend it.
'And since the mind of Man has a Natu-
'ral Bent to Extravagance; how is it
'likely to hold out under Example, and
'Invitation? If you push that which tot-
'ters already, whether will it tumble?
'In earnest, we must draw off our Incli-
'nations from these Vanities. A Christian
'has much better *Sights* than these to
'look at. He has solid Satisfactions in his

'Power,

'Power, which will please, and improve
'him at the same time.

'Would a Christian be agreeably Re-
'fresh'd? Let him read the *Scriptures*:
'Here the Entertainment will suit his
'Character, and be big enough for his Qua-
'lity.—Beloved, how noble, how moving
'how profitable a pleasure is it to be thus
'employed? To have our Expectations al-
'ways in prospect, and be intent
'on the Glories of Heaven?

He has a great deal more upon this Subject in his *Epistles* to *Donatus* and *Eucra-
tius*, which are undoubtedly genuine. The
later being somewhat remarkable, I shall
Translate part of it for the *Reader*.

*Ad Euv-
crat.*

'Dear Brother, your usual Kindness,
'together with your desire of releiving
'your own Modesty and mine, has put
'you upon asking my Thoughts concer-
'ning a certain *Player* in your Neighbour-
'hood; whether such a Person ought to
'be allow'd the Privilege of *Communion*.
'This Man it seems continues in his Scan-
'dalous Profession, and keeps a Nursery
'under him. He teaches that which 'twas
'a Crime in him to learn, sets up for a
'Master of Debauch, and Propagates the
'lewd Mystery. The case standing thus,
''tis my Opinion that the Admission of
'such a *Member* would be a Breach of the
'Discipline

' Discipline of the Gospel, and a Presump-
' tion upon the Divine Majesty : Neither
' do I think it fit the Honour of the Church
' should suffer by so Infamous a Cor-
' respondence.

Lactantius's Testimony shall come next.
This Author in his *Divine Institutions*, Lib. 6.
which he Dedicates to *Constantine* the cap. 20.
Great, cautions the Christians against the
Play-House, from the Disorder, and dan-
ger of those places. For as he observes.

' The debauching of Virgins, and the
' Amours of Strumpets, are the Subject
' of *Comedy*. And here the Rule is, the
' more Rhetorick the more Mischeif, and
' the best *Poets* are the worst Common-
' Wealths-men. For the Harmony and
' Ornament of the Composition serves
' only to recommend the Argument, to
' fortifie the Charm, and engage the Me-
' mory. At last he concludes with this
' advice.

' Let us avoid therefore these Diversions,
' least somewhat of the Malignity should
' seize us. Our Minds should be quiet
' and Compos'd, and not over-run with A-
' musements. Besides a Habit of Plea-
' sure is an ensnaring Circumstance. 'Tis *Ibid. cap.*
' apt to make us forget God, and grow 21.
' cool in the Offices of Virtue.

' Should

'Should a Man have a Stage at Home,
'would not his Reputation suffer extream-
'ly, and all people count him a notorious
'Libertine? most undoubtedly. Now the
'Place does not alter the Property. The
'Practise at the *Play-House* is the same
'thing, only there he has more Compa-
'ny to keep him in Countenance.

'A well work'd *Poem* is a powerful
'piece of Imposture: It masters the Fan-
'cy, and hurries it no Body knows whi-
'ther.——If therefore we would be go-
'vern'd by Reason let us stand off from
'the Temptation, such Pleasures can have
'no good Meaning. Like delicious Mor-
'sels they subdue the Palate, and flatter
'us only to cut our Throats. Let us pre-
Ibid. cap. 'fer Reality to Appearance, Service, to
22. 'Show; and Eternity to Time.

'As God makes Virtue the Condition
'of Glory, and trains men up to Hap-
'piness by Hardship and Industry.
'So the Devils road to Destruction lies
'through Sensuality and *Epicurism*. And
'as pretended Evils lead us on to un-
'counterfeited Bliss; So Visionary Satis-
'factions are the causes of Real Misery.
'In short, These Inviting Things are all
'stratagem. Let us, take care the soft-
'ness and Importunity of the Pleasure
'does not surprise us, nor the Bait bring
'us

'us within the snare. The Senses are
'more than *Out-Works*, and should be
'defended accordingly.

I shall pass over St. *Ambrose*, and go *In Psal:*
on to St. *Chrisostome*. This *Father* is copi- 119.
ous upon the Subject, I could translate
some *Sheets* from him were it necessary.
But length being not my Business, a few
Lines may serve to discover his Opinion.
His 15 *Homily ad Popalum Antiochenum*,
runs thus.

'Most People fancy the Unlawfulness
'of going to *Plays* is not clear. But by their
'favour, a world of Disorders are the
'Consequences of such a Liberty. For
'frequenting the *Play-House* has brought
'Whoring and Ribaldry into Vogue, and
'finish'd all the parts of Debauchery.

Afterwards he seems to make the supposition better than the *Fact*, and
argues upon a feign'd Case.

'Let us not only avoid downright Sin-
'ning, but the Tendencies to it. Some Indiffe-
'rent Things are fatal in the Consequence,
'and strike us at the Rebound. Now
'who would chuse his standing within an
'Inch of a Fall ; or swim upon the Verge
'of a Whirlpool ? He that walks upon
'a Precipice, shakes tho' he does not tum-
'ble. And commonly his Concern brings
'him to the Bottom. The Case is much

'the

' the same in reference to Conscience, and
' Morality. He that won't keep his Di-
' stance from the Gulph, is oftentimes
' suck'd in by the Eddy; and the least
' oversight is enough to undo Him.

In his 37 Homily upon the Eleventh
Chapter of St. *Matthew* he declaims more
at large against the Stage.

' Smutty Songs (says he) are much
' more abominable than Stench and Or-
' dure. And which is most to be lamen-
' ted, you are not at all uneasy at such
' Licentiousness. You Laugh when you
' should Frown; and Commend what
' you ought to abhor.—— Heark you, you
' can keep the Language of your own
' House in order : If your Servants or
' your Childrens Tongues run Riot, they
' presently smart for't. And yet at the
' *Play-House* you are quite another Thing.
' These little Buffoons have a strange As-
' cendant ! A luscious Sentence is huge-
' ly welcome from their Mouth : And in-
' stead of Censure, they have thanks and
' encouragement for their Pains. Now
' if a Man would be so just as to won-
' der at himself, here's Madness, and Con-
' tradiction in Abundance.

' But I know you'l say what's this to
' me, I neither sing nor pronounce any of
' this Lewd stuff? Granting your Plea,
' what

'what do you get by't? If you don't re-
'peat these Scurrilities, you are very wil-
'ling to hear them. Now whether the
'Ear, or the Tongue is mismanaged, comes
'much to the same reckoning. The diffe-
'rence of the *Organ*, does not alter the
'Action so mightily, as you may imagine.
'But pray how do you prove you don't
'repeat them? They may be your Dif-
'course, or the Entertainments of your
'Closet for ought we know to the con-
'trary. This is certain; you hear them
'with pleasure in your Face, and make
'it your business to run after them: And
'to my Mind, these are strong Arguments
'of your Approbation.

'I desire to ask you a Question. Sup-
'pose you hear any wretches Blaspheme,
'are you in any Rapture about it? And
'do your Gestures appear airy, and obliged?
'Far from it. I doubt not but your blood
'grows chill, and your Ears are stopt at
'the Presumption. And what's the Rea-
'son of this Aversion in your Behaviour?
'Why 'tis because you don't use to Blaf-
'pheme, your self. Pray clear your self
'the same way from the Charge of Ob-
'scenity, Wee'l then believe you don't
'talk Smut, when we percieve you care-
'ful not to hear it. Lewd Sonnets, and
'Serenades are quite different from the
'Pre-

' Prescriptions of Virtue. This is strange
' Nourishment for a Christian to take in!
' I don't wonder you should lose your
' Health, when you feed thus Foul. It
' may be Chastity is no such easy Task!
' Innocence moves upon an Ascent, at least
' for sometime. Now those who are al-
' ways Laughing can never strain up Hill.
' If the best preparations of Care will just
' do, what must become of those that are
' dissolv'd in Pleasure, and lie under the In-
' structions of Debauchery? ——Have you
' not heard how that St. *Paul* exhorts us *to*
' *rejoyce in the Lord*? He said *in the Lord*;
' not in the Devil. But alas! what
' leisure have you to Mind St. *Paul*?
' How should you be sensible of your
' Faults, when your Head is always kept
' Hot, and as it were intoxicated with
' Buffooning? —— —— He goes on, and
lashes the Impudence of the *Stage* with a
great deal of Satir and Severity; and at
last proposes this Objection.

' You'l say, I can give you many Instan=
' ces where the *Play-House* has done no
' Harm. Don't mistake. Throwing a-
' way of Time and ill example, has a great
' deal of Harm in't; And thus far you are
' guilty at the best. For granting your
own Virtue impenetrable, and out of
Reach, Granting the Protection of your
Temper has brought you off unhurt,

are

are all People thus Fortified? By no
' means. However, many a weak
' Brother has ventur'd after you, and mif-
' carried upon your *Precedent*. And fince
' you make others thus *Faulty*, how can
' you be *Innocent* your felf? All the Peo-
' ple undone There, will lay their Ruine at
' your Door. The Company are all Ac-
' ceffary to the Mifcheif of the Place.
' For were there no *Audience*, we fhould
' have no *Acting*. And therefore thofe
' who joyn in the Crime, will ne're be par-
' ted in the Punifhment. Granting your
' Modefty has fecur'd you, which by the
' way I believe nothing of; yet fince ma-
' ny have been debauch'd by the *Play-
' Houfe*, you muft expect a fevere Reck-
' ning for giving them Encouragement.
' Tho' after all, as Virtuous as you are,
' I doubt not, you wou'd have been much
' Better, had you kept away.

   ' In fine, Let us not difpute to no pur-
' pofe; The practife won't bear a Defence!
' Where the Caufe is naught 'tis in vain
' to rack our Reafon, and ftrain for Pre-
' tences. The beft excufe for what is
' paft, is to ftand clear from the danger,
' and do fo no more.

   One citation more from St. *Chryfoſtom*,
and I take Leave. In the Preface of his
Commentary upon St. *John*'s Gofpel fpeak-
ing of *Plays* and other Publick *Shews*, he
has thefe words.   ' But

' But what need I branch out the Lewd-
' ness of those *Spectacles*, and be particu-
' lar in Description? For what's there to
' be met with but Lewd Laughing, but
' Smut, Railing, and Buffoonry? In a
' word. 'Tis all Scandal and Confusion.
' Observe me, I speak to you all; Let
' none who partake of this *Holy-Table*,
' unqualifie himself with such Mortal
' Diversions.

St. *Hierom* on the 1*st*. Verse 32 *Psal*.
makes this Exposition upon the *Text*.

' Some are delighted with the Satisfac-
' tions of this World, some with the *Circus*,
' and some with the *Theatre* : But the
' Psalmist commands every good Man *to*
' *delight himself in the Lord*.——For as
' *Isaiah* speaks, *woe to them that put bitter*
' *for sweet , and sweet for bitter.* And in

Ep: 9. 12.
Advers.
Jovinian.
Lib. 2.
cap, 7.

his *Epistles* he cautions the Ladies against
having any thing to do with the *Play-
House*, against Lewd Songs, and Ill Conversation. Because they set ill Humours
at work, Caress the Fancy, and make
pleasure a Conveyance for Destruction.

In the 6*th*. Book of his Comentary on

Chap. 20.

Ezechiel he lets us understand; ' That
' when we depart out of *Ægypt* we must
' refine our Inclinations, and change our
' Delights into Aversion. And after some
' other Instances, He tells us we must
                                    ' decline

' decline the *Theatres*, and all other dan-
' gerous Diversions, which stain the In-
' nocence of the Soul, and slip into the
' *Will* through the Senses.

St. *Augustine* in his 5th. Epistle to *Mar-
cellinus* will afford us something upon the
same Argument.

' The prosperity of Sinners is their grea-
' test Unhappiness. If one may say so,
' They are most Punish'd when they are
' overlook'd. By this means their bad
' Temper is encourag'd, and they are more
' Inclin'd to be false to themselves ; And
' we know an Enemy *within*, is more dan-
' gerous than one *without*. But the per-
' verse Reasonings of the Generality, make
' different Conclusions. They fancy the
' World goes wonderfully well when
' People make a Figure. When a Man
' is a Prince in his Fortune, but a Begger
' in his Vertue ; Has a great many fine
' Things about him, but not so much as
' one good Quality to deserve them. When
' the *Play-Houses* go up, and Religion go's
' down. When Prodigality is admir'd,
' and Charity laugh'd at. When the *Players* can revel with the Rich Man's purse,
' And the Poor have scarse enough to keep
' Life and Soul together.——When God
' suffers these Things to flourish, we may
' be sure he is most Angry. Present Im-
' punity, is the deepest Revenge. But

T   When

'when he cuts off the Supplies of Lux-
'ury, and difables the Powers of Extra-
'vagance, then as one may fay, he is mer-
'cifully fevere.

cap. 33.

In his 1ft. Book *de confensu Evange-
liftarum*, He anfwers an objection of the
Heathens, and comes up to the Cafe in
Hand.

'Their Complaint as if the Times
'were lefs happy fince the Appearance of
'Chriftianity is very unreafonable. Let them
'read their own Philofophers: There they'l
'find thofe very Things cenfured, which
'they now are fo uneafy to part with;
'This Remark muft fhut up their Mouths,
'and convince them of the Excellency of
'our Religion. For pray what Satisfa-
'ctions have they loft? None that I know
'of, excepting fome Licentious ones,
'which they abufed to the Difhonour of
'their Creatour. But it may be the Times
'are bad becaufe the *Theatres* are Tum-
'bling almoft every where. The *Thea-
'ters* thofe *Cages* of *Uncleanefs*, and pub-
'lick Schools of Debauchery.——And
'what's the Reafon of their running to
'Ruine? Why 'tis the Reformation of
'the Age : 'Tis becaufe thofe Lewd Prac-
'tifes are out of Fafhion, which firft built
'and kept them in Countenance. Their
'own *Tully*'s Commendation of the *Actor
'Rofcius* is remarkable. He was fo much

a

' a Mafter (fays he) that none but him-
' felf was worthy to Tread the *Stage*. And
' on the other hand, fo good a Man, that
' he was the moft unfit Perfon of the Gang
' to come There. And is not this a plain
' Confeffion of the Lewdnefs of the *Play-*
' *Houfe*; And that the better a Man was,
' the more he was obliged to forbear it?

I could go on, much farther with St.
Auguftine, but I love to be as brief as may
be. I could likewife run through the
fucceeding *Centuries*, and collect Evidence
all along. But I conceive the beft Ages,
and the biggeft Authorities, may be sufficient : And thefe the *Reader* has had already.
However, one Inftance more from the
Moderns may not be amifs. *Didacus de
Tapia* an eminent *Spaniard*, fhall clofe the
Evidence. This Author in debating the
Queftion whether *Players* might be admitted to the *Sacrament*, amongft other
things encounters an Objection. Some People it feems pretended there was fome good
to be learn'd at the *Play-Houfe*. To thefe,
he makes this reply.

'Granting your Suppofition, (fays He)
'your Inference is naught. Do People ufe
'to fend their Daughters to the *Stews* for
'Difcipline? And yet it may be, they
'might meet fome there lamenting their
'own Debauchery. No Man will breed
'his Son upon the *High-way*, to harden his

'Courage

'Courage; Neither will any one go on
'board a Leaky Vessel, to learn the Art of
'shifting in a Wreck the better. My con-
'clusion is, let no body go to the Infamous
'*Play-House*. A place of such staring Con-
'tradiction to the Strictness and Sobriety
'of Religion: A Place hated by God, and
'haunted by the Devil. Let no man I say
Didac, &c. 'learn to relish any thing that's said there;
in D. Thom. 'For 'tis all but Poyson handsomly pre-
p. 546. 'pared.

    Thus I have presented the *Reader* with
a short View of the Sense of *Christianity*.
This was the opinion of the *Church* for
the first 500 Years. And thus she has
Censured the *Stage* both in *Councils*,
and Single *Authorities*. And since the Satir of the *Fathers* comes full upon the
Modern Poets, their Caution must be ap-
plicable. The parity of the Case makes
their Reasons take place, and their Authority revive upon us. If we are *Christians*,
the *Canons* of *Councils*, and the Sense of the
Primitive *Church* must have a weight. The
very Time is a good argument of it self.
Then the *Apostolical Traditions* were fresh,
and undisputed; and the *Church* much better agreed than she has been since. Then,
Discipline was in Force, and Virtue Flourish'd, and People lived up to their *Profession*. And as for the *Persons*, they are beyond all exception. Their *Station*, their
Learning,

Learning, and Sufficiency was very Confiderable; Their Piety and Refolution, extraordinary. They acted generoufly, and wrote freely, and were always above the little Regards of Intereft or Danger. To be fhort; They were, as we may fay the *Worthies* of *Chriftendom*, the Flower of Humane Nature, and the Top of their *Species*. Nothing can be better eftablifh'd than the Credit of thefe *Fathers*: Their Affirmation goes a great way in a proof; And we might argue upon the ftrength of their *Character*.

But fuppofing them contented to wave their Privilege, and difpute upon the Level. Granting this, the *Stage* would be undone by them. The Force of their Reafoning, and the bare *Intrinfick* of the Argument, would be abundantly fufficient to carry the Caufe.

But it may be objected, is the Refemblance exact between Old *Rome* and *London*, will the Paralel hold out, and has the *Englifh Stage* any Thing fo bad as the *Dancing* of the *Pantomimi*? I don't fay that: The *Modern Geftures* tho' bold, and Lewd too fometimes, are not altogether fo fcandalous as the *Roman*. Here then we can make them fome little Abatement.

And to go as far in their *Excufe* as we can, 'tis probable their *Mufick* may not be altogether fo exceptionable as that of the

Antients. I don't say this part of the Entertainment is directly vitious, because I am not willing to Censure at Uncertainties. Those who frequent the *Play-House* are the most competent Judges : But this I must say, the Performances of this kind are much too fine for the *Place*. 'Twere to be wish'd that either the *Plays* were better, or the *Musick* worse. I'm sorry to see *Art* so meanly Prostituted : Atheism ought to have nothing Charming in its *Retinue*. 'Tis great Pity *Debauchery* should have the Assistance of a fine Hand, to whet the Appetite, and play it down.

Now granting the *Play-House-Musick* not vitious in the Composition, yet the design of it is to refresh the *Idea*'s of the *Action*, to keep *Time* with the *Poem*, and be true to the *Subject*. For this Reason among others the *Tunes* are generally Airy and Gailliardizing : They are contriv'd on purpose to excite a sportive Humour, and spread a Gaity upon the Spirits. To banish all Gravity and Scruple, and lay Thinking and Reflection a sleep. This sort of Musick warms the Passions, and unlocks the Fancy, and makes it open to Pleasure like a Flower to the Sun. It helps a Luscious Sentence to slide, drowns the Discords of *Atheism*, and keeps off the Aversions of Conscience. It throws a Man off his Guard, makes way for an ill Impression and is most Commodiously

modiouſly planted to do Mischief. A Lewd *Play* with good Muſick is like a Load-ſtone *Arm'd*, it draws much ſtronger than before.

Now why ſhould it be in the power of a few mercenary Hands to play People out of their Senſes, to run away with their Under-ſtandings, and wind their Paſſions about their Fingers as they liſt? Muſick is al-moſt as dangerous as Gunpowder; And it may be requires looking after no leſs than the *Preſs*, or the *Mint*. 'Tis poſſible a Publick Regulation might not be amiſs. No leſs a Philoſopher than *Plato* ſeems to be of this Opinion. He is clearly for keep-ing up the old grave, and ſolemn way of *Playing*. He lays a mighty ſtreſs upon this Obſervation: He does not ſtick to af-firm, that to extend the *Science*, and alter the *Notes*, is the way to have the *Laws* repeal'd and to unſettle the *Conſtitution*. I ſuppoſe He imagined that if the Power of *Sounds*, the Temper of Conſtitutions, and the Diverſities of Age, were well ſtu-died; If this were done, and ſome general Permiſſions formed upon the Enquiry, the *Commonwealth* might find their Account in't. *D: Repub. L. 4.*

Tully does not carry the Speculation thus high: However, he owns it has a weight in't, and ſhould not be overlook'd. He de-nies not but that when the Muſick is ſoft, *Cic. de Leg. L. 2.*

T 4   exqui-

exquisite, and airy, 'tis dangerous and ensnaring. He commends the Discipline of
the antient *Greeks*, for fencing against this
Inconvenience. He tells us the *Lacedemonians* fixt the number of Strings for the
Harp, by express *Law*. And afterwards si-
lenc'd *Timotheus*, * and seiz'd his Harp,
for having One String above publick Allowance. To return. If the *English Stage*
is more reserv'd than the *Roman* in the
Case above mention'd: If they have any
advantage in their *Instrumental* Musick,
they loose it in their *Vocal*. Their *Songs*
are often rampantly Lewd, and Irreligious to a flaming Excess. Here you have
the very *Spirit* and *Essence* of Vice drawn
off strong scented, and thrown into a little
Compass. Now the *Antients* as we have
seen already were inoffensive in this respect.

** a Famous
Musitian.*

Ibid.

*See Chap.
1st:*

To go on. *As* to Rankness of Language we have seen how deeply the *Moderns* stand charged upon the Comparison.
And as for their Caressing of Libertines,
their ridiculing of Vertue, their horrible
Profaness, and Blasphemies, there's nothing
in *Antiquity* can reach them.

Now were the *Stage* in a Condition
to wipe off any of these Imputations, which
They are not, there are two Things behind, which would stick upon them, and
have an ill Effect upon the *Audience*.

The

The firſt is their dilating ſo much upon the ʼArgument of Love.

This Subject is generally treated Home, and in the moſt tender and paſſionate manner imaginable. Tis often the governing Concern : The Incidents make way, and the *Plot* turns upon't. As matters go, the Company expect it : And it may be the *Poets* can neither Write, nor Live without it. This is a cunning way enough of ſtealing upon the Blind Side, and Practiſing upon the Weakneſs of humane Nature. People love to ſee their *Paſſions* painted no leſs than their *Perſons* : And like *Narciſſus* are apt to dote on their own Image. This Bent of ſelf Admiration recommends the Buſineſs of *Amours,* and engages the Inclination. And which is more, theſe Love-repreſentations oftentimes call up the Spirits, and ſet them on work. The *Play* is acted over again in the *Scene* of Fancy, and the firſt Imitation becomes a Model. *Love* has generally a *Party Within* ; And when the Wax is prepared, the Impreſſion is eaſily made. Thus the Diſeaſe of the *Stage* grows Catching : It throws its own *Amours* among the Company, and forms theſe Paſſions when it does not find them. And when they are born before, they thrive extreamly in this *Nurſery.* Here they ſeldom fail either of Grouth, or Complexion.

They

They grow ftrong, and they grow Charming too. This is the beft Place to recover a Languifhing Amour, to rowfe it from Sleep, and retrieve it from Indifference. And thus Defire becomes Abfolute, and forces the Oppofitions of Decency and Shame. And if the Misfortune does not go thus far, the confequences are none of the beft. The Paffions are up in Arms, and there's a mighty Conteft between Duty, and Inclination. The Mind is over-run with Amufements, and commonly good for nothing fometime after.

I don't fay the *Stage* Fells all before them, and difables the whole *Audience* : 'Tis a hard Battle where none efcapes. However, Their *Triumphs* and their *Tropheys* are unfpeakable. Neither need we much wonder at the Matter. They are dangeroufly Prepar'd for Conqueft, and Empire. There's Nature, and Paffion, and Life, in all the Circumftances of their *Action*. Their Declamation, their *Mein* their Geftures, and their Equipage, are very moving and fignificant. Now when the Subject is agreeable, a lively Reprefentation, and a Paffionate way of Expreffion, make wild work, and have a ftrange Force upon the Blood, and Temper.

And then as for the General Strains of Courtfhip, there can be nothing more Profane and extravagant. The Hero's Miftrefs

is

is no less than his Deity. She disposes of his Reason, prescribes his Motions, and Commands his Interest. What Soveraign Respect, what Religious Address, what Idolizing Raptures are we pester'd with? *Shrines* and *Offerings*, and Adorations, are nothing upon such solemn Occasions. Thus Love and Devotion, Ceremony and Worship, are Confounded; And God, and his Creatures treated both alike! These Shreds of Distraction are often brought from the *Play-House* into Conversation: And thus the *Sparks* are taught to Court their Mistresses, in the same Language they say their *Prayers*.

A Second Thing which I have to object against the *Stage* is their encouraging Revenge. What is more Common than Duels and Quarrelling in their *Characters* of Figure? Those Practises which are infamous in Reason, *Capital* in *Law*, and Damnable in Religion, are the Credit of the *Stage*. Thus Rage and Resentment, Blood and Barbarity, are almost Deified: Pride goes for Greatness, and *Fiends* and *Hero's* are made of the same Mettal. To give Instances were needless, nothing is more frequent. And in this respect the *French Dramatists* have been to blame no less than the *English*. And thus the Notion *Vid. Corneille Cid.* of Honour is mistated, the Maxims of *Cinna &* Christianity despised, and the Peace of the *Pompee*.

World

World diſturb'd. I grant this deſperate
Cuſtom is no *Original* of the *Stage*. But
then why was not the Growth of it
check'd? I thought the *Poets* buſineſs had
not been to back falſe Reaſoning and ill
Practiſe; and to fix us in Frenſy and Miſtake! Yes. They have done their endeavour to cheriſh the Malignity, and keep
the Diſorder in Countenance. They have
made it both the Mark, and the Merit of
a Man of Honour; and ſet it off with *Qua-*
lity, and Commendation. But I have diſ-
courſ'd on this Subject elſwhere, and
therefore ſhall purſue it no farther.

Moral
Eſſ.ꝯ s.

To draw towards an End. And here I
muſt obſerve that theſe two later Exceptions are but Petty Miſmanagements with
reſpect to the Former. And when the
beſt are thus bad, what are the worſt?
What muſt we ſay of the more foul Re-
preſentations, of all the Impudence in Language and Geſture? Can this Stuff be the
Inclination of *Ladies*? Is a *Reading* upon
Vice ſo Entertaining, and do they love to
ſee the *Stews Diſſected* before them? One
would think the Diſhonour of their own
Sex, the Diſcovery of ſo much Lewdneſs,
and the treating Human Nature ſo very
Coarſly, could have little Satisfaction in't.
Let us ſet Conſcience aſide, and throw the
other World out of the Queſtion: Theſe In-
tereſts are far the greateſt, but not all. The
Ladies

Ladies have other Motives to confine them. The Reftraints of Decency, and the Confiderations of Honour, are fufficient to keep them at Home. But hoping They will be juft to themfelves I fhall wave this unacceptable Argument. I fhall only add, that a Surprize ought not to be Cenfured. Accidents are no Faults. The ftricteft Virtue may fometimes ftumble upon an *Ill Sight.* But Choife, and Frequency, and ill Ground, conclude ftrongly for Inclination. To be affured of the inoffenfivenefs of the *Play* is no more than a Neceffary Precaution. Indeed the *Players* fhould be generally difcouraged. They have no relifh of Modefty, nor any fcruples upon the Quality of the Treat. The groffeft *Difh* when 'twill down is as ready as the Beft. To fay Money is their Bufinefs and they muft *Live,* is the Plea of *Pick pockets,* and *High way men.* Thefe later may as well pretend their *Vocation* for a Lewd practife as the other. But

To give the Charge its due Compafs: To comprehend the whole *Audience,* and take in the Motives of Religon.

And here I can't imagine how we can reconcile fuch Liberties with our Proffeffion. Thefe Entertainments are as it were Litterally renounc'd in *Baptifm.* They are the *Vanities of the wicked World, and the Works of the Devil,* in the moft open, and emphatical Signification. *What Communion*

2 Cor. 6.
14.

has Light with Darkness, *and what concord has Christ with Belial.* Call you this Diversion? Can Profaneſs be ſuch an irreſiſtable Delight? Does the Crime of the Performance make the Spirit of the Satisfaction, and is the Scorn of Chriſtianity the Entertainment of Chriſtians? Is it ſuch a Pleaſure to hear the *Scriptures* burleſqu'd? Is Ribaldry ſo very obliging, and *Atheiſm* ſo Charming a Quality? Are we indeed willing to quit the Privilege of our Nature; to ſurrender our *Charter* of Immortality, and throw up the Pretences to another Life? It may be ſo! But then we ſhould do well to remember that *Nothing* is not in our Power. Our Deſires did not make us, neither can they unmake us. But I hope our wiſhes are not ſo mean, and that we have a better ſenſe of the Dignity of our *Being.* And if ſo, how can we be pleas'd with thoſe Things which would degrade us into Brutes, which ridicule our *Creed,* and turn all our Expectations into *Romance.*

And after all, the Jeſt on't is, theſe Men would make us believe their deſign is Virtue and Reformation. In good time! They are likely to combat Vice with ſucceſs, who deſtroy the Principles of Good and Evil! Take them at the beſt, and they do no more than expoſe a little Humour, and Formality. But then, as the Matter is manag'd, the Correction is much worſe

than

than the Fault. They laugh at *Pedantry*, and teach *Atheism*, cure a Pimple, and give the Plague. I heartily wish they would have let us alone. To exchange Virtue for Behaviour is a hard Bargain. Is not plain Honesty much better than Hypocrify well Dres'd? What's Sight good for without Subftance? What is a well Bred Libertine but a well bred Knave? One that can't prefer Confcience to Pleafure, without calling himfelf Fool: And will fell his Friend, or his Father, if need be, for his Convenience.

In fhort: Nothing can be more differviceable to Probity and Religion, than the management of the *Stage*. It cherifhes thofe Paffions, and rewards thofe Vices, which 'tis the bufinefs of Reafon to difcountenance. It ftrikes at the Root of Principle, draws off the Inclinations from Virtue, and fpoils good Education: 'Tis the moft effectual means to baffle the Force of Difcipline, to emafculate peoples Spirits, and Debauch their Manners. How *many* of the Unwary have thefe *Syrens* devour'd? And how often has the beft Blood been tainted, with this Infection? What Difappointment of Parents, what Confufion in Families, and what Beggery in Eftates have been hence occafion'd? And which is ftill worfe, the Mifchief fpreads dayly, and the Malignity grows more envenom'd.

The

The Feavour works up towards Madness,
and will scarcely endure to be touch'd:
And what hope is there of Health when
the *Patient* strikes in with the Disease,
and flies in the Face of the *Remedy*? Can
Religion retrive us? Yes, when we don't
despise it. But while our *Notions* are
naught, our *Lives* will hardly be otherwise. What can the Assistance of the
Church signify to those who are more
ready to Rally the *Preacher*, than Practise
the *Sermon*? To those who are overgrown
with Pleasure, and hardned in Ill Custom?
Who have neither Patience to hear, nor
Conscience to take hold of? You may almost as well feed a Man without a Mouth,
as give Advice where there's no dispositi-
on to receive it. 'Tis true; as long as
there is Life there's Hope. Sometimes
the Force of Argument, and the Grace of
God, and the anguish of Affliction, may
strike through the Prejudice, and make
their way into the Soul. But these circumstances don't always meet, and then
the Case is extreamly dangerous. For
this miserable Temper, we may thank the
Stage in a great Measure. And therefore,
if I mistake not, They have the least pretence to Favour, and the most need of Repentance, of all Men Living.

THE END.